OECD/G20 Base Erosion and Profit Shifting Project

Prevention of Tax Treaty Abuse – Third Peer Review Report on Treaty Shopping

INCLUSIVE FRAMEWORK ON BEPS: ACTION 6

OECD
BETTER POLICIES FOR BETTER LIVES

This document, as well as any data and map included herein, are without prejudice to the status of or sovereignty over any territory, to the delimitation of international frontiers and boundaries and to the name of any territory, city or area.

The statistical data for Israel are supplied by and under the responsibility of the relevant Israeli authorities. The use of such data by the OECD is without prejudice to the status of the Golan Heights, East Jerusalem and Israeli settlements in the West Bank under the terms of international law.

Note by Turkey
The information in this document with reference to "Cyprus" relates to the southern part of the Island. There is no single authority representing both Turkish and Greek Cypriot people on the Island. Turkey recognises the Turkish Republic of Northern Cyprus (TRNC). Until a lasting and equitable solution is found within the context of the United Nations, Turkey shall preserve its position concerning the "Cyprus issue".

Note by all the European Union Member States of the OECD and the European Union
The Republic of Cyprus is recognised by all members of the United Nations with the exception of Turkey. The information in this document relates to the area under the effective control of the Government of the Republic of Cyprus.

Please cite this publication as:
OECD (2021), *Prevention of Tax Treaty Abuse – Third Peer Review Report on Treaty Shopping : Inclusive Framework on BEPS: Action 6*, OECD/G20 Base Erosion and Profit Shifting Project, OECD Publishing, Paris, *https://doi.org/10.1787/d6cecbb8-en*.

ISBN 978-92-64-70701-6 (print)
ISBN 978-92-64-95098-6 (pdf)

OECD/G20 Base Erosion and Profit Shifting Project
ISSN 2313-2604 (print)
ISSN 2313-2612 (online)

Photo credits: Cover © ninog-Fotolia.com.

Corrigenda to publications may be found on line at: *www.oecd.org/about/publishing/corrigenda.htm*.

Foreword

The integration of national economies and markets has increased substantially in recent years, putting a strain on the international tax rules, which were designed more than a century ago. Weaknesses in the current rules create opportunities for base erosion and profit shifting (BEPS), requiring bold moves by policy makers to restore confidence in the system and ensure that profits are taxed where economic activities take place and value is created.

Following the release of the report *Addressing Base Erosion and Profit Shifting* in February 2013, OECD and G20 countries adopted a 15-point Action Plan to address BEPS in September 2013. The Action Plan identified 15 actions along three key pillars: introducing coherence in the domestic rules that affect cross-border activities, reinforcing substance requirements in the existing international standards, and improving transparency as well as certainty.

After two years of work, measures in response to the 15 actions were delivered to G20 Leaders in Antalya in November 2015. All the different outputs, including those delivered in an interim form in 2014, were consolidated into a comprehensive package. The BEPS package of measures represents the first substantial renovation of the international tax rules in almost a century. Once the new measures become applicable, it is expected that profits will be reported where the economic activities that generate them are carried out and where value is created. BEPS planning strategies that rely on outdated rules or on poorly co-ordinated domestic measures will be rendered ineffective.

Implementation is now the focus of this work. The BEPS package is designed to be implemented via changes in domestic law and practices, and in tax treaties. With the negotiation of a multilateral instrument (MLI) having been finalised in 2016 to facilitate the implementation of the treaty related BEPS measures, over 90 jurisdictions are covered by the MLI. The entry into force of the MLI on 1 July 2018 paves the way for swift implementation of the treaty related measures. OECD and G20 countries also agreed to continue to work together to ensure a consistent and co-ordinated implementation of the BEPS recommendations and to make the project more inclusive. Globalisation requires that global solutions and a global dialogue be established which go beyond OECD and G20 countries.

A better understanding of how the BEPS recommendations are implemented in practice could reduce misunderstandings and disputes between governments. Greater focus on implementation and tax administration should therefore be mutually beneficial to governments and business. Proposed improvements to data and analysis will help support ongoing evaluation of the quantitative impact of BEPS, as well as evaluating the impact of the countermeasures developed under the BEPS Project.

As a result, the OECD established the OECD/G20 Inclusive Framework on BEPS (Inclusive Framework), bringing all interested and committed countries and jurisdictions on an equal footing in the Committee on Fiscal Affairs and all its subsidiary bodies. The Inclusive Framework, which already has more than 135 members, is monitoring and peer reviewing the implementation of the minimum standards as well as completing the work on standard setting to address BEPS issues. In addition to BEPS members, other international organisations and regional tax bodies are involved in the work of the Inclusive Framework, which also consults business and the civil society on its different work streams.

This report was approved by the Inclusive Framework on 17 February 2021 and prepared for publication by the OECD Secretariat.

Table of contents

TABLES

Executive Summary

1. Action 6 of the BEPS Project identified treaty abuse, and in particular treaty shopping, as one of the principal sources of BEPS concerns. Owing to the seriousness of treaty shopping, jurisdictions have agreed to adopt, as a minimum standard, measures to address it, and to subject their efforts to an annual peer review. This 2020 peer review report contains the results of the third yearly peer review, background information on treaty shopping, and the "jurisdictional sections" which provide detailed information on the implementation of the minimum standard for each member of the Inclusive Framework.

2. The efforts made by most Inclusive Framework members in tackling treaty shopping started to come to light in the 2020 peer review, in particular for those that ratified the *Multilateral Convention to Implement Tax Treaty Related Measures to Prevent Base Erosion and Profit Shifting* (MLI). Although very few of the reported agreements met the minimum standard at the time of the first two peer reviews conducted in 2018 and 2019,[1] the MLI, which has been the main tool used to implement the minimum standard, has started to have a significant effect and is now strengthening the bilateral tax treaty network of jurisdictions that ratified it. The MLI did not offer a way for jurisdictions to implement the minimum standard through a detailed limitation on benefits provision instead of the principal purpose test (PPT).

3. Thus, because of the ratification of the MLI by those jurisdictions, the number of compliant agreements[2] covered by the MLI has increased by nearly 500% since the last peer review. This year's peer review, however, reveals an important difference in the progress made on the implementation of the minimum standard between the jurisdictions that have ratified the MLI and other jurisdictions that have not.

4. In fact, the jurisdictions that had not signed or ratified the MLI have still generally made no or very little progress in implementing the minimum standard. This report acknowledges, though, that the starting point for a jurisdiction's exposure to treaty abuse may be different based on whether its existing agreements or domestic law already contain anti-treaty shopping tools.

5. A new feature of this year's peer review is to provide additional information on some jurisdictions' progress towards the implementation of the minimum standard and to encourage signatories to the MLI to ratify it as soon as possible. This information does not give rise to formal recommendations. The additional information on jurisdictions' progress can be found in the section "Implementation Issues" of each of the jurisdictional sections in Chapter 5.

6. The key objectives of this year's peer review and the additional information provided in the section "Implementation issues" of the jurisdictional sections are to encourage signatories to the MLI to ratify it, close the gaps in the MLI's coverage and provide support to other jurisdictions to strengthen their tax treaty network.

Ratification of the MLI

7. The treaty networks of jurisdictions that ratified the MLI and for which the MLI started to take effect in January 2020[3] were on average about 30% compliant with the minimum standard in 2020. In

comparison, those that had not signed or ratified the MLI before that time had generally made no or very little progress in implementing the minimum standard (their treaty networks were on average about 1.5% compliant with the minimum standard).

8. The 2020 peer review thus shows that ratification of the MLI is important for the effective implementation of the minimum standard, and all signatories to the MLI that have not yet ratified it are encouraged to do so.

Gaps in the MLI coverage

9. The 2020 peer review also identifies gaps in the coverage of the MLI and agreements of signatories or parties to the MLI that are neither covered under the MLI nor subject to bilateral renegotiations.[4] While the MLI did not offer a way for jurisdictions to implement the minimum standard through a detailed limitation on benefits provision, it now covers 94 jurisdictions[5] and will implement the minimum standard in over 1,700 agreements once it is fully in effect (i.e. after a period once it has been ratified by all signatories). However, about 200 agreements, concluded between pairs of MLI signatories that are members of the Inclusive Framework, would still not be modified by the MLI because, at this stage, at least one treaty partner has not listed the agreement under the MLI. An additional 325 agreements have been concluded between pairs of jurisdictions where only one of them has signed the MLI; none of these agreements would, at this stage, be modified by the MLI.

10. As part of the additional information provided on jurisdictions' progress, the jurisdictional sections identify these "non-covered agreements" concluded between pairs of the signatories to the MLI that are members of the Inclusive Framework and are not subject to bilateral negotiations.

11. Listing the agreements under the MLI[6] or entering into bilateral renegotiations to implement the minimum standard would ensure that the minimum standard could be implemented in those non-covered agreements.

Support to jurisdictions to strengthen their network of agreements

12. The OECD Secretariat stands ready to discuss with all jurisdictions that are members of the Inclusive Framework and that have not signed the MLI nor implemented compliant anti-treaty-shopping measures in their agreements to see how support could be provided to bring those agreements into compliance with the minimum standard.

13. The section "Implementation issues" in the jurisdictional sections in Chapter 5 of this report provides additional information on jurisdictions' progress towards the implementation of the minimum standard and identifies those jurisdictions with which the Secretariat would want to discuss a plan for the implementation of the minimum standard. Those discussions could provide useful insights for the ongoing review of the peer review methodology.

14. As noted at paragraph 14 of the Peer Review Documents,[7] the methodology for the review of the implementation of the minimum standard would be reviewed in light of the experience in conducting the first three peer reviews in 2018, 2019 and 2020.

15. The Inclusive Framework on BEPS, together with Working Party No. 1, will carry out the 2020 review and the implementation of the minimum standard will continue to be monitored. The next peer review exercise will be launched in the first half of 2021.

Notes

[1] The MLI had not started to show its effect at the time where the 2018 and 2019 peer reviews were conducted.

[2] For the purpose of this report, a compliant agreement contains provisions that meet the Action 6 minimum standard. As indicated in paragraph 23 of the final Report on Action 6, it is understood that jurisdictions only need to implement those provisions if requested to do so by another jurisdiction member of the Inclusive Framework.

[3] The MLI generally started to take effect with respect to agreements concluded by jurisdictions that ratified it before the end of September 2019.

[4] The MLI allows its signatories and parties to list the agreements they want to modify via the MLI. There could be reasons why a jurisdiction would not sign or list a specific agreement under the MLI (e.g. because a jurisdiction wishes to implement the minimum standard through detailed LOBs, because the treaty partners have agreed that an agreement is going to be renegotiated bilaterally, or because the agreement is too old and contains too much non-standard language to be easily modified by the MLI). Parties to those agreements, although not listed under the MLI, are still under the obligation to implement the minimum standard if both parties to the agreement are members of the Inclusive Framework, but it is expected that they would do so through bilateral renegotiations.

[5] Ninety-one of those jurisdictions are currently members of the Inclusive Framework.

[6] This way, should the other treaty partner sign the MLI and list that agreement to be covered under the MLI, it would become a covered tax agreement.

[7] Paragraph 14, OECD (2017), *BEPS Action 6 on Preventing the Granting of Treaty Benefits in Inappropriate Circumstances – Peer Review Documents*, OECD/G20 Base Erosion and Profit Shifting Project, OECD, Paris. www.oecd.org/tax/beps/beps-action-6-preventing-the-granting-of-treaty-benefits-in-inappropriate-circumstance-peer-review-documents.pdf.

1 Implementation issues, the minimum standard and the MLI

22. The minimum standard requires jurisdictions to do two things in their tax treaties: include an express statement on non-taxation (generally in the preamble); and adopt one of three methods of addressing treaty shopping. It does not specify how these two things should be achieved (e.g. through the MLI or bilaterally).[1]

23. The MLI has proven to be an effective way of implementing the minimum standard. However, a jurisdiction that prefers to implement the minimum standard through a detailed limitation on benefits provision cannot use the MLI to do so. Ninety-four jurisdictions have joined the MLI, 54 have ratified it, and the MLI would, once fully in effect, implement the minimum standard in about 1,700 bilateral agreements (thus modifying the majority of agreements concluded between members of the Inclusive Framework).

24. The efforts made by most members of the Inclusive Framework in tackling treaty shopping started to come to light in 2020 for those that ratified the MLI. The number of compliant agreements covered by the MLI has increased by nearly 500% since the last peer review.

25. Jurisdictions that have not signed or ratified the MLI have still generally made no or very little progress in implementing the minimum standard. This report acknowledges, though, that the starting point for a jurisdiction's exposure to treaty abuse may be different based on whether its existing agreements or domestic law already contain anti-treaty shopping tools.

26. Additional information is provided on jurisdictions' progress towards the implementation of the minimum standard in the jurisdictional sections in Chapter 5. As mentioned above, this information does not give rise to formal recommendations.

27. The information that can be found in the section "Implementation Issues" in some of the jurisdictional sections in Chapter 5 highlights the fact that:

- As the listed agreements under the MLI of jurisdictions that are members of the Inclusive Framework that are signatories to the MLI but that have not yet ratified it will only start to be compliant after their ratification of the MLI, those jurisdictions are encouraged to ratify the MLI as soon as possible (section 2.1 below);
- "Non-covered agreements" under the MLI (agreements concluded between pairs of signatories to the MLI where one treaty partner has not listed the agreement under the MLI; and agreements concluded between jurisdictions only one of which has signed the MLI)[2] will only be compliant if they are listed under the MLI or if their parties enter into bilateral renegotiations to implement the minimum standard (section 2.2 below); and
- The OECD Secretariat stands ready to discuss with any jurisdiction that is a member of the Inclusive Framework that has neither signed the MLI nor implemented anti-treaty-shopping measures in its agreements to see how support could be provided to bring those agreements into compliance with the minimum standard (section 2.3 below).

- Jurisdictions that are parties to the CARICOM Agreement are encouraged to bring that agreement up to date by commencing talks among all the treaty partners (see section 4 below).

Ratification of the MLI: the key to the effective implementation of the minimum standard

28. The MLI started to show its effect and to strengthen the bilateral tax treaty network of jurisdictions that ratified it in the course of 2020. The number of agreements that became compliant with the MLI increased from 60 to over 350. The peer review, however, reveals an important difference in the progress made on implementing the minimum standard by jurisdictions that have ratified the MLI compared with other jurisdictions.

29. In fact, on average, approximately 30% of the treaty networks of jurisdictions for which the MLI started to take effect as of 1 January 2020,[3] are compliant with the minimum standard in 2020, as shown in the table below.

Table 1.1. Treaty networks and ratification of the MLI

Jurisdiction	Date of MLI Ratification	Agreements in force	Compliant agreements on 1 July 2020	% of network compliant	% of network with IF members compliant
Australia	26 September 2018	45	18	40%	44%
Austria	22 September 2017	91	20	22%	26%
Belgium	27 June 2019	95	24	25%	31%
Canada	29 August 2019	94	24	26%	31%
Curaçao	29 March 2019	3	1	33%	33%
Denmark	30 September 2019	71	19	27%	32%
Finland	25 February 2019	73	25	34%	40%
France	26 September 2018	119	25	21%	28%
Georgia	29 March 2019	56	16	29%	33%
Guernsey	12 February 2019	13	6	46%	50%
Iceland	26 September 2019	41	19	46%	48%
India	25 June 2019	95	34	36%	43%
Ireland	29 January 2019	73	26	36%	39%
Isle of Man	25 October 2017	10	4	40%	40%
Israel	13 September 2018	58	25	43%	49%
Japan	26 September 2018	73	30	41%	48%
Jersey	15 December 2017	15	6	40%	46%
Lithuania	11 September 2018	57	25	44%	51%
Luxembourg	9 April 2019	83	32	39%	39%
Malta	18 December 2018	77	27	35%	38%
Monaco	10 January 2019	10	4	40%	44%
Netherlands	29 March 2019	92	25	27%	30%
New Zealand	27 June 2018	40	16	40%	42%
Norway	17 July 2019	84	15	18%	21%
Poland	23 January 2018	82	24	29%	36%
Russia4	18 June 2019	85	2	2%	3%
Serbia	5 June 2018	60	22	37%	42%
Singapore	21 December 2018	88	28	32%	38%
Slovak Republic	20 September 2018	70	23	33%	39%
Slovenia	22 March 2018	59	24	41%	47%
Sweden5	22 June 2018	81	2	2%	3%

Switzerland6	29 August 2019	106	4	4%	3%
Ukraine	8 August 2019	76	20	26%	33%
United Arab Emirates	29 May 2019	94	21	22%	29%
United Kingdom	29 June 2018	131	35	27%	32%

30. Albania, Barbados, Bosnia and Herzegovina, Burkina Faso Chile, Costa Rica, the Czech Republic, Germany, Egypt, Indonesia, Jordan, Kazakhstan, Korea, Latvia, Liechtenstein, Mauritius, Oman, Pakistan, Panama, Portugal, Qatar, San Marino, Saudi Arabia and Uruguay also ratified the MLI, but they did so between October 2019 and December 2020. As a result, the MLI had not yet started to take effect for their agreements in July 2020. This is because the MLI can only start to take effect for an agreement after a period of time that follows the latest of the dates on which the MLI enters into force for each of the treaty partners to an agreement. This period could roughly amount to a year from the latest ratification.[7]

31. While the jurisdictions that ratified the MLI made good progress in the implementation of the minimum standard, those that did not sign or ratify the MLI generally made no or very little progress in implementing the minimum standard. On average, their treaty networks are generally about 1.5% compliant.

32. The 2020 peer review thus shows the importance of swift ratification of the MLI. All signatories to the MLI that have not yet ratified it are therefore encouraged to do so.

33. The OECD Secretariat has liaised with the signatories of the MLI that, at the time of the drafting of this report, had not yet ratified it and notes that Bulgaria, Cameroon, Colombia, Croatia, Estonia, Greece, Hungary, Jamaica, Malaysia, Mexico, Morocco, North Macedonia, Romania, Senegal, South Africa, Spain and Turkey are aiming to deposit their instrument of ratification of the MLI by mid-2021.

Gaps in the coverage of the MLI

34. Throughout the 2020 peer review, gaps in the coverage of the MLI were identified. These gaps exist because the MLI is a flexible instrument that allows each signatory to decide which of its agreements it wishes to cover under the MLI. Thus, at the time of signature, signatories are required to deposit lists of agreements they want to modify. The MLI only modifies bilateral agreements listed by both treaty partners.

One-way agreements

35. The 2020 peer review reveals that about 200 bilateral agreements, concluded between pairs of signatories to the MLI that are members of the Inclusive Framework, would not be modified by the MLI because, at this stage, only one jurisdiction had listed the agreement under the MLI ("one-way agreements").[8]

36. In the course of the peer review, the OECD Secretariat liaised with some of the jurisdictions that are parties to those "one-way agreements" and asked why they had not been listed. In general, those agreements had not been listed under the MLI because their parties were planning renegotiations beyond the implementation of the BEPS treaty- related measures.

37. The jurisdictional sections identify those one-way agreements and recognise that, when no bilateral renegotiations are planned or envisaged for the implementation of the minimum standard, those agreements will not be compliant unless they are listed under the MLI or their parties enter into bilateral renegotiations to implement the minimum standard.

Waiting agreements

38. The 2020 peer review reveals that there are about 325 agreements concluded between pairs of jurisdictions that are members of the Inclusive Framework where only one of them has signed the MLI ("waiting agreements"). None of these agreements would, at this stage, be modified by the MLI because one treaty partner has not signed the MLI. Nearly all these agreements would become covered under the MLI if the treaty partner that has not yet signed the MLI would join it and would list the agreement.

39. The jurisdictional sections identify those "waiting agreements" and recognise that, when no bilateral renegotiations are planned or envisaged, those agreements will not be compliant unless they are listed under the MLI[9] or their parties enter into bilateral renegotiations to implement the minimum standard.

40. In the course of this peer review, the OECD Secretariat liaised with some of the jurisdictions that were working towards signature of the MLI. Those included Bahrain, Mongolia, Thailand and Viet Nam, which between them had over 125 waiting agreements that would become covered agreements under the MLI following their signatures.[10] Thus, the signature of the MLI by jurisdictions with large treaty networks would materially improve the coverage of the MLI.

Support to jurisdictions to strengthen their network of agreements

41. The 2020 peer review shows that jurisdictions that are members of the Inclusive Framework that did not sign the MLI or otherwise implement anti-treaty-shopping measures in their agreements have made no or very little progress in the implementation of the minimum standard.

42. Those jurisdictions are invited to contact the OECD Secretariat if they need support in planning the implementation of the minimum standard across their treaty networks, including, where relevant, towards the signature and ratification of the MLI.

Notes

[1] See the BEPS Action 6 Final Report (2015). The Action 6 Final Report further states that (i) a jurisdiction is required to implement the minimum standard in a treaty only if asked to do so by another member of the Inclusive Framework; (ii) the decision on which of the three methods to adopt has to be agreed (a solution cannot be imposed); and (iii) reflecting treaties' bilateral nature, there is no time limit within which a jurisdiction has to attain the minimum standard.

[2] The non-covered agreements identified in this report are agreements concluded between pairs of signatories to the MLI that are members of the Inclusive Framework and are not subject to bilateral negotiations where one treaty partner has not listed the agreement under the MLI; and agreements concluded between jurisdictions that are members of the Inclusive Framework where only one of the jurisdictions has signed the MLI.

[3] The MLI generally started to take effect as of 1 January 2020, with respect to agreements of jurisdictions that ratified it before the end of September 2019.

[4] The Russia Federation made a reservation under Article 35(7) of the MLI to delay the entry into effect of the MLI after completing its domestic procedures.

[5] Sweden made a reservation under Article 35(7) of the MLI to delay the entry into effect of the MLI after completing its domestic procedures.

[6] Switzerland made a reservation under Article 35(7) of the MLI to delay the entry into effect of the MLI after completing its domestic procedures.

[7] Article 35 of the MLI provides for the rules on its entry into effect and divides modifications into two categories based on the type of taxation to which they apply. In general, under Article 35(1)(a), with respect to taxes withheld at source on amounts paid or credited to non- residents, the MLI enters into effect on or after the first day of the next calendar year that begins on or after the latest of the dates on which the Convention enters into force for each of the Contracting Jurisdictions to a Covered Tax Agreement. As for all the other taxes levied by a jurisdiction, Article 35(1)(b) provides that the MLI generally enters into effect with respect to taxable periods beginning on or after the expiration of a period of six calendar months from the latest of the dates on which the Convention enters into force for each of the Contracting Jurisdictions to a Covered Tax Agreement.

[8] The MLI can only modify bilateral agreements that have been listed by both treaty partners under the MLI.

[9] This way, should the other treaty partner sign the MLI and list that agreement to be covered under the MLI, it would become a covered tax agreement.

[10] Bahrain has since signed the MLI on 27 November 2020, and listed 44 of its treaties under the MLI.

2 Aggregate data on the implementation of the minimum standard

43. The data collected on the implementation of the Action 6 minimum standard showed that, on 1 July 2020, 98 jurisdictions of the Inclusive Framework had some agreements that already complied with the minimum standard or that were subject to a complying instrument and would therefore become compliant shortly.[1] An additional seven jurisdictions had no comprehensive tax agreements in force subject to the peer review.[2] Thirty-seven jurisdictions had not implemented anti-abuse measures in their treaty network. As mentioned above, those jurisdictions are encouraged to liaise with the OECD Secretariat to discuss their plan for the implementation of the minimum standard.

44. In total, the 137 jurisdictions of the Inclusive Framework reported 2,295 agreements in force between members of the Inclusive Framework, and about 905 agreements between members of the Inclusive Framework and non-members.[3]

45. The agreements between members of the Inclusive Framework and non-members are not subject to the peer review and the aggregate results in this chapter focus on the 2,295 agreements entered into among members of the Inclusive Framework. The jurisdictional sections in Chapter 5 nevertheless indicate where agreements outside the peer review comply with the minimum standard or are subject to a complying instrument.[4]

Compliant agreements

46. On 1 July 2020, over 350 bilateral agreements between members of the Inclusive Framework complied with the minimum standard. An additional 20 agreements not subject to this review (i.e. agreements between members of the Inclusive Framework and non-members) also complied with the minimum standard.

47. In all compliant agreements, the preamble statement and the principal purpose test (PPT) were implemented to meet the minimum standard. Thirty-one of those agreements supplemented the PPT with a limitation on benefits (LOB) provision.

Agreements subject to a complying instrument that will be compliant

48. Many jurisdictions in the Inclusive Framework have agreements currently subject to a signed complying instrument that is not yet in force, but that would implement the minimum standard.

49. On 1 July 2020, over 1,300 bilateral agreements (of the 2 295 bilateral) between members of the Inclusive Framework were set to become covered tax agreements under the MLI (i.e. both Contracting Jurisdictions had listed the agreement under the MLI and, as a result, the MLI will modify the agreement

once in effect) and were thereby set to become compliant with the minimum standard.[5] These agreements, to be modified by the MLI, will comply with the minimum standard once its provisions take effect, following ratification by both Contracting Jurisdictions.[6]

50. A further 17 agreements are subject to a bilateral amending instrument that is not yet in force.[7] The number of agreements subject to a bilateral amending instrument, when compared with those that are subject to the MLI, shows the comparative effectiveness of the MLI in implementing the minimum standard.

51. For the agreements listed under the MLI, all members of the Inclusive Framework that are parties and signatories to the MLI are implementing the preamble statement and the PPT. Thirteen jurisdictions have also opted to apply the simplified LOB through the MLI to supplement the PPT when possible. Six additional jurisdictions agreed to accept a simplified LOB in agreements with partners that opted for it under the MLI.

Notes

[1] On 1 July 2020, 94 jurisdictions were signatories or parties to the MLI, but three of them (Cyprus, Fiji and Kuwait) are not members of the Inclusive Framework. As of 1 July 2020, 91 members of the Inclusive Framework were signatories or parties to the MLI. Seven additional members of the Inclusive Framework (Angola, Brazil, the Faroe Islands, Gibraltar, Greenland, Paraguay and Zambia), although not signatories or parties to the MLI, have concluded one or two amending protocols to implement the minimum standard.

[2] The Bahamas, the Cayman Islands, the Cook Islands, Djibouti, Haiti, Honduras and Turks and Caicos Islands have no agreements in force.

[3] In 2018, the Inclusive Framework reported 1 940 agreements entered into between members of the Inclusive Framework. The additional 205 agreements reviewed in 2019 include new agreements entered into between members of the Inclusive Framework between 30 June 2018, and 30 June 2019, and the relevant existing agreements of the 13 new members of the Inclusive Framework, which agreements were not subject to the 2018 Peer Review.

[4] A "complying instrument" could be the MLI or a suitable new amending protocol yet to enter into force. It could also be a completely new agreement that has not yet entered into force.

[5] On 1 July 2020, most signatories' MLI positions, including the list of notified tax agreements, were provisional and could be subject to future changes.

[6] Article 35 of the MLI governs its entry into effect. The provisions of the MLI take effect for covered tax agreements on different dates.

[7] Some agreements subject to a bilateral complying instrument were also listed under the MLI as the MLI allows jurisdictions to implement other (non-minimum standard) treaty-related BEPS measures.

3 Difficulties in implementing the minimum standard

52. The peer review also provides jurisdictions that encounter difficulties in reaching agreement with another jurisdiction to implement the Action 6 minimum standard with an opportunity to raise concerns in writing to the OECD Secretariat. This process, which is set out in paragraph 19 of the Peer Review Documents, was put in place to identify cases where a jurisdiction is facing a treaty partner that is a member of the Inclusive Framework that is unwilling to respect its commitment to implement the minimum standard.

53. In the course of the 2019 peer review, a jurisdiction raised a concern about the Agreement among the Member States of the Caribbean Community (CARICOM), a multilateral agreement concluded by eleven jurisdictions, ten of which are members of the Inclusive Framework. This concern remained this year as the parties to the CARICOM Agreement have not yet modernised it.

54. The CARICOM Agreement was concluded in 1994 to encourage regional trade and investment within the CARICOM, and contains several unusual features,[1] not found in the OECD Model Tax Convention or UN Model Double Taxation Convention, which could lead to certain income flows escaping tax altogether. These departures from standard tax treaty provisions may have encouraged greater economic integration within the CARICOM at the time, but they may also have made the Agreement more vulnerable to treaty shopping and other forms of abuse.

55. Previous attempts to renegotiate the CARICOM Agreement have proven to be difficult. Recent events (e.g. hurricanes in the region, the Covid-19 pandemic) have also made it difficult to launch discussions on the modernisation of the Agreement. The impetus of the Inclusive Framework and the commitment of its members to implement the BEPS minimum standards, could now provide an opportune time to modernise the Agreement.

56. The process through which a jurisdiction can report difficulties in getting agreement from another jurisdiction to amend an existing agreement in order to implement the minimum standard would also be examined as part of the ongoing review of the peer review methodology.

Notes

[1] The CARICOM Agreement provides for an almost exclusive source-based taxation of all income, gains and profits. Some income – for instance, dividends – are also entirely exempted from tax under the CARICOM Agreement.

4 Conclusion and next steps

57. The 2020 peer review shows that the MLI, which has been the main tool used to implement the minimum standard, has started to have a significant effect and is now strengthening the bilateral tax treaty network of jurisdictions that have ratified it.

58. This year's peer review, however, reveals that the Action 6 minimum standard is being implemented unevenly and, in particular, that there is an important difference in the progress made on its implementation between jurisdictions that have ratified the MLI and other jurisdictions that have not.

59. Importantly, the peer review shows that jurisdictions that have not signed or ratified the MLI have still generally made no or very little progress in implementing the minimum standard. The 2020 peer review thus highlights that ratification of the MLI is an effective tool for jurisdictions that want to implement the minimum standard through the PPT.

60. The 2020 peer review also identifies gaps in the coverage of the MLI and the agreements of signatories or parties to the MLI that are neither covered under the MLI nor subject to bilateral renegotiations. In total, over 500 agreements concluded between jurisdictions that are members of the Inclusive Framework will not at this stage be modified by the MLI as one partner has either not listed the agreement under the MLI or signed the MLI.

61. Finally, the 2020 peer review identifies jurisdictions that made no or very little progress in the implementation of the minimum standard to ensure those jurisdictions can be provided with support when needed. In general, those jurisdictions have not signed the MLI or implemented anti-treaty-shopping measures in their treaties.

62. The 2020 peer review and the implementation issues identified provide useful insights for the ongoing review of the peer review methodology.

Next steps for certain members of the Inclusive Framework

63. This year's peer review provides additional information on some jurisdictions' progress towards the implementation of the minimum standard. The information provided could help jurisdictions in identifying the immediate next steps to take towards the implementation of the minimum standard. Those could include ratifying the MLI for signatories that had not done so, closing gaps in the MLI coverage or establishing a negotiation plan for the implementation of the minimum standard.

Next steps for the Inclusive Framework

64. The implementation of the minimum standard will continue to be monitored and, as set out in the Peer Review Documents, the next peer review exercise will be launched in the first half of 2021.

65. As noted at paragraph 14 of the Peer Review Documents, the methodology for the review of the implementation of the minimum standard would be reviewed in light of the experience in conducting the first three peer reviews conducted in 2018, 2019 and 2020.

66. At the time this report was written, the review was being discussed by Working Party 1 and it is expected that the 2021 peer review will be conducted under a revised peer review methodology, which the Inclusive Framework will have an opportunity to approve in the first part of 2021.

Background on the Action 6 Minimum Standard and Peer Review

Context of the peer review

67. Over the last decades, bilateral tax agreements, concluded by nearly every jurisdiction in the world, have served to prevent harmful double taxation and remove obstacles to cross-border trade in goods and services, and movements of capital, technology and persons. This extensive network of tax agreements has, however, also given rise to so-called "treaty-shopping" arrangements.

68. As set out in the Action 6 Final Report, treaty shopping typically involves the attempt by a person to indirectly access the benefits of a tax agreement between two jurisdictions without being a resident of one of those jurisdictions.[1]

69. Treaty shopping is undesirable for several reasons, including:

- Treaty benefits negotiated between the parties to an agreement are economically extended to residents of a third jurisdiction in a way the parties did not intend. The principle of reciprocity is therefore breached and the balance of concessions that the parties make is altered;
- Income may escape taxation altogether or be subject to inadequate taxation in a way the parties did not intend; and
- The jurisdiction of residence of the ultimate income beneficiary has less incentive to enter into a tax agreement with the jurisdiction of source, because residents of the jurisdiction of residence can indirectly receive treaty benefits from the jurisdiction of source without the need for the jurisdiction of residence to provide reciprocal benefits.

Some previous attempts to tackle treaty shopping

70. Concerns about treaty shopping are not new. For example, in 1977, the concept of "beneficial owner" was introduced into the dividends, interest, and royalties articles of the OECD Model Tax Convention to clarify the meaning of the words "paid to", and deal with simple treaty-shopping situations where income is paid to an intermediary resident of a treaty country who is not treated as the owner of that income for tax purposes (such as an agent or nominee).[2]

71. In 1977, the Commentary on Article 1 of the OECD Model Tax Convention was also updated to include a section on the improper use of tax agreements.[3] In 1986, the Committee on Fiscal Affairs (CFA) published two reports: Double Taxation and the Use of Base Companies and Double Taxation and the Use of Conduit Companies. In 2002, the Committee published the report, Restricting the Entitlement to Treaty Benefits. The Commentary on Article 1 of the OECD Model Tax Convention was expanded on several occasions, notably in 2003, with the inclusion of sample provisions that countries could use to counter treaty shopping.

72. A review of jurisdictions' practices shows that they have tried to address treaty shopping in the past and have used different approaches to do so. Some have relied on specific anti-abuse rules based on the legal nature, ownership, and general activities of residents of a jurisdiction party to a tax agreement.[4] Others have favoured a general anti-abuse rule based on the purpose of transactions or arrangements.

BEPS and treaty shopping

73. The BEPS Action Plan, developed by the CFA and endorsed by the G20 Leaders in September 2013, identified 15 actions to address base erosion and profit shifting (BEPS). It identified treaty abuse, and in particular treaty shopping, as one of the most important sources of BEPS concerns.

74. Action 6 (Prevent Treaty Abuse) of the BEPS Action Plan called for the development of treaty provisions to prevent the granting of treaty benefits in inappropriate circumstances. In parallel, Action 15 of the BEPS Action Plan called for an analysis of the possible development of a multilateral instrument "to enable jurisdictions that wish to do so to implement measures developed in the course of the work on BEPS and amend bilateral tax treaties".

75. After two years of work, the CFA, in which OECD and G20 countries work on an equal footing, produced the final BEPS Package,[5] which was endorsed by the OECD Council and the G20 Leaders in November 2015.

76. Jurisdictions agreed that four of the BEPS measures would be minimum standards that participating jurisdictions would commit to implement. The Action 6 Report sets out one of these minimum standards. The Action 6 minimum standard requires jurisdictions to commit to include in their tax treaties provisions dealing with treaty shopping to ensure a minimum level of protection against treaty abuse.

The Action 6 minimum standard

77. The minimum standard on treaty shopping requires jurisdictions to include two components in their tax agreements: an express statement on non-taxation (generally in the preamble) and one of three methods of addressing treaty shopping.

78. The minimum standard does not provide how these two components should be implemented (i.e. through the MLI or amending instruments). It recognises, however, that these provisions need to be agreed bilaterally and that a jurisdiction will be required to implement the minimum standard when requested to do so by another member of the Inclusive Framework.

The express statement

79. As set out in paragraphs 22 and 23 of the Final Report on Action 6, jurisdictions have agreed to include in their tax agreements an express statement that their common intention is to eliminate double taxation without creating opportunities for non-taxation or reduced taxation through tax evasion or avoidance, including through treaty-shopping arrangements. The following provision now appears in the 2017 OECD Model Tax Convention: "Intending to conclude a Convention for the elimination of double taxation with respect to taxes on income and on capital without creating opportunities for non- taxation or reduced taxation through tax evasion or avoidance (including through treaty-shopping arrangements aimed at obtaining reliefs provided in this Convention for the indirect benefit of residents of third States)."

Three methods of addressing treaty shopping

80. Jurisdictions have also committed to implement that "common intention" through the inclusion of treaty provisions in one of the following three forms:

i. a principal purpose test (PPT) equivalent to paragraph 9 of Article 29 of the 2017 OECD Model Tax Convention, together with either a simplified or a detailed version of the limitation on benefits (LOB) rule that appears in paragraphs 1 to 7 of the 2017 OECD Model Tax Convention; or

ii. the PPT alone; or

iii. a detailed version of the LOB rule together with a mechanism (such as a treaty rule that might take the form of a PPT rule restricted to conduit arrangements, or domestic anti-abuse rules or judicial doctrines that would achieve a similar result) that would deal with conduit arrangements not already dealt with in tax treaties.

The obligation to implement the minimum standard

81. The Action 6 Report recognised that "some flexibility in the implementation of the Action 6 minimum standard [would be] required, as these provisions need to be adapted to each country's specificities and to the circumstances of the negotiation of bilateral conventions." In particular:

- a jurisdiction is required to implement the minimum standard in a treaty only if asked to do so by another member of the Inclusive Framework;
- its form (which of the three options used) has to be agreed (a solution cannot be imposed); and
- the commitment to adopt in bilateral treaties measures that implement the minimum standard should not be interpreted as a commitment to conclude new treaties or amend existing treaties within a specified period of time.

82. The Action 6 Report itself recognised that since participation in the multilateral instrument (see next section) was not mandatory and because jurisdictions could have different preferences about how the minimum standard should be met, monitoring its implementation would be necessary.

83. In May 2017, the Inclusive Framework agreed the Terms of Reference for the peer review and its methodology, and decided that the methodology would be reviewed in 2020.[6]

The 2018 peer review

84. The first peer review was conducted in 2018 and covered the 116 jurisdictions that were members of the Inclusive Framework on 30 June 2018. The Peer Review Report, which was adopted by the Inclusive Framework in January 2019, was published on 14 February 2019.

85. The 2018 peer review revealed that, as the provisions of the MLI had not taken effect at the time of the first peer review, nearly all of the agreements reviewed for this report did not at that time comply with the minimum standard. Substantial progress had, however, been made in 2017 and 2018 towards its implementation and a large majority of members of the Inclusive Framework had begun to translate their commitment on treaty shopping into actions and were in the process of modifying their treaty networks.

86. In total, on 30 June 2018, the peer review showed that 82 jurisdictions had some agreements that were already compliant with the minimum standard or were subject to a complying instrument that would bring their agreements into compliance.[7] The first peer review highlighted the effectiveness of the MLI in implementing the treaty-related BEPS measures. It was by far the preferred tool of members of the Inclusive Framework for implementing the minimum standard.

87. In the course of the first peer review, all concerns raised by jurisdictions on the implementation of the minimum standard in their agreements had been resolved when the 2018 report was approved by the Inclusive Framework and therefore no recommendation was made under the first peer review.

The 2019 peer review

88. The second peer review was conducted in 2019 and covered the 129 jurisdictions that were members of the Inclusive Framework on 30 June 2019. The peer review report, which was adopted by the Inclusive Framework in January 2020, was published on 24 March 2020.

89. The 2019 peer review revealed that, by 30 June 2019, 91 members of the Inclusive Framework had begun to update their bilateral treaty network and were implementing the minimum standard. The data compiled for this peer review demonstrated that the MLI had been the tool used by the vast majority of jurisdictions that had begun to implement the minimum standard.

90. By 30 June 2019, the MLI had already modified around 60 bilateral agreements. The MLI's impact was expected to increase quickly as jurisdictions ratified it.

91. In the course of the second peer review, a jurisdiction had raised a concern with respect to the CARICOM Agreement, a multilateral agreement concluded by eleven jurisdictions, ten of which were members of the Inclusive Framework. The CARICOM Agreement had been concluded in 1994 to encourage regional trade and investment within the CARICOM, and contains several unusual features,[8] not found in the OECD Model Tax Convention or UN Model Double Taxation Convention, which could lead to certain income flows escaping tax altogether. These departures from standard tax treaty provisions may have encouraged greater economic integration within the CARICOM at the time, but they may also have made the CARICOM Agreement more vulnerable to treaty shopping and other forms of abuse. Previous renegotiation attempts of the CARICOM Agreement had proven to be difficult.

Conduct of the 2020 peer review

92. The review started with a questionnaire sent to members of the Inclusive Framework in March 2020. The questionnaire was based on the 2018 Action 6 peer review questionnaire with a few modifications. In 2018, each jurisdiction was asked to list all of its comprehensive income tax agreements in force. Those lists indicated whether each agreement included the provisions of the minimum standard, i.e. a complying preamble and the necessary anti-abuse provision(s), whether it was subject to a "complying instrument" that would soon bring it into compliance, what that instrument was, and which of the three methods of meeting the minimum standard had been used.

93. In 2020, each jurisdiction was invited to update its 2019 questionnaire taking into consideration any new agreements that had entered into force by adding them to their list of agreements. Jurisdictions that joined the Inclusive Framework after 30 June 2019, were asked to complete the original questionnaire.

94. Each jurisdiction was also asked to answer additional questions on the ratification of complying instruments and issues described in Sections D and E of the Peer Review Documents on difficulties encountered in getting agreement from another jurisdiction to implement the minimum standard. Jurisdictions were also free to add any further comments. The list of the 137 jurisdictions that were subject to the peer review and full details by jurisdiction are contained in Chapter 5.

95. The Secretariat analysed jurisdictions' responses to verify and reconcile any divergent information and produced a first draft of this report.

Notes

[1] See paragraph 17 of the BEPS Action 6 Final Report (2015). As the Report also notes, cases where a resident of the Contracting State in which income originates seeks to obtain treaty benefits (e.g. through a transfer of residence to the other Contracting State or through the use of an entity established in that other State) could also be considered a form of treaty shopping.

[2] See paragraph 2 of Articles 10 and 11, and paragraph 1 of Article 12 of the OECD Model Tax Convention.

[3] See paragraphs 7-10 of the Commentary on Article 1 of the 1977 Model Tax Convention.

[4] "Limitation on benefits" provisions commonly found in treaties concluded by the United States are the best-known example.

[5] In October 2015, the CFA, including OECD and G20 countries working on an equal footing, produced the Final BEPS Package, in the form of reports on each of the 15 actions accompanied by an Explanatory Statement. The Final BEPS Package gives countries and economies the tools they need to ensure that profits are taxed where economic activities generating the profits are performed and where value is created, while at the same time giving businesses greater certainty by reducing disputes over the application of international tax rules and standardising compliance requirements.

[6] The review of the peer review methodology was being conducted at the time this report was written, in light of the experience in conducting the peer reviews.

[7] A further seven jurisdictions had no comprehensive tax agreements and were outside the scope of this exercise.

[8] The CARICOM Agreement provides for an almost exclusive source-based taxation of all income, gains and profits. Some income – for instance dividends – are also entirely exempted from tax under the CARICOM Agreement.

5 Data for each jurisdiction of the Inclusive Framework

Jurisdictional Sections

Explanation of the jurisdictional data

The jurisdictional sections provide specific information for each of the 137 jurisdictions in the Inclusive Framework subject to the Peer Review. The information is based on the lists of tax agreements provided by those jurisdictions.

Each jurisdictional section contains information on the progress made in the implementation of the minimum standard (A) and on implementation issues (B). It also includes a summary of the jurisdiction's response to the Peer Review questionnaire (i.e. the list of tax agreements provided). The summary of the jurisdiction's response is presented in the form of a table in which all its tax agreements in force are listed.

Although the tax agreements between Inclusive Framework members and non-members are not subject to the Peer Review, to recognise the progress made by some jurisdictions, and for the sake of completeness, information on these agreements is also reported.

This section includes a list of the 137 jurisdictions subject to the Peer Review.

Explanations of the data shown in the jurisdictional sections

A. Progress in the implementation of the minimum standard

The first subsection of each of the jurisdictional sections provides specific information on the progress made in the implementation of the minimum standard.

It presents information on:

- the tax agreements in force;
- the tax agreements compliant with the minimum standard;
- the tax agreements subject to a complying instrument; and
- the tax agreements not listed under the MLI.

The number of tax agreements:

- The jurisdictional sections indicate the number of tax agreements for each jurisdiction and include tax agreements with jurisdictions that are not members of the Inclusive Framework. Such agreements are indicated with an asterisk.

- For the purpose of the Peer Review, a tax agreement is a comprehensive agreement for the avoidance of double taxation with respect to taxes on income (whether or not other taxes are also covered) that is presently in force. It does not include other types of agreements such as inheritance tax treaties, tax information exchange agreements (TIEAs) or other administrative agreements, shipping and air transport agreements, nor does it include non-comprehensive agreements covering only individuals.
- The term "agreement" should also be interpreted to mean a treaty relationship. For example, if a state has split into two and each successor state is honouring an agreement concluded by the predecessor state, each successor state is treated as having a separate agreement. In this example, the number of bilateral treaty relationships therefore exceeds the number of signed agreements.

The tax agreements compliant with the minimum standard:

- The jurisdictional sections indicate the number of tax agreements that fully comply with the minimum standard for each jurisdiction. Partially compliant agreements, i.e. agreements that contain only one element of the minimum standard, are shown as non-compliant.
- Where a jurisdiction has concluded a new tax agreement or an amending protocol that complies with the minimum standard, it is shown as meeting the minimum standard only when the provisions implementing the minimum standard are in force.
- Where the minimum standard has been implemented through the MLI, *the relevant provisions of the MLI (Article 6 and Article 7) must have started to take effect as of 1 July 2020 for this agreement to meet the minimum standard (Article 35 of the MLI).*

The tax agreements subject to a complying instrument:

- The jurisdictional sections indicate the number of tax agreements that do not comply with the minimum standard but that are subject to a complying instrument.
- A "complying instrument" can be the MLI or an amending protocol that has not entered into force and that could bring the tax agreement into compliance with the minimum standard. It can also be a completely new agreement that complies with the minimum standard that has not yet entered into force.
- The complying instrument can only be the MLI if the agreement is notified as an agreement the jurisdiction wishes to cover under the MLI *irrespective of whether or not its treaty partner has notified the tax agreement.*
- MLI information shown for each jurisdiction is generally based on its latest publicly available positions, which will be the definitive position for those jurisdictions that have already deposited their instrument of ratification and provisional for those that have not yet done so.

The tax agreements not listed under the MLI:

When the jurisdiction has signed the MLI, the jurisdictional section indicates the number of tax agreements concluded with members of the Inclusive Framework that have not been notified as agreements the jurisdiction wishes to cover under the MLI and that are not otherwise compliant with the minimum standard. It also indicates whether the relevant treaty partners, if they have signed the MLI, have notified their agreement.

B. Implementation issues

When implementation issues have been identified with respect to a jurisdiction, the second subsection of the jurisdictional sections contains encouragements for the implementation of the minimum standard.

Four different types of targeted encouragement are inserted in the jurisdictional sections:

- Jurisdictions that are members of the Inclusive Framework that are signatories to the MLI and that have not yet ratified it are encouraged to do so as soon as possible, noting that their listed agreements under the MLI will start to be compliant after their ratification of the MLI;
- "Non-covered agreements" under the MLI (agreements concluded between pairs of signatories to the MLI where one treaty partner has not listed the agreement under the MLI; and agreements concluded between jurisdictions only one of which has signed the MLI)[1] will only be compliant if they are listed under the MLI or if their parties enter into bilateral renegotiations to implement the minimum standard;
- The OECD Secretariat stands ready to discuss with any jurisdiction that is a member of the Inclusive Framework that has neither signed the MLI nor implemented anti-treaty-shopping measures in its agreements to see how support could be provided to bring those agreements into compliance with the minimum standard; and,
- Jurisdictions that are parties to multilateral agreements not compliant with the minimum standard are encouraged to bring the agreement up to date by commencing talks among all the treaty partners, to the extent that no renegotiations are planned or envisaged for the implementation of the minimum standard.

Table 5.1. List of jurisdictions in the Inclusive Framework subject to the Peer Review

On 1 July 2020, the following jurisdictions were members of the Inclusive Framework

1.	Albania	51.	Georgia	101.	Papua New Guinea
2.	Andorra	52.	Germany	102.	Paraguay
3.	Angola	53.	Gibraltar	103.	Peru
4.	Anguilla	54.	Greece	104.	Poland
5.	Antigua and Barbuda	55.	Greenland	105.	Portugal
6.	Argentina	56.	Grenada	106.	Qatar
7.	Armenia	57.	Guernsey	107.	Romania
8.	Aruba	58.	Haiti	108.	Russian Federation
9.	Australia	59.	Honduras	109.	Saint Kitts and Nevis
10.	Austria	60.	Hong Kong, China	110.	Saint Lucia
11.	The Bahamas	61.	Hungary	111.	Saint Vincent and the Grenadines
12.	Bahrain	62.	Iceland	112.	San Marino
13.	Barbados	63.	India	113.	Saudi Arabia
14.	Belgium	64.	Indonesia	114.	Senegal
15.	Belize	65.	Ireland	115.	Serbia
16.	Benin	66.	Isle of Man	116.	Seychelles
17.	Bermuda	67.	Israel	117.	Sierra Leone
18.	Bosnia-Herzegovina	68.	Italy	118.	Singapore
19.	Botswana	69.	Jamaica	119.	Slovak Republic
20.	Brazil	70.	Japan	120.	Slovenia

[1] The non-covered agreements identified in this report are agreements concluded between pairs of signatories to the MLI that are members of the Inclusive Framework and are not subject to bilateral negotiations where one treaty partner has not listed the agreement under the MLI; and agreements concluded between jurisdictions that are members of the Inclusive Framework where only one of the jurisdictions has signed the MLI.

21.	British Virgin Islands	71.	Jersey	121.	South Africa
22.	Brunei Darussalam	72.	Jordan	122.	Spain
23.	Bulgaria	73.	Kazakhstan	123.	Sri Lanka
24.	Burkina Faso	74.	Kenya	124.	Sweden
25.	Cabo Verde	75.	Korea	125.	Switzerland
26.	Cameroon	76.	Latvia	126.	Thailand
27.	Canada	77.	Liberia	127.	Trinidad and Tobago
28.	Cayman Islands	78.	Liechtenstein	128.	Tunisia
29.	Chile	79.	Lithuania	129.	Turks and Caicos Islands
30.	China (People's Republic of)	80.	Luxembourg	130	Turkey
31.	Colombia	81.	Macau, China	131	Ukraine
32.	Congo	82.	Malaysia	132	United Arab Emirates
33.	Cook Islands	83.	Maldives	133	United Kingdom
34.	Costa Rica	84.	Malta	134	United States
35.	Côte d'Ivoire	85.	Mauritius	135	Uruguay
36.	Croatia	86.	Mexico	136	Viet Nam
37.	Curaçao	87.	Monaco	137	Zambia
38.	Czech Republic	88.	Mongolia		
39.	Democratic Republic of the Congo	89.	Montenegro		
40.	Denmark	90.	Montserrat		
41.	Djibouti	91.	Morocco		
42.	Dominica	92.	Namibia		
43.	Dominican Republic	93.	Netherlands		
44.	Egypt	94.	New Zealand		
45.	Estonia	95.	Nigeria		
46.	Eswatini	96.	North Macedonia		
47.	Faroe Islands	97.	Norway		
48.	Finland	98.	Oman		
49.	France	99.	Pakistan		
50.	Gabon	100.	Panama		

Albania

A. Progress in the implementation of the minimum standard

Albania has 42 tax agreements in force, as reported in its response to the Peer Review questionnaire.

Albania signed the MLI in 2019 and deposited its instrument of ratification on 22 September 2020. The MLI will enter into force for Albania on 1 January 2021. Albania has not listed its agreement with Saudi Arabia. This agreement will not, at this stage, be modified by the MLI. Saudi Arabia has listed its agreement with Albania under the MLI.

Albania is implementing the minimum standard in its tax agreements through the inclusion of the preamble statement and the PPT.[2]

The agreements that will be modified by the MLI will come into compliance with the minimum standard once the provisions of the MLI take effect.

B. Implementation issues

As mentioned above, Albania has not listed its agreement with Saudi Arabia under the MLI. Listing the agreement under the MLI or entering into bilateral renegotiations to implement the minimum standard would ensure that the minimum standard could be implemented in that non-covered agreement.

Summary of the jurisdiction response - Albania

	Treaty partners	Compliance with the standard	If compliant, the alternative implemented	Signature of a complying instrument	The alternative implemented through the complying instrument (if not the MLI)	Comments
1	Austria	No	N/A	Yes	N/A	
2	Belgium	No	N/A	Yes	N/A	
3	Bosnia-Herzegovina	No	N/A	Yes	N/A	
4	Bulgaria	No	N/A	Yes	N/A	
5	China (People's Republic of)	No	N/A	Yes	N/A	
6	Croatia	No	N/A	Yes	N/A	
7	Czech Republic	No	N/A	Yes	N/A	
8	Egypt	No	N/A	Yes	N/A	
9	Estonia	No	N/A	Yes	N/A	
10	France	No	N/A	Yes	N/A	
11	Germany	No	N/A	Yes	N/A	
12	Greece	No	N/A	Yes	N/A	
13	Hungary	No	N/A	Yes	N/A	
14	Iceland	No	N/A	Yes	N/A	
15	India	No	N/A	Yes	N/A	

[2] For its agreements listed under the MLI, Armenia is implementing the preamble statement (Article 6 of the MLI) and the PPT (Article 7 of the MLI).

16	Ireland	No	N/A	Yes	N/A	
17	Italy	No	N/A	Yes	N/A	
18	Korea	No	N/A	Yes	N/A	
19	Kosovo*	No	N/A	Yes	N/A	
20	Kuwait*	No	N/A	Yes	N/A	
21	Latvia	No	N/A	Yes	N/A	
22	Malaysia	No	N/A	Yes	N/A	
23	Malta	No	N/A	Yes	N/A	
24	Moldova*	No	N/A	Yes	N/A	
25	Montenegro	No	N/A	Yes	N/A	
26	Netherlands	No	N/A	Yes	N/A	
27	North Macedonia	No	N/A	Yes	N/A	
28	Norway	No	N/A	Yes	N/A	
29	Poland	No	N/A	Yes	N/A	
30	Qatar	No	N/A	Yes	N/A	
31	Romania	No	N/A	Yes	N/A	
32	Russia	No	N/A	Yes	N/A	
33	Saudi Arabia	No	N/A	No	N/A	
34	Serbia	No	N/A	Yes	N/A	
35	Singapore	No	N/A	Yes	N/A	
36	Slovenia	No	N/A	Yes	N/A	
37	Spain	No	N/A	Yes	N/A	
38	Sweden	No	N/A	Yes	N/A	
39	Switzerland	No	N/A	Yes	N/A	
40	Turkey	No	N/A	Yes	N/A	
41	United Arab Emirates	No	N/A	Yes	N/A	
42	United Kingdom	No	N/A	Yes	N/A	

Andorra

A. Progress in the implementation of the minimum standard

Andorra has eight tax agreements in force, as reported in its response to the Peer Review questionnaire. One of those agreements, the agreement with Cyprus*, complies with the minimum standard.

Andorra signed the MLI in 2017, listing its non-compliant agreements.

Andorra is implementing the minimum standard in its tax agreements through the inclusion of the preamble statement and the PPT.[3]

The agreements that will be modified by the MLI will come into compliance with the minimum standard once the provisions of the MLI take effect.

B. Implementation issues

Andorra's listed agreements under the MLI will start to be compliant after Andorra's ratification of the MLI. Andorra is encouraged to ratify the MLI as soon as possible.

Summary of the jurisdiction response - Andorra

	Treaty partners	Compliance with the standard	If compliant, the alternative implemented	Signature of a complying instrument	The alternative implemented through the complying instrument (if not the MLI)	Comments
1	Cyprus*	Yes	PPT alone	N/A	N/A	
2	France	No	N/A	Yes	N/A	
3	Liechtenstein	No	N/A	Yes	N/A	
4	Luxembourg	No	N/A	Yes	N/A	
5	Malta	No	N/A	Yes	N/A	
6	Portugal	No	N/A	Yes	N/A	
7	Spain	No	N/A	Yes	N/A	
8	United Arab Emirates	No	N/A	Yes	N/A	

[3] For all of its agreements listed under the MLI, Andorra is implementing the preamble statement (Article 6 of the MLI). For five of its agreements listed under the MLI, Andorra is implementing the PPT (Article 7 of the MLI). Andorra made a reservation pursuant to Article 7(15)(b) of the MLI not to apply Article 7(1) of the MLI with respect to agreements which already contain a PPT. Two of Andorra's agreements are within the scope of this reservation.

Angola

A. Progress in the implementation of the minimum standard

Angola has two tax agreement in force with Portugal and the United Arab Emirates, as reported in its response to the Peer Review questionnaire. Its agreements comply with the minimum standard.

Angola is implementing the minimum standard through the inclusion of the preamble statement and the PPT.

B. Implementation issues

No jurisdiction has raised any concerns about Angola.

Summary of the jurisdiction response - Angola

	Treaty partners	Compliance with the standard	If compliant, the alternative implemented	Signature of a complying instrument	The alternative implemented through the complying instrument (if not the MLI)	Comments
1	Portugal	Yes	PPT alone	N/A	N/A	
2	United Arab Emirates	Yes	PPT alone	N/A	N/A	

Anguilla

A. Progress in the implementation of the minimum standard

Anguilla has one tax agreement in force with Switzerland, as reported in its response to the Peer Review questionnaire.

Anguilla's agreement does not comply with the minimum standard and is not subject to a complying instrument.

Anguilla has not joined the MLI.

B. Implementation issues

As Anguilla has not joined the MLI or implemented anti-treaty-shopping measures in its agreement, the Secretariat will offer its support to design a plan for the implementation of the minimum standard to strengthen its treaty network.

Summary of the jurisdiction response - Anguilla

	Treaty partners	Compliance with the standard	If compliant, the alternative implemented	Signature of a complying instrument	The alternative implemented through the complying instrument (if not the MLI)	Comments
1	Switzerland	No	N/A	No	N/A	

Antigua and Barbuda

A. Progress in the implementation of the minimum standard

Antigua and Barbuda has three tax agreements in force, as reported in its response to the Peer Review questionnaire, including the multilateral agreement among the members of the CARICOM concluded with ten treaty partners (the CARICOM Agreement).[4]

None of Antigua and Barbuda's agreements comply with the minimum standard or are subject to a complying instrument.

Antigua and Barbuda has not signed the MLI.

B. Implementation issues

As Antigua and Barbuda has not signed the MLI or implemented anti-treaty-shopping measures in its agreements, the Secretariat will offer its support to design a plan for the implementation of the minimum standard to strengthen its network of agreements.

Antigua and Barbuda is encouraged to bring the CARICOM Agreement up to date by commencing talks among all the treaty partners.[5]

Summary of the jurisdiction response – Antigua and Barbuda

	Treaty partners	Compliance with the standard	If compliant, the alternative implemented	Signature of a complying instrument	The alternative implemented through the complying instrument (if not the MLI)	Comments
1	Barbados	No	N/A	No	N/A	CARICOM
2	Belize	No	N/A	No	N/A	CARICOM
3	Dominica	No	N/A	No	N/A	CARICOM
4	Grenada	No	N/A	No	N/A	CARICOM
5	Guyana*	No	N/A	No	N/A	CARICOM
6	Jamaica	No	N/A	No	N/A	CARICOM
7	Saint Kitts and Nevis	No	N/A	No	N/A	CARICOM
8	Saint Lucia	No	N/A	No	N/A	CARICOM
9	Saint Vincent and the Grenadines	No	N/A	No	N/A	CARICOM
10	Switzerland	No	N/A	No	N/A	
11	Trinidad and Tobago	No	N/A	No	N/A	CARICOM
12	United Kingdom	No	N/A	No	N/A	

[4] In total, Antigua and Barbuda identified twelve "agreements" in its List of Tax agreements: two bilateral agreements and the CARICOM Agreement concluded with ten of its treaty partners.

[5] Revisions to the CARICOM Agreement require an agreement from its eleven treaty partners.

Argentina

A. Progress in the implementation of the minimum standard

Argentina has 20 tax agreements in force, as reported in its response to the Peer Review questionnaire. Three of those agreements, the agreements with Brazil, Chile and Mexico, comply with the minimum standard.

Argentina signed the MLI in 2017 and has not listed its agreement with Germany. It indicated in its response to the Peer Review questionnaire that bilateral negotiations would be pursued to bring this agreement into compliance with the minimum standard.

Argentina is implementing the minimum standard through the inclusion of the preamble statement and the PPT combined with the LOB.[6]

The agreements that will be modified by the MLI will come into compliance with the minimum standard once the provisions of the MLI take effect.

B. Implementation issues

Argentina's listed agreements under the MLI will start to be compliant after Argentina's ratification of the MLI. Argentina is encouraged to ratify the MLI as soon as possible.

Summary of the jurisdiction response - Argentina

	Treaty partners	Compliance with the standard	If compliant, the alternative implemented	Signature of a complying instrument	The alternative implemented through the complying instrument (if not the MLI)	Comments
1	Australia	No	N/A	Yes	N/A	
2	Belgium	No	N/A	Yes	N/A	
3	Bolivia*	No	N/A	No	N/A	
4	Brazil	Yes	PPT and LOB	N/A	N/A	
5	Canada	No	N/A	Yes	N/A	
6	Chile	Yes	PPT and LOB	N/A	N/A	
7	Denmark	No	N/A	Yes	N/A	
8	Finland	No	N/A	Yes	N/A	
9	France	No	N/A	Yes	N/A	
10	Germany	No	N/A	No	N/A	
11	Italy	No	N/A	Yes	N/A	
12	Mexico	Yes	PPT and LOB	N/A	N/A	
13	Netherlands	No	N/A	Yes	N/A	
14	Norway	No	N/A	Yes	N/A	
15	Russia	No	N/A	Yes	N/A	
16	Spain	No	N/A	Yes	N/A	

[6] For 15 of its agreements listed under the MLI, Argentina is implementing the preamble statement (Article 6 of the MLI) and the PPT (Article 7 of the MLI). Two of Argentina's agreements, the agreements with Chile and Mexico, are within the scope of reservations made by Argentina pursuant to Article 6(4) and Article 7(15)(b) of the MLI. Argentina also opted for the simplified LOB under Article 7(6) of the MLI.

17	Sweden	No	N/A	Yes	N/A	
18	Switzerland	No	N/A	Yes	N/A	
19	United Arab Emirates	No	N/A	Yes	N/A	
20	United Kingdom	No	N/A	Yes	N/A	

Armenia

A. Progress in the implementation of the minimum standard

Armenia has 48 tax agreements in force, as reported in its response to the Peer Review questionnaire.

Armenia signed the MLI in 2017 and has not listed its agreements with Denmark and Israel. These agreements will therefore not, at this stage, be modified by the MLI. Denmark indicated in its response to the Peer Review questionnaire that it will add its agreement with Armenia under the MLI. Israel has listed its agreement with Armenia under the MLI.

Armenia is implementing the minimum standard through the inclusion of the preamble statement and the PPT combined with the LOB.[7]

The agreements that will be modified by the MLI will come into compliance with the minimum standard once the provisions of the MLI take effect.

B. Implementation issues

Armenia's listed agreements under the MLI will start to be compliant after Armenia's ratification of the MLI. Armenia is encouraged to ratify the MLI as soon as possible.

As mentioned above, Armenia has not listed its agreements with Denmark and Israel under the MLI. Listing the agreements under the MLI or entering into bilateral renegotiations to implement the minimum standard would ensure that the minimum standard could be implemented in those non-covered agreements.

Summary of the jurisdiction response - Armenia

	Treaty partners	Compliance with the standard	If compliant, the alternative implemented	Signature of a complying instrument	The alternative implemented through the complying instrument (if not the MLI)	Comments
1	Austria	No	N/A	Yes	N/A	
2	Belarus*	No	N/A	Yes	N/A	
3	Belgium	No	N/A	Yes	N/A	
4	Bulgaria	No	N/A	Yes	N/A	
5	Canada	No	N/A	Yes	N/A	
6	China (People's Republic of)	No	N/A	Yes	N/A	
7	Croatia	No	N/A	Yes	N/A	
8	Cyprus*	No	N/A	Yes	N/A	
9	Czech Republic	No	N/A	Yes	N/A	
10	Denmark	No	N/A	No	N/A	
11	Estonia	No	N/A	Yes	N/A	
12	Finland	No	N/A	Yes	N/A	
13	France	No	N/A	Yes	N/A	
14	Georgia	No	N/A	Yes	N/A	
15	Germany	No	N/A	Yes	N/A	

[7] For its agreements listed under the MLI, Armenia is implementing the preamble statement (Article 6 of the MLI) and the PPT (Article 7 of the MLI). Armenia also opted for the simplified LOB under Article 7(6) of the MLI.

16	Greece	No	N/A	Yes	N/A	
17	Hungary	No	N/A	Yes	N/A	
18	India	No	N/A	Yes	N/A	
19	Indonesia	No	N/A	Yes	N/A	
20	Iran*	No	N/A	Yes	N/A	
21	Ireland	No	N/A	Yes	N/A	
22	Israel	No	N/A	No	N/A	
23	Italy	No	N/A	Yes	N/A	
24	Kazakhstan	No	N/A	Yes	N/A	
25	Kuwait*	No	N/A	Yes	N/A	
26	Latvia	No	N/A	Yes	N/A	
27	Lebanon*	No	N/A	Yes	N/A	
28	Lithuania	No	N/A	Yes	N/A	
29	Luxembourg	No	N/A	Yes	N/A	
30	Moldova*	No	N/A	Yes	N/A	
31	Netherlands	No	N/A	Yes	N/A	
32	Poland	No	N/A	Yes	N/A	
33	Qatar	No	N/A	Yes	N/A	
34	Romania	No	N/A	Yes	N/A	
35	Russia	No	N/A	Yes	N/A	
36	Serbia	No	N/A	Yes	N/A	
37	Slovak Republic	No	N/A	Yes	N/A	
38	Slovenia	No	N/A	Yes	N/A	
39	Spain	No	N/A	Yes	N/A	
40	Sweden	No	N/A	Yes	N/A	
41	Switzerland	No	N/A	Yes	N/A	
42	Syrian Arab Republic*	No	N/A	Yes	N/A	
43	Tajikistan*	No	N/A	Yes	N/A	
44	Thailand	No	N/A	Yes	N/A	
45	Turkmenistan*	No	N/A	Yes	N/A	
46	Ukraine	No	N/A	Yes	N/A	
47	United Arab Emirates	No	N/A	Yes	N/A	
48	United Kingdom	No	N/A	Yes	N/A	

Aruba

A. Progress in the implementation of the minimum standard

Aruba has one tax agreement in force, as reported in its response to the Peer Review questionnaire.

Aruba's agreement does not comply with the minimum standard and is not subject to a complying instrument.

Aruba has not joined the MLI.

Aruba's agreement with the Netherlands is an arrangement governed by the domestic law of the Kingdom of the Netherlands.

B. Implementation issues

As Aruba has not joined the MLI or implemented anti-treaty-shopping measures in its agreements, the Secretariat will offer its support to design a plan for the implementation of the minimum standard to strengthen its network of agreements.

Summary of the jurisdiction response - Aruba

	Treaty partners	Compliance with the standard	If compliant, the alternative implemented	Signature of a complying instrument	The alternative implemented through the complying instrument (if not the MLI)	Comments
1	Netherlands	No	N/A	No	N/A	A new treaty is under negotiation

Australia

A. Progress in the implementation of the minimum standard

Australia has 45 tax agreements in force, as reported in its response to the Peer Review questionnaire. 18 of those agreements, the agreements with Belgium, Canada, Denmark, Finland, France, Germany, India, Ireland, Israel, Japan, Malta, the Netherlands, New Zealand, Norway, Poland, Singapore, the Slovak Republic and the United Kingdom, comply with the minimum standard.

Australia signed the MLI in 2017 and deposited its instrument of ratification on 26 September 2018.[8] The MLI entered into force for Australia on 1 January 2019.

Australia is implementing the minimum standard through the inclusion of the preamble statement and the PPT.[9]

The agreements modified by the MLI come into compliance with the minimum standard once the provisions of the MLI take effect.

B. Implementation issues

No jurisdiction has raised any concerns about their agreements with Australia.

Summary of the jurisdiction response - Australia

	Treaty partners	Compliance with the standard	If compliant, the alternative implemented	Signature of a complying instrument	The alternative implemented through the complying instrument (if not the MLI)	Comments
1	Argentina	No	N/A	Yes	N/A	
2	Austria	No	N/A	Yes	N/A	Austria has not listed this agreement as a CTA.
3	Belgium	Yes	PPT alone	N/A	N/A	MLI entered into force on 1/10/2019.
4	Canada	Yes	PPT alone	N/A	N/A	MLI entered into force on 1/12/2019.
5	Chile	No	N/A	Yes	N/A	
6	China (People's Republic of)	No	N/A	Yes	N/A	
7	Chinese Taipei*	No	N/A	No	N/A	
8	Czech Republic	No	N/A	Yes	N/A	MLI will enter into force on 1/9/2020.
9	Denmark	Yes	PPT alone	N/A	N/A	MLI entered into force on 1/1/2020.
10	Fiji*	No	N/A	Yes	N/A	
11	Finland	Yes	PPT alone	N/A	N/A	MLI entered into force on 1/6/2019.
12	France	Yes	PPT alone	N/A	N/A	MLI entered into force on 1/1/2019.
13	Germany	Yes	PPT alone	N/A	N/A	Amending protocol entered into force

[8] The agreement with Germany, already compliant with the minimum standard, has not been listed under the MLI. A new agreement with Israel entered into force in December 2019 and also complies with the minimum standard.

[9] For its agreements listed under the MLI, Australia is implementing the preamble statement (Article 6 of the MLI) and the PPT (Article 7 of the MLI).

						on 7/12/2016.
14	Hungary	No	N/A	Yes	N/A	
15	India	Yes	PPT alone	N/A	N/A	MLI entered into force on 1/10/2019.
16	Indonesia	No	N/A	Yes	N/A	MLI will enter into force on 1/8/2020.
17	Ireland	Yes	PPT alone	N/A	N/A	MLI entered into force on 1/5/2019.
18	Israel	Yes	PPT alone	N/A	N/A	New treaty entered into force on 6/12/2019.
19	Italy	No	N/A	Yes	N/A	
20	Japan	Yes	PPT and LOB	N/A	N/A	MLI entered into force on 1/1/2019.
21	Kiribati*	No	N/A	Yes	N/A	
22	Korea	No	N/A	Yes	N/A	MLI will enter into force on 1/9/2020.
23	Malaysia	No	N/A	Yes	N/A	
24	Malta	Yes	PPT alone	N/A	N/A	MLI entered into force on 1/4/2019.
25	Mexico	No	N/A	Yes	N/A	
26	Netherlands	Yes	PPT alone	N/A	N/A	MLI entered into force on 1/7/2019.
27	New Zealand	Yes	PPT alone	N/A	N/A	MLI entered into force on 1/1/2019.
28	Norway	Yes	PPT alone	N/A	N/A	MLI entered into force on 1/11/2019.
29	Papua New Guinea	No	N/A	Yes	N/A	
30	Philippines*	No	N/A	Yes	N/A	
31	Poland	Yes	PPT alone	N/A	N/A	MLI entered into force on 1/1/2019.
32	Romania	No	N/A	Yes	N/A	
33	Russia	No	N/A	Yes	N/A	MLI entered into force on 1/10/2019.
34	Singapore	Yes	PPT alone	N/A	N/A	MLI entered into force on 1/4/2019.
35	Slovak Republic	Yes	PPT alone	N/A	N/A	MLI entered into force on 1/1/2019.
36	South Africa	No	N/A	Yes	N/A	
37	Spain	No	N/A	Yes	N/A	
38	Sri Lanka	No	N/A	Yes	N/A	
39	Sweden	No	N/A	Yes	N/A	Sweden has not listed this agreement as a CTA.
40	Switzerland	No	N/A	Yes	N/A	Switzerland has not listed this agreement as a CTA.
41	Thailand	No	N/A	Yes	N/A	
42	Turkey	No	N/A	Yes	N/A	
43	United Kingdom	Yes	PPT alone	N/A	N/A	MLI entered into force on 1/1/2019.
44	United States	No	N/A	Yes	N/A	
45	Viet Nam	No	N/A	Yes	N/A	

Austria

A. Progress in the implementation of the minimum standard

Austria has 91 tax agreements in force, as reported in its response to the Peer Review questionnaire. 20 of those agreements,[10] the agreements with Belgium, Canada, Finland, France, India,[11] Ireland, Israel, Japan, Kosovo*, Liechtenstein, Lithuania, Luxembourg,[12] Malta, the Netherlands, Poland, Serbia, Singapore, the Slovak Republic, Slovenia and the United Kingdom, comply with the minimum standard.

Austria signed the MLI in 2017 and deposited its instrument of ratification on 22 September 2017. The MLI entered into force for Austria on 1 July 2018. Austria has not listed its agreements with Albania, Armenia, Australia, Bahrain, Barbados, Belize, Bosnia-Herzegovina, Brazil, Denmark, Egypt, Georgia, Iceland, Indonesia, Kazakhstan, Korea, Malaysia, Mongolia, Montenegro, Morocco, New Zealand, North Macedonia, Norway, Qatar, San Marino, Saudi Arabia, Sweden, Thailand, Tunisia, Ukraine, the United Arab Emirates, and Viet Nam. These agreements will therefore not, at this stage, be modified by the MLI. Albania, Armenia, Australia, Barbados, Belize, Bosnia-Herzegovina, Denmark, Egypt, Kazakhstan, Malaysia, Morocco, New Zealand, North Macedonia, San Marino, Saudi Arabia, Tunisia, Ukraine and the United Arab Emirates have listed their agreements with Austria under the MLI.

Austria has also signed bilateral complying instruments with respect to its agreements with Korea and Ukraine. The complying instrument with respect to its agreement with Ukraine has been ratified and the complying instrument with respect to its agreement with Korea is pending ratification.

Austria further indicated that bilateral negotiations would be pursued with respect to its agreements with Australia, Bahrain, Brazil, Egypt, Indonesia, New Zealand, Norway, Qatar and the United Arab Emirates.

Austria is implementing the minimum standard through the inclusion of the preamble statement and the PPT.[13]

The agreements modified by the MLI come into compliance with the minimum standard once the provisions of the MLI take effect.[14]

---

[10] Since Russia made use of Art 35 (7) MLI and has only recently confirmed completion of the necessary procedures, the MLI only enters into effect for the treaty between Austria and Russia for the taxable period 2021.Moreover, Switzerland also made use of Art 35 (7) MLI and has not yet notified the MLI's entry into effect for Austria. Switzerland has informed Austria that Switzerland can only notify the completion of internal procedures with respect to a jurisdiction if Switzerland have reached agreement with that jurisdiction that the MLI applies to a tax treaty in the same way as a new protocol to the treaty and have also reached agreement on the exact wording of the changes made by the MLI to the treaty text, including the addition of new articles and paragraphs to the treaty (for instance in the case of the PPT). Since this is not in line with Austria's current understanding of the legal effects of the MLI, Austria is currently in the process of determining the best way forward. It is therefore not to be expected that the MLI will enter into effect between Switzerland and Austria before 30 June 2020.

[11] The MLI only enters into effect for other taxes levied by Austria in 2021, however, it is in force for Austrian withholding taxes beginning in 2020 and it is in force for all taxes levied by India beginning in 2020.

[12] The MLI only enters into effect for other taxes levied by Austria in 2021, however, it is in force for Austrian withholding taxes beginning in 2020 and it is in force for all taxes levied by Luxembourg beginning in 2020.

[13] For its agreements listed under the MLI, Austria is implementing the preamble statement (Article 6 of the MLI) and the PPT (Article 7 of the MLI).

[14] Austria made a reservation under Article 35(3) of the MLI (Entry into Effect).

B. Implementation issues

As mentioned above, Austria has not listed its agreements with Albania, Armenia, Barbados, Belize, Bosnia-Herzegovina, Denmark, Georgia, Iceland, Kazakhstan, Malaysia, Mongolia, Montenegro, Morocco, North Macedonia, Norway, San Marino, Saudi Arabia, Sweden, Thailand, Tunisia and Viet Nam under the MLI. Listing the agreements under the MLI or entering into bilateral renegotiations to implement the minimum standard would ensure that the minimum standard could be implemented in those non-covered agreements.

Summary of the jurisdiction response - Austria

	Treaty partners	Compliance with the standard	If compliant, the alternative implemented	Signature of a complying instrument	The alternative implemented through the complying instrument (if not the MLI)	Comments
1	Albania	No	N/A	No	N/A	
2	Algeria*	No	N/A	No	N/A	
3	Armenia	No	N/A	No	N/A	
4	Australia	No	N/A	No	N/A	
5	Azerbaijan*	No	N/A	No	N/A	
6	Bahrain	No	N/A	No	N/A	
7	Barbados	No	N/A	No	N/A	
8	Belarus*	No	N/A	No	N/A	
9	Belgium	Yes	PPT alone	N/A	N/A	
10	Belize	No	N/A	No	N/A	
11	Bosnia-Herzegovina	No	N/A	No	N/A	
12	Brazil	No	N/A	No	N/A	
13	Bulgaria	No	N/A	Yes	N/A	
14	Canada	Yes	PPT alone	N/A	N/A	
15	Chile	No	N/A	Yes	N/A	
16	China (People's Republic of)	No	N/A	Yes	N/A	
17	Chinese Taipei*	No	N/A	No	N/A	
18	Croatia	No	N/A	Yes	N/A	
19	Cuba*	No	N/A	No	N/A	
20	Cyprus*	No	N/A	Yes	N/A	
21	Czech Republic	No	N/A	Yes	N/A	
22	Denmark	No	N/A	No	N/A	
23	Egypt	No	N/A	No	N/A	
24	Estonia	No	N/A	Yes	N/A	
25	Finland	Yes	PPT alone	N/A	N/A	
26	France	Yes	PPT alone	N/A	N/A	
27	Georgia	No	N/A	No	N/A	
28	Germany	No	N/A	Yes	N/A	
29	Greece	No	N/A	Yes	N/A	
30	Hong Kong (China)	No	N/A	Yes	N/A	
31	Hungary	No	N/A	Yes	N/A	
32	Iceland	No	N/A	No	N/A	
33	India	Yes	PPT alone	N/A	N/A	
34	Indonesia	No	N/A	No	N/A	
35	Iran*	No	N/A	No	N/A	
36	Ireland	Yes	PPT alone	N/A	N/A	
37	Israel	Yes	PPT alone	N/A	N/A	
38	Italy	No	N/A	Yes	N/A	

39	Japan	Yes	PPT and LOB	N/A	N/A	
40	Kazakhstan	No	N/A	No	N/A	
41	Korea	No	N/A	Yes	PPT alone	
42	Kosovo*	Yes	PPT alone	N/A	N/A	
43	Kuwait*	No	N/A	No	N/A	
44	Kyrgyzstan*	No	N/A	No	N/A	
45	Latvia	No	N/A	Yes	N/A	
46	Libya*	No	N/A	No	N/A	
47	Liechtenstein	Yes	PPT alone	N/A	N/A	
48	Lithuania	Yes	PPT alone	N/A	N/A	
49	Luxembourg	Yes	PPT alone	N/A	N/A	
50	Malaysia	No	N/A	No	N/A	
51	Malta	Yes	PPT alone	N/A	N/A	
52	Mexico	No	N/A	Yes	N/A	
53	Moldova*	No	N/A	No	N/A	
54	Mongolia	No	N/A	No	N/A	
55	Montenegro	No	N/A	No	N/A	
56	Morocco	No	N/A	No	N/A	
57	Nepal*	No	N/A	No	N/A	
58	Netherlands	Yes	PPT alone	N/A	N/A	
59	New Zealand	No	N/A	No	N/A	
60	North Macedonia	No	N/A	No	N/A	
61	Norway	No	N/A	No	N/A	
62	Pakistan	No	N/A	Yes	N/A	
63	Philippines*	No	N/A	No	N/A	
64	Poland	Yes	PPT alone	N/A	N/A	
65	Portugal	No	N/A	Yes	N/A	
66	Qatar	No	N/A	No	N/A	
67	Romania	No	N/A	Yes	N/A	
68	Russia	No	N/A	Yes	N/A	
69	San Marino	No	N/A	No	N/A	
70	Saudi Arabia	No	N/A	No	N/A	
71	Serbia	Yes	PPT alone	N/A	N/A	
72	Singapore	Yes	PPT alone	N/A	N/A	
73	Slovak Republic	Yes	PPT alone	N/A	N/A	
74	Slovenia	Yes	PPT alone	N/A	N/A	
75	South Africa	No	N/A	Yes	N/A	
76	Spain	No	N/A	Yes	N/A	
77	Sweden	No	N/A	No	N/A	
78	Switzerland	No	N/A	Yes	N/A	
79	Syrian Arab Republic*	No	N/A	No	N/A	
80	Tajikistan*	No	N/A	No	N/A	
81	Thailand	No	N/A	No	N/A	
82	Tunisia	No	N/A	No	N/A	
83	Turkey	No	N/A	Yes	N/A	
84	Turkmenistan*	No	N/A	No	N/A	
85	Ukraine	No	N/A	Yes	PPT alone	
86	United Arab Emirates	No	N/A	No	N/A	
87	United Kingdom	Yes	PPT alone	N/A	N/A	
88	United States	No	N/A	No	N/A	
89	Uzbekistan*	No	N/A	No	N/A	
90	Venezuela*	No	N/A	No	N/A	
91	Viet Nam	No	N/A	No	N/A	

The Bahamas

A. Progress in the implementation of the minimum standard

The Bahamas has no tax agreements, as reported in its response to the Peer Review questionnaire.

B. Implementation issues

No jurisdiction has raised any concerns about the Bahamas.

Bahrain

A. Progress in the implementation of the minimum standard

Bahrain has 44 tax agreements in force, as reported in its response to the Peer Review questionnaire.

Bahrain signed the MLI in 2020, listing its non-compliant bilateral agreements.

Bahrain further indicated that bilateral negotiations would be used with respect to several agreements.[15]

Bahrain is implementing the minimum standard through the inclusion of the preamble statement and the PPT.[16]

The agreements that will be modified by the MLI will come into compliance with the minimum standard once the provisions of the MLI take effect.

B. Implementation issues

Bahrain's listed agreements under the MLI will start to be compliant after Bahrain's ratification of the MLI. Bahrain is encouraged to ratify the MLI as soon as possible.

Summary of the jurisdiction response - Bahrain

	Treaty partners	Compliance with the standard	If compliant, the alternative implemented	Signature of a complying instrument	The alternative implemented through the complying instrument (if not the MLI)	Comments
1	Algeria*	No	N/A	No	N/A	
2	Austria	No	N/A	No	N/A	
3	Bangladesh*	No	N/A	No	N/A	
4	Barbados	No	N/A	No	N/A	
5	Belarus*	No	N/A	No	N/A	
6	Belgium	No	N/A	No	N/A	
7	Bermuda	No	N/A	No	N/A	
8	Brunei Darussalam	No	N/A	No	N/A	
9	Bulgaria	No	N/A	No	N/A	
10	China (People's Republic of)	No	N/A	No	N/A	
11	Cyprus*	No	N/A	No	N/A	
12	Czech Republic	No	N/A	No	N/A	
13	Egypt	No	N/A	No	N/A	
14	Estonia	No	N/A	No	N/A	
15	France	No	N/A	No	N/A	
16	Georgia	No	N/A	No	N/A	
17	Hungary	No	N/A	No	N/A	
18	Iran*	No	N/A	No	N/A	

[15] On 23 November 2019, Bahrain signed an agreement with Switzerland. The agreement is compliant with the minimum standard both has not yet been ratified.

[16] For its agreements listed under the MLI, Bahrain is implementing the preamble statement (Article 6 of the MLI) and the PPT (Article 7 of the MLI).

19	Ireland	No	N/A	No	N/A	
20	Isle of Man	No	N/A	No	N/A	
21	Jordan	No	N/A	No	N/A	
22	Korea	No	N/A	No	N/A	
23	Lebanon*	No	N/A	No	N/A	
24	Luxembourg	No	N/A	No	N/A	
25	Malaysia	No	N/A	No	N/A	
26	Malta	No	N/A	No	N/A	
27	Mexico	No	N/A	No	N/A	
28	Morocco	No	N/A	No	N/A	
29	Netherlands	No	N/A	No	N/A	
30	Pakistan	No	N/A	No	N/A	
31	Philippines*	No	N/A	No	N/A	
32	Portugal	No	N/A	No	N/A	
33	Seychelles	No	N/A	No	N/A	
34	Singapore	No	N/A	No	N/A	
35	Sri Lanka	No	N/A	No	N/A	
36	Sudan*	No	N/A	No	N/A	
37	Syrian Arab Republic*	No	N/A	No	N/A	
38	Tajikistan*	No	N/A	No	N/A	
39	Thailand	No	N/A	No	N/A	
40	Turkey	No	N/A	No	N/A	
41	Turkmenistan*	No	N/A	No	N/A	
42	United Kingdom	No	N/A	No	N/A	
43	Uzbekistan*	No	N/A	No	N/A	
44	Yemen*	No	N/A	No	N/A	

Barbados

A. Progress in the implementation of the minimum standard

Barbados has 31 tax agreements in force, including the multilateral agreement among the members of the CARICOM concluded with ten treaty partners (the CARICOM Agreement).[17]

Barbados signed the MLI in 2018 and deposited its instrument of ratification on 21 December 2020. The MLI will enter into force for Barbados on 1 April 2021.

Barbados is implementing the minimum standard through the inclusion of the preamble statement and the PPT.[18]

The agreements that will be modified by the MLI will come into compliance with the minimum standard once the provisions of the MLI take effect.

B. Implementation issues

No jurisdiction has raised any concerns about their agreements with Barbados.

Barbados is encouraged to bring the CARICOM Agreement up to date by commencing talks among all the treaty partners.[19]

Summary of the jurisdiction response - Barbados

	Treaty partners	Compliance with the standard	If compliant, the alternative implemented	Signature of a complying instrument	The alternative implemented through the complying instrument (if not the MLI)	Comments
1	Antigua and Barbuda	No	N/A	No	N/A	CARICOM
2	Austria	No	N/A	Yes	N/A	
3	Bahrain	No	N/A	Yes	N/A	
4	Belize	No	N/A	No	N/A	CARICOM
5	Botswana	No	N/A	Yes	N/A	
6	Canada	No	N/A	Yes	N/A	
7	China (People's Republic of)	No	N/A	Yes	N/A	
8	Cuba*	No	N/A	No	N/A	
9	Cyprus*	No	N/A	Yes	N/A	
10	Czech Republic	No	N/A	Yes	N/A	
11	Dominica	No	N/A	No	N/A	CARICOM
12	Finland	No	N/A	Yes	N/A	
13	Grenada	No	N/A	No	N/A	CARICOM
14	Guyana*	No	N/A	No	N/A	CARICOM

[17] In total, Barbados identified 40 "agreements" in its List of Tax agreements: 30 bilateral agreements and the CARICOM Agreement concluded with ten of its treaty partners.

[18] For its agreements listed under the MLI, Barbados is implementing the preamble statement (Article 6 of the MLI) and the PPT (Article 7 of the MLI).

[19] Revisions to the CARICOM Agreement require an agreement from its eleven treaty partners.

15	Iceland	No	N/A	Yes	N/A	
16	Italy	No	N/A	Yes	N/A	
17	Jamaica	No	N/A	No	N/A	CARICOM
18	Luxembourg	No	N/A	Yes	N/A	
19	Malta	No	N/A	Yes	N/A	
20	Mauritius	No	N/A	Yes	N/A	
21	Mexico	No	N/A	Yes	N/A	
22	Netherlands	No	N/A	Yes	N/A	
23	Norway	No	N/A	Yes	N/A	
24	Panama	No	N/A	Yes	N/A	
25	Portugal	No	N/A	Yes	N/A	
26	Qatar	No	N/A	Yes	N/A	
27	Saint Kitts and Nevis	No	N/A	No	N/A	CARICOM
28	Saint Lucia	No	N/A	No	N/A	CARICOM
29	Saint Vincent and the Grenadines	No	N/A	No	N/A	CARICOM
30	San Marino	No	N/A	Yes	N/A	
31	Seychelles	No	N/A	Yes	N/A	
32	Singapore	No	N/A	Yes	N/A	
33	Spain	No	N/A	Yes	N/A	
34	Sweden	No	N/A	Yes	N/A	
35	Switzerland	No	N/A	Yes	N/A	
36	Trinidad and Tobago	No	N/A	No	N/A	CARICOM
37	United Arab Emirates	No	N/A	Yes	N/A	
38	United Kingdom	No	N/A	Yes	N/A	
39	United States	No	N/A	Yes	N/A	
40	Venezuela*	No	N/A	Yes	N/A	

Belgium

A. Progress in the implementation of the minimum standard

Belgium has 95 tax agreements in force, as reported in its response to the Peer Review questionnaire. 24 of those agreements, the agreements with Australia, Austria, Canada, Denmark, Finland, France, Georgia, Iceland, India, Ireland, Israel, Japan, Lithuania, Luxembourg, Malta, New Zealand, Poland, Serbia, Singapore, the Slovak Republic, Slovenia, Ukraine, the United Arab Emirates and the United Kingdom, comply with the minimum standard.

Belgium signed the MLI in 2017 and deposited its instrument of ratification on 26 June 2019. The MLI entered into force for Belgium on 1 October 2019. Belgium has not listed its agreements with Germany, Norway and Switzerland but indicated in its response of the Peer Review questionnaire that bilateral negotiations would be pursued to bring those agreements into compliance with the minimum standard.

Belgium is generally implementing the minimum standard through the inclusion of the preamble statement and the PPT.[20]

The agreements modified by the MLI come into compliance with the minimum standard once the provisions of the MLI take effect.

B. Implementation issues

No jurisdiction has raised any concerns about their agreements with Belgium.

Summary of the jurisdiction response - Belgium

	Treaty partners	Compliance with the standard	If compliant, the alternative implemented	Signature of a complying instrument	The alternative implemented through the complying instrument (if not the MLI)	Comments
1	Albania	No	N/A	Yes	N/A	
2	Algeria*	No	N/A	Yes	N/A	
3	Argentina	No	N/A	Yes	N/A	
4	Armenia	No	N/A	Yes	N/A	
5	Australia	Yes	PPT alone	N/A	N/A	
6	Austria	Yes	PPT alone	N/A	N/A	
7	Azerbaijan*	No	N/A	Yes	N/A	
8	Bahrain	No	N/A	Yes	N/A	
9	Bangladesh*	No	N/A	Yes	N/A	
10	Belarus*	No	N/A	Yes	N/A	
11	Bosnia-Herzegovina	No	N/A	Yes	N/A	
12	Brazil	No	N/A	Yes	N/A	
13	Bulgaria	No	N/A	Yes	N/A	
14	Canada	Yes	PPT alone	N/A	N/A	
15	Chile	No	N/A	Yes	N/A	

[20] For its agreements listed under the MLI, Belgium is implementing the preamble statement (Article 6 of the MLI) and the PPT (Article 7 of the MLI).

16	China (People's Republic of)	No	N/A	Yes	N/A
17	Chinese Taipei*	No	N/A	No	N/A
18	Democratic Republic of the Congo	No	N/A	Yes	N/A
19	Côte d'Ivoire	No	N/A	Yes	N/A
20	Croatia	No	N/A	Yes	N/A
21	Cyprus*	No	N/A	Yes	N/A
22	Czech Republic	No	N/A	Yes	N/A
23	Denmark	Yes	PPT alone	N/A	N/A
24	Ecuador*	No	N/A	Yes	N/A
25	Egypt	No	N/A	Yes	N/A
26	Estonia	No	N/A	Yes	N/A
27	Finland	Yes	PPT alone	N/A	N/A
28	France	Yes	PPT alone	N/A	N/A
29	Gabon	No	N/A	Yes	N/A
30	Georgia	Yes	PPT alone	N/A	N/A
31	Germany	No	N/A	No	N/A
32	Ghana*	No	N/A	Yes	N/A
33	Greece	No	N/A	Yes	N/A
34	Hong Kong (China)	No	N/A	Yes	N/A
35	Hungary	No	N/A	Yes	N/A
36	Iceland	Yes	PPT alone	N/A	N/A
37	India	Yes	PPT alone	N/A	N/A
38	Indonesia	No	N/A	Yes	N/A
39	Ireland	Yes	PPT alone	N/A	N/A
40	Israel	Yes	PPT alone	N/A	N/A
41	Italy	No	N/A	Yes	N/A
42	Japan	Yes	PPT and LOB	N/A	N/A
43	Kazakhstan	No	N/A	Yes	N/A
44	Korea	No	N/A	Yes	N/A
45	Kosovo*	No	N/A	Yes	N/A
46	Kuwait*	No	N/A	Yes	N/A
47	Kyrgyzstan*	No	N/A	Yes	N/A
48	Latvia	No	N/A	Yes	N/A
49	Lithuania	Yes	PPT alone	N/A	N/A
50	Luxembourg	Yes	PPT alone	N/A	N/A
51	Malaysia	No	N/A	Yes	N/A
52	Malta	Yes	PPT alone	N/A	N/A
53	Mauritius	No	N/A	Yes	N/A
54	Mexico	No	N/A	Yes	N/A
55	Moldova*	No	N/A	Yes	N/A
56	Mongolia	No	N/A	Yes	N/A
57	Montenegro	No	N/A	Yes	N/A
58	Morocco	No	N/A	Yes	N/A
59	Netherlands	No	N/A	Yes	N/A
60	New Zealand	Yes	PPT alone	N/A	N/A
61	Nigeria	No	N/A	Yes	N/A
62	North Macedonia	No	N/A	Yes	N/A
63	Norway	No	N/A	No	N/A
64	Pakistan	No	N/A	Yes	N/A
65	Philippines*	No	N/A	Yes	N/A
66	Poland	Yes	PPT alone	N/A	N/A
67	Portugal	No	N/A	Yes	N/A
68	Romania	No	N/A	Yes	N/A

69	Russia	No	N/A	Yes	N/A	
70	Rwanda*	No	N/A	Yes	N/A	
71	San Marino	No	N/A	Yes	N/A	
72	Senegal	No	N/A	Yes	N/A	
73	Serbia	Yes	PPT alone	N/A	N/A	
74	Seychelles	No	N/A	Yes	N/A	
75	Singapore	Yes	PPT alone	N/A	N/A	
76	Slovak Republic	Yes	PPT alone	N/A	N/A	
77	Slovenia	Yes	PPT alone	N/A	N/A	
78	South Africa	No	N/A	Yes	N/A	
79	Spain	No	N/A	Yes	N/A	
80	Sri Lanka	No	N/A	Yes	N/A	
81	Sweden	No	N/A	Yes	N/A	
82	Switzerland	No	N/A	No	N/A	
83	Tajikistan*	No	N/A	Yes	N/A	
84	Thailand	No	N/A	Yes	N/A	
85	Tunisia	No	N/A	Yes	N/A	
86	Turkey	No	N/A	Yes	N/A	
87	Turkmenistan*	No	N/A	Yes	N/A	
88	Ukraine	Yes	PPT alone	N/A	N/A	
89	United Arab Emirates	Yes	PPT alone	N/A	N/A	
90	United Kingdom	Yes	PPT alone	N/A	N/A	
91	United States	No	N/A	Yes	N/A	
92	Uruguay	No	N/A	Yes	N/A	
93	Uzbekistan*	No	N/A	Yes	N/A	
94	Venezuela*	No	N/A	Yes	N/A	
95	Viet Nam	No	N/A	Yes	N/A	

Belize

A. Progress in the implementation of the minimum standard

Belize has four tax agreements in force, as reported in its response to the Peer Review questionnaire, including the multilateral agreement among the members of the CARICOM concluded with ten of its treaty partners (the CARICOM Agreement).[21]

Belize signed the MLI in 2019, listing its non-compliant bilateral agreements.

Belize is implementing the minimum standard through the inclusion of the preamble statement and the PPT.

The agreements that will be modified by the MLI will come into compliance with the minimum standard once the provisions of the MLI take effect.

B. Implementation issues

Belize's listed agreements under the MLI will start to be compliant after Belize's ratification of the MLI. Belize is encouraged to ratify the MLI as soon as possible.

Belize is encouraged to bring the CARICOM Agreement up to date by commencing talks among all the treaty partners.[22]

Summary of the jurisdiction response - Belize

	Treaty partners	Compliance with the standard	If compliant, the alternative implemented	Signature of a complying instrument	The alternative implemented through the complying instrument (if not the MLI)	Comments
1	Antigua and Barbuda	No	N/A	Yes	N/A	CARICOM
2	Austria	No	N/A	Yes	N/A	
3	Barbados	No	N/A	Yes	N/A	CARICOM
4	Dominica	No	N/A	Yes	N/A	CARICOM
5	Grenada	No	N/A	Yes	N/A	CARICOM
6	Guyana*	No	N/A	Yes	N/A	CARICOM
7	Jamaica	No	N/A	Yes	N/A	CARICOM
8	Saint Kitts and Nevis	No	N/A	Yes	N/A	CARICOM
9	Saint Lucia	No	N/A	Yes	N/A	CARICOM
10	Saint Vincent and the Grenadines	No	N/A	Yes	N/A	CARICOM
11	Switzerland	No	N/A	Yes	N/A	
12	Trinidad and Tobago	No	N/A	Yes	N/A	CARICOM
13	United Kingdom	No	N/A	Yes	N/A	

[21] In total, Belize identified thirteen "agreements" in its List of Tax agreements: three bilateral agreements and the CARICOM Agreement concluded with ten of its treaty partners.

[22] Revisions to the CARICOM Agreement require an agreement from its eleven treaty partners.

Benin

A. Progress in the implementation of the minimum standard

Benin has three tax agreements in force, as reported in its response to the Peer Review questionnaire, including the multilateral Regulation 08/2008/COM adopting the rules for the avoidance of double taxation within the West African Economic and Monetary Union and the rule for assistance in tax matters (the UEMOA) concluded with seven partners.[23]

None of Benin's agreements comply with the minimum standard or are subject to a complying instrument.

Benin has not signed the MLI.

B. Implementation issues

As Benin has not signed the MLI or implemented anti-treaty-shopping measures in its agreements, the Secretariat will offer its support to design a plan for the implementation of the minimum standard to strengthen its network of agreements.

Summary of the jurisdiction response - Benin

	Treaty partners	Compliance with the standard	If compliant, the alternative implemented	Signature of a complying instrument	The alternative implemented through the complying instrument (if not the MLI)	Comments
1	Burkina Faso	No	N/A	No	N/A	UEMOA
2	Côte d'Ivoire	No	N/A	No	N/A	UEMOA
3	France	No	N/A	No	N/A	
4	Guinea-Bissau*	No	N/A	No	N/A	UEMOA
5	Mali*	No	N/A	No	N/A	UEMOA
6	Niger*	No	N/A	No	N/A	UEMOA
7	Norway	No	N/A	No	N/A	
8	Senegal	No	N/A	No	N/A	UEMOA
9	Togo*	No	N/A	No	N/A	UEMOA

[23] Règlement n°08/2008/CM des pays de l'Union économique et monétaire Ouest Africaine (UEMOA) du 26 septembre 2008 portant adoption des règles visant à éviter la double imposition au sein de l'UEMOA et des règles d'assistance en matière fiscale. In total, Benin identified nine "agreements" in its list of tax agreements: two bilateral agreements and the UEMOA.

Bermuda

A. Progress in the implementation of the minimum standard

Bermuda has two tax agreements in force as reported in its response to the Peer Review questionnaire.

Neither of Bermuda's agreements comply with the minimum standard or are subject to a complying instrument.

Bermuda has not joined the MLI.

B. Implementation issues

As Bermuda has not joined the MLI or implemented anti-treaty-shopping measures in its agreements, the Secretariat will offer its support to design a plan for the implementation of the minimum standard to strengthen its network of agreements.

Summary of the jurisdiction response - Bermuda

	Treaty partners	Compliance with the standard	If compliant, the alternative implemented	Signature of a complying instrument	The alternative implemented through the complying instrument (if not the MLI)	Comments
1	Bahrain	No	N/A	No	N/A	
2	Seychelles	No	N/A	No	N/A	

Bosnia-Herzegovina

A. Progress in the implementation of the minimum standard

Bosnia-Herzegovina has 37 tax agreements in force as reported in its response to the Peer Review questionnaire.

Bosnia-Herzegovina signed the MLI in 2019 and deposited its instrument of ratification on 16 September 2020. The MLI will enter into force for Bosnia-Herzegovina on 1 January 2021.

Bosnia-Herzegovina is implementing the minimum standard through the inclusion of the preamble statement and the PPT.[24]

The agreements that will be modified by the MLI will come into compliance with the minimum standard once the provisions of the MLI take effect.

B. Implementation issues

No jurisdiction has raised any concerns about their agreements with Bosnia-Herzegovina.

Summary of the jurisdiction response – Bosnia-Herzegovina

	Treaty partners	Compliance with the standard	If compliant, the alternative implemented	Signature of a complying instrument	The alternative implemented through the complying instrument (if not the MLI)	Comments
1	Albania	No	N/A	Yes	N/A	
2	Algeria*	No	N/A	Yes	N/A	
3	Austria	No	N/A	Yes	N/A	
4	Azerbaijan*	No	N/A	Yes	N/A	
5	Belgium	No	N/A	Yes	N/A	
6	China (People's Republic of)	No	N/A	Yes	N/A	
7	Croatia	No	N/A	Yes	N/A	
8	Cyprus*	No	N/A	Yes	N/A	
9	Czech Republic	No	N/A	Yes	N/A	
10	Finland	No	N/A	Yes	N/A	
11	France	No	N/A	Yes	N/A	
12	Germany	No	N/A	Yes	N/A	
13	Greece	No	N/A	Yes	N/A	
14	Hungary	No	N/A	Yes	N/A	
15	Ireland	No	N/A	Yes	N/A	
16	Italy	No	N/A	Yes	N/A	
17	Jordan	No	N/A	Yes	N/A	
18	Kuwait*	No	N/A	Yes	N/A	
19	Malaysia	No	N/A	Yes	N/A	
20	Moldova*	No	N/A	Yes	N/A	

[24] For its agreements listed under the MLI, Bosnia-Herzegovina is implementing the preamble statement (Article 6 of the MLI) and the PPT (Article 7 of the MLI).

21	Montenegro	No	N/A	Yes	N/A	
22	Netherlands	No	N/A	Yes	N/A	
23	North Macedonia	No	N/A	Yes	N/A	
24	Norway	No	N/A	Yes	N/A	
25	Pakistan	No	N/A	Yes	N/A	
26	Poland	No	N/A	Yes	N/A	
27	Qatar	No	N/A	Yes	N/A	
28	Romania	No	N/A	Yes	N/A	
29	Serbia	No	N/A	Yes	N/A	
30	Slovak Republic	No	N/A	Yes	N/A	
31	Slovenia	No	N/A	Yes	N/A	
32	Spain	No	N/A	Yes	N/A	
33	Sri Lanka	No	N/A	Yes	N/A	
34	Sweden	No	N/A	Yes	N/A	
35	Turkey	No	N/A	Yes	N/A	
36	United Arab Emirates	No	N/A	Yes	N/A	
37	United Kingdom	No	N/A	Yes	N/A	

Botswana

A. Progress in the implementation of the minimum standard

Botswana has 17 tax agreements in force, as reported in its response to the Peer Review questionnaire.

None of Botswana's agreements comply with the minimum standard or are subject to a complying instrument.

Botswana has not signed the MLI.

B. Implementation issues

As Botswana has not signed the MLI or implemented anti-treaty-shopping measures in its agreements, the Secretariat will offer its support to design a plan for the implementation of the minimum standard to strengthen its network of agreements.

Summary of the jurisdiction response - Botswana

	Treaty partners	Compliance with the standard	If compliant, the alternative implemented	Signature of a complying instrument	The alternative implemented through the complying instrument (if not the MLI)	Comments
1	Barbados	No	N/A	No	N/A	
2	China (People's Republic of)	No	N/A	No	N/A	
3	Eswatini	No	N/A	No	N/A	
4	France	No	N/A	No	N/A	
5	India	No	N/A	No	N/A	
6	Ireland	No	N/A	No	N/A	
7	Malta	No	N/A	No	N/A	
8	Mauritius	No	N/A	No	N/A	
9	Mozambique*	No	N/A	No	N/A	
10	Namibia	No	N/A	No	N/A	
11	Russia	No	N/A	No	N/A	
12	Seychelles	No	N/A	No	N/A	
13	South Africa	No	N/A	No	N/A	
14	Sweden	No	N/A	No	N/A	
15	United Kingdom	No	N/A	No	N/A	
16	Zambia	No	N/A	No	N/A	
17	Zimbabwe*	No	N/A	No	N/A	

Brazil

A. Progress in the implementation of the minimum standard

Brazil has 33 tax agreements in force, as reported in its response to the Peer Review questionnaire. One of those agreements, the agreement with Argentina, complies with the minimum standard.

Brazil has not signed the MLI.

Brazil is implementing the minimum standard through the inclusion of the preamble statement and the PPT combined with the LOB.

Brazil has signed one bilateral complying instrument with respect to its agreement with Sweden.

Brazil indicated in its response to the Peer Review questionnaire that bilateral negotiations would be used with respect to its agreements and that it already contacted its treaty partners for negotiations.

B. Implementation issues

As Brazil has not signed the MLI or implemented anti-treaty-shopping measures in its agreements, the Secretariat will offer its support to design a plan for the implementation of the minimum standard to strengthen its network of agreements.

Summary of the jurisdiction response - Brazil

	Treaty partners	Compliance with the standard	If compliant, the alternative implemented	Signature of a complying instrument	The alternative implemented through the complying instrument (if not the MLI)	Comments
1	Argentina	Yes	PPT and LOB	N/A	N/A	
2	Austria	No	N/A	No	N/A	
3	Belgium	No	N/A	No	N/A	
4	Canada	No	N/A	No	N/A	
5	Chile	No	N/A	No	N/A	
6	China (People's Republic of)	No	N/A	No	N/A	
7	Czech Republic	No	N/A	No	N/A	
8	Denmark	No	N/A	No	N/A	
9	Ecuador*	No	N/A	No	N/A	
10	Finland	No	N/A	No	N/A	
11	France	No	N/A	No	N/A	
12	Hungary	No	N/A	No	N/A	
13	India	No	N/A	No	N/A	
14	Israel	No	N/A	No	N/A	
15	Italy	No	N/A	No	N/A	
16	Japan	No	N/A	No	N/A	
17	Korea	No	N/A	No	N/A	
18	Luxembourg	No	N/A	No	N/A	
19	Mexico	No	N/A	No	N/A	
20	Netherlands	No	N/A	No	N/A	
21	Norway	No	N/A	No	N/A	

22	Peru	No	N/A	No	N/A	
23	Philippines*	No	N/A	No	N/A	
24	Portugal	No	N/A	No	N/A	
25	Russia	No	N/A	No	N/A	
26	Slovak Republic	No	N/A	No	N/A	
27	South Africa	No	N/A	No	N/A	
28	Spain	No	N/A	No	N/A	
29	Sweden	No	N/A	Yes	PPT and LOB	
30	Trinidad and Tobago	No	N/A	No	N/A	
31	Turkey	No	N/A	No	N/A	
32	Ukraine	No	N/A	No	N/A	
33	Venezuela*	No	N/A	No	N/A	

British Virgin Islands

A. Progress in the implementation of the minimum standard

The British Virgin Islands has one tax agreement in force, as reported in its response to the Peer Review questionnaire.

The British Virgin Islands' agreement does not comply with the minimum standard and is not subject to any complying instruments.

The British Virgin Islands has not joined the MLI.

B. Implementation issues

As the British Virgin Islands has not joined the MLI or implemented anti-treaty-shopping measures in its agreement, the Secretariat will offer its support to design a plan for the implementation of the minimum standard to strengthen its treaty network.

Summary of the jurisdiction response – British Virgin Islands

	Treaty partners	Compliance with the standard	If compliant, the alternative implemented	Signature of a complying instrument	The alternative implemented through the complying instrument (if not the MLI)	Comments
1	Switzerland	No	N/A	No	N/A	

Brunei Darussalam

A. Progress in the implementation of the minimum standard

Brunei Darussalam has 18 tax agreements in force, as reported in its response to the Peer Review questionnaire.

None of Brunei Darussalam's agreements comply with the minimum standard or are subject to a complying instrument.

Brunei Darussalam has not signed the MLI.

Brunei Darussalam indicated in its response to the Peer Review questionnaire that it is updating its Model Tax Convention with the treaty-related BEPS minimum standards and it is considering signing the MLI.

B. Implementation issues

As Brunei Darussalam has not signed the MLI or implemented anti-treaty-shopping measures in its agreements, the Secretariat will offer its support to design a plan for the implementation of the minimum standard to strengthen its network of agreements.

Summary of the jurisdiction response – Brunei Darussalam

	Treaty partners	Compliance with the standard	If compliant, the alternative implemented	Signature of a complying instrument	The alternative implemented through the complying instrument (if not the MLI)	Comments
1	Bahrain	No	N/A	No	N/A	
2	Cambodia*	No	N/A	No	N/A	
3	China (People's Republic of)	No	N/A	No	N/A	
4	Hong Kong (China)	No	N/A	No	N/A	
5	Indonesia	No	N/A	No	N/A	
6	Japan	No	N/A	No	N/A	
7	Korea	No	N/A	No	N/A	
8	Kuwait*	No	N/A	No	N/A	
9	Lao People's Democratic Republic*	No	N/A	No	N/A	
10	Luxembourg	No	N/A	No	N/A	
11	Malaysia	No	N/A	No	N/A	
12	Oman	No	N/A	No	N/A	
13	Pakistan	No	N/A	No	N/A	
14	Qatar	No	N/A	No	N/A	
15	Singapore	No	N/A	No	N/A	
16	United Arab Emirates	No	N/A	No	N/A	
17	United Kingdom	No	N/A	No	N/A	
18	Viet Nam	No	N/A	No	N/A	

Bulgaria

A. Progress in the implementation of the minimum standard

Bulgaria has 71 tax agreements in force, as reported in its response to the Peer Review questionnaire. Two of those agreements, the agreements with Pakistan and Saudi Arabia, comply with the minimum standard.

Bulgaria signed the MLI in 2017 and has not listed its agreements with Finland, Malta and the Netherlands. It indicated in its response to the Peer Review questionnaire that bilateral negotiations would be used for those agreements.

Bulgaria is implementing the minimum standard through the inclusion of the preamble statement and the PPT combined with the LOB.[25]

The agreements that will be modified by the MLI will come into compliance with the minimum standard once the provisions of the MLI take effect.

B. Implementation issues

Bulgaria's listed agreements under the MLI will start to be compliant after Bulgaria's ratification of the MLI. Bulgaria indicated that it expected to deposit its instrument of ratification of the MLI early in 2021.

Summary of the jurisdiction response - Bulgaria

	Treaty partners	Compliance with the standard	If compliant, the alternative implemented	Signature of a complying instrument	The alternative implemented through the complying instrument (if not the MLI)	Comments
1	Albania	No	N/A	Yes	N/A	
2	Algeria*	No	N/A	Yes	N/A	
3	Armenia	No	N/A	Yes	N/A	
4	Austria	No	N/A	Yes	N/A	
5	Azerbaijan*	No	N/A	Yes	N/A	
6	Bahrain	No	N/A	Yes	N/A	
7	Belarus*	No	N/A	Yes	N/A	
8	Belgium	No	N/A	Yes	N/A	
9	Canada	No	N/A	Yes	N/A	
10	China (People's Republic of)	No	N/A	Yes	N/A	
11	Croatia	No	N/A	Yes	N/A	
12	Cyprus*	No	N/A	Yes	N/A	

[25] For 65 of its agreements listed under the MLI, Bulgaria is implementing the preamble statement (Article 6 of the MLI). For its 66 agreements listed under the MLI, Bulgaria is implementing the PPT (Article 7 of the MLI). Bulgaria also opted for the simplified LOB under Article 7(6) of the MLI. Bulgaria made a reservation pursuant to Article 6(4) of the MLI not to apply Article 6(1) of the MLI with respect to agreements, which already contain the relevant preamble language. One of Bulgaria's agreements, the agreement with Romania, is within the scope of this reservation.

13	Czech Republic	No	N/A	Yes	N/A	
14	Democratic People's Republic of Korea*	No	N/A	Yes	N/A	
15	Denmark	No	N/A	Yes	N/A	
16	Egypt	No	N/A	Yes	N/A	
17	Estonia	No	N/A	Yes	N/A	
18	Finland	No	N/A	No	N/A	
19	France	No	N/A	Yes	N/A	
20	Georgia	No	N/A	Yes	N/A	
21	Germany	No	N/A	Yes	N/A	Amending protocol to be signed. Germany will be excluded from the Bulgarian list of CTAs.
22	Greece	No	N/A	Yes	N/A	
23	Hungary	No	N/A	Yes	N/A	
24	India	No	N/A	Yes	N/A	
25	Indonesia	No	N/A	Yes	N/A	
26	Iran*	No	N/A	Yes	N/A	
27	Ireland	No	N/A	Yes	N/A	
28	Israel	No	N/A	Yes	N/A	
29	Italy	No	N/A	Yes	N/A	
30	Japan	No	N/A	Yes	N/A	
31	Jordan	No	N/A	Yes	N/A	
32	Kazakhstan	No	N/A	Yes	N/A	
33	Korea	No	N/A	Yes	N/A	
34	Kuwait*	No	N/A	Yes	N/A	
35	Latvia	No	N/A	Yes	N/A	
36	Lebanon*	No	N/A	Yes	N/A	
37	Lithuania	No	N/A	Yes	N/A	
38	Luxembourg	No	N/A	Yes	N/A	Possible bilateral negotiations for a new treaty to be scheduled
39	Malta	No	N/A	No	N/A	Scheduled negotiations for a new treaty postponed due to COVID-19 outbreak
40	Moldova*	No	N/A	Yes	N/A	
41	Mongolia	No	N/A	Yes	N/A	
42	Montenegro	No	N/A	Yes	N/A	
43	Morocco	No	N/A	Yes	N/A	
44	Netherlands	No	N/A	No	N/A	
45	North Macedonia	No	N/A	Yes	N/A	
46	Norway	No	N/A	Yes	N/A	
47	Pakistan	Yes	PPT alone	N/A	N/A	In force as of 20 February 2020
48	Poland	No	N/A	Yes	N/A	
49	Portugal	No	N/A	Yes	N/A	
50	Qatar	No	N/A	Yes	N/A	
51	Romania	No	N/A	Yes	N/A	
52	Russia	No	N/A	Yes	N/A	
53	Saudi Arabia	Yes	PPT alone	N/A	N/A	
54	Serbia	No	N/A	Yes	N/A	
55	Singapore	No	N/A	Yes	N/A	
56	Slovak Republic	No	N/A	Yes	N/A	
57	Slovenia	No	N/A	Yes	N/A	
58	South Africa	No	N/A	Yes	N/A	
59	Spain	No	N/A	Yes	N/A	
60	Sweden	No	N/A	Yes	N/A	
61	Switzerland	No	N/A	Yes	N/A	

62	Syrian Arab Republic*	No	N/A	Yes	N/A	
63	Thailand	No	N/A	Yes	N/A	
64	Turkey	No	N/A	Yes	N/A	
65	Ukraine	No	N/A	Yes	N/A	
66	United Arab Emirates	No	N/A	Yes	N/A	
67	United Kingdom	No	N/A	Yes	N/A	
68	United States	No	N/A	Yes	N/A	
69	Uzbekistan*	No	N/A	Yes	N/A	Bilateral negotiations for Amending protocol to be scheduled.
70	Viet Nam	No	N/A	Yes	N/A	
71	Zimbabwe*	No	N/A	Yes	N/A	

Burkina Faso

A. Progress in the implementation of the minimum standard

Burkina Faso has three tax agreements in force, as reported in its response to the Peer Review questionnaire, including the multilateral Regulation 08/2008/COM adopting the rules for the avoidance of double taxation within the West African Economic and Monetary Union and the rule for assistance in tax matters (the UEMOA) concluded with seven partners.[26]

Burkina Faso signed the MLI in 2017 and deposited its instrument of ratification on 30 October 2020. The MLI will enter into force for Burkina Faso on 1 February 2021.

Burkina Faso indicated in its response to the Peer Review questionnaire that the UEMOA has not been listed under the MLI as it is a regulation of the West African Economic and Monetary Union.

Burkina Faso is implementing the minimum standard through the inclusion of the preamble statement and the PPT.[27]

The agreements that will be modified by the MLI will come into compliance with the minimum standard once the provisions of the MLI take effect.

B. Implementation issues

No jurisdiction has raised any concerns about their agreements with Burkina Faso.

Burkina Faso is encouraged to consider entering into negotiations with respect to the UEMOA to implement the minimum standard.

Summary of the jurisdiction response – Burkina Faso

	Treaty partners	Compliance with the standard	If compliant, the alternative implemented	Signature of a complying instrument	The alternative implemented through the complying instrument (if not the MLI)	Comments
1	Benin	No	N/A	No	N/A	UEMOA
2	Côte d'Ivoire	No	N/A	No	N/A	UEMOA
3	France	No	N/A	Yes	N/A	
4	Guinea-Bissau*	No	N/A	No	N/A	UEMOA
5	Mali*	No	N/A	No	N/A	UEMOA
6	Niger*	No	N/A	No	N/A	UEMOA
7	Senegal	No	N/A	No	N/A	UEMOA
8	Togo*	No	N/A	No	N/A	UEMOA
9	Tunisia	No	N/A	Yes	N/A	

26 Règlement n°08/2008/CM des pays de l'Union économique et monétaire Ouest Africaine (UEMOA) du 26 septembre 2008 portant adoption des règles visant à éviter la double imposition au sein de l'UEMOA et des règles d'assistance en matière fiscale. In total, Burkina Faso identified nine "agreements" in its List of Tax agreements: two bilateral agreements and the UEMOA concluded with seven of its treaty partners.

27 For its agreements listed under the MLI, Burkina Faso is implementing the preamble statement (Article 6 of the MLI) and the PPT (Article 7 of the MLI).

Cabo Verde

A. Progress in the implementation of the minimum standard

Cabo Verde has three tax agreements in force, as reported in its response to the Peer Review questionnaire.

None of Cabo Verde's agreements comply with the minimum standard or are subject to a complying instrument.

Cabo Verde has not signed the MLI.

B. Implementation issues

As Cabo Verde has not signed the MLI or implemented anti-treaty-shopping measures in its agreements, the Secretariat will offer its support to design a plan for the implementation of the minimum standard to strengthen its network of agreements.

Summary of the jurisdiction response – Cabo Verde

	Treaty partners	Compliance with the standard	If compliant, the alternative implemented	Signature of a complying instrument	The alternative implemented through the complying instrument (if not the MLI)	Comments
1	Macau (China)	No	N/A	No	N/A	
2	Mauritius	No	N/A	No	N/A	
3	Portugal	No	N/A	No	N/A	

Cameroon

A. Progress in the implementation of the minimum standard

Cameroon has four tax agreements in force, as reported in its response to the Peer Review questionnaire.

Cameroon signed the MLI in 2017, listing its non-compliant agreements.

Cameroon is implementing the minimum standard through the inclusion of the preamble statement and the PPT.[28]

The agreements that will be modified by the MLI will come into compliance with the minimum standard once the provisions of the MLI take effect.

B. Implementation issues

Cameroon's listed agreements under the MLI will start to be compliant after Cameroon's ratification of the MLI. Cameroon is encouraged to ratify the MLI as soon as possible. Cameroon's National Assembly had approved a draft bill for the ratification of the MLI on 20 November 2020. Cameroon is expected to deposit its instrument of ratification of the MLI early in 2021.

Summary of the jurisdiction response - Cameroon

	Treaty partners	Compliance with the standard	If compliant, the alternative implemented	Signature of a complying instrument	The alternative implemented through the complying instrument (if not the MLI)	Comments
1	Canada	No	N/A	Yes	N/A	
2	France	No	N/A	Yes	N/A	
3	South Africa	No	N/A	Yes	N/A	
4	Tunisie	No	N/A	Yes	N/A	

[28] For its agreements listed under the MLI, Cameroon is implementing the preamble statement (Article 6 of the MLI) and the PPT (Article 7 of the MLI).

Canada

A. Progress in the implementation of the minimum standard

Canada has 94 tax agreements in force, as reported in its response to the Peer Review questionnaire. 24 of those agreements, the agreements with Australia, Austria, Belgium, Denmark, Finland, France, Iceland, India, Ireland, Israel, Japan, Lithuania, Luxembourg, Malta, the Netherlands, New Zealand, Poland, Serbia, Singapore, the Slovak Republic, Slovenia, Ukraine, the United Arab Emirates and the United Kingdom, comply with the minimum standard.

Canada signed the MLI in 2017 and deposited its instrument of ratification on 28 August 2019. The MLI entered into force for Canada on 1 December 2019. Canada has not listed its agreements with Germany and Switzerland but indicated in its response to the Peer Review questionnaire that bilateral negotiations would be pursued with respect to its agreements with Germany and Switzerland.

Canada is implementing the minimum standard through the inclusion of the preamble statement and the PPT.[29]

The agreements modified by the MLI come into compliance with the minimum standard once the provisions of the MLI take effect.

B. Implementation issues

No jurisdiction has raised any concerns about their agreements with Canada.

Summary of the jurisdiction response - Canada

	Treaty partners	Compliance with the standard	If compliant, the alternative implemented	Signature of a complying instrument	The alternative implemented through the complying instrument (if not the MLI)	Comments
1	Algeria*	No	N/A	Yes	N/A	
2	Argentina	No	N/A	Yes	N/A	
3	Armenia	No	N/A	Yes	N/A	
4	Australia	Yes	PPT alone	N/A	N/A	
5	Austria	Yes	PPT alone	N/A	N/A	
6	Azerbaijan*	No	N/A	Yes	N/A	
7	Bangladesh*	No	N/A	Yes	N/A	
8	Barbados	No	N/A	Yes	N/A	
9	Belgium	Yes	PPT alone	N/A	N/A	
10	Brazil	No	N/A	Yes	N/A	
11	Bulgaria	No	N/A	Yes	N/A	
12	Cameroon	No	N/A	Yes	N/A	
13	Chile	No	N/A	Yes	N/A	

29 For its agreements listed under the MLI, Canada is implementing the preamble statement (Article 6 of the MLI) and the PPT (Article 7 of the MLI). Canada also expressed a statement, in accordance with Article 7(17)(a) of the MLI, that while it accepts the application of the PPT under the MLI, it intends where possible to adopt an LOB provision in addition to or in replacement of the PPT through bilateral negotiation.

14	China (People's Republic of)	No	N/A	Yes	N/A	
15	Chinese Taipei*[30]	No	N/A	No	N/A	
16	Colombia	No	N/A	Yes	N/A	
17	Côte d'Ivoire	No	N/A	Yes	N/A	
18	Croatia	No	N/A	Yes	N/A	
19	Cyprus*	No	N/A	Yes	N/A	
20	Czech Republic	No	N/A	Yes	N/A	
21	Denmark	Yes	PPT alone	N/A	N/A	
22	Dominican Republic	No	N/A	Yes	N/A	
23	Ecuador*	No	N/A	No	N/A	
24	Egypt	No	N/A	Yes	N/A	
25	Estonia	No	N/A	Yes	N/A	
26	Finland	Yes	PPT alone	N/A	N/A	
27	France	Yes	PPT alone	N/A	N/A	
28	Gabon	No	N/A	Yes	N/A	
29	Germany	No	N/A	No	N/A	
30	Greece	No	N/A	Yes	N/A	
31	Guyana*	No	N/A	No	N/A	
32	Hong Kong (China)	No	N/A	Yes	N/A	
33	Hungary	No	N/A	Yes	N/A	
34	Iceland	Yes	PPT alone	N/A	N/A	
35	India	Yes	PPT alone	N/A	N/A	
36	Indonesia	No	N/A	Yes	N/A	
37	Ireland	Yes	PPT alone	N/A	N/A	
38	Israel	Yes	PPT alone	N/A	N/A	
39	Italy	No	N/A	Yes	N/A	
40	Jamaica	No	N/A	Yes	N/A	
41	Japan	Yes	PPT alone	N/A	N/A	
42	Jordan	No	N/A	Yes	N/A	
43	Kazakhstan	No	N/A	Yes	N/A	
44	Kenya	No	N/A	Yes	N/A	
45	Korea	No	N/A	Yes	N/A	
46	Kuwait*	No	N/A	Yes	N/A	
47	Kyrgyzstan*	No	N/A	No	N/A	
48	Latvia	No	N/A	Yes	N/A	
49	Lithuania	Yes	PPT alone	N/A	N/A	
50	Luxembourg	Yes	PPT alone	N/A	N/A	
51	Madagascar*	No	N/A	No	N/A	
52	Malaysia	No	N/A	Yes	N/A	
53	Malta	Yes	PPT alone	N/A	N/A	
54	Mexico	No	N/A	Yes	N/A	
55	Moldova*	No	N/A	Yes	N/A	
56	Mongolia	No	N/A	Yes	N/A	
57	Morocco	No	N/A	Yes	N/A	
58	Netherlands	Yes	PPT alone	N/A	N/A	
59	New Zealand	Yes	PPT alone	N/A	N/A	
60	Nigeria	No	N/A	Yes	N/A	
61	Norway	No	N/A	Yes	N/A	
62	Oman	No	N/A	Yes	N/A	

[30] This is an Arrangement for the Avoidance of Double Taxation and the Prevention of Fiscal Evasion with Respect to Taxes on Income between the Canadian Trade Office in Taipei and the Taipei Economic and Cultural Office in Canada.

63	Pakistan	No	N/A	Yes	N/A	
64	Papua New Guinea	No	N/A	Yes	N/A	
65	Peru	No	N/A	Yes	N/A	
66	Philippines*	No	N/A	Yes	N/A	
67	Poland	Yes	PPT alone	N/A	N/A	
68	Portugal	No	N/A	Yes	N/A	
69	Romania	No	N/A	Yes	N/A	
70	Russia	No	N/A	Yes	N/A	
71	Senegal	No	N/A	Yes	N/A	
72	Serbia	Yes	PPT alone	N/A	N/A	
73	Singapore	Yes	PPT alone	N/A	N/A	
74	Slovak Republic	Yes	PPT alone	N/A	N/A	
75	Slovenia	Yes	PPT alone	N/A	N/A	
76	South Africa	No	N/A	Yes	N/A	
77	Spain	No	N/A	Yes	N/A	
78	Sri Lanka	No	N/A	Yes	N/A	
79	Sweden	No	N/A	Yes	N/A	
80	Switzerland	No	N/A	No	N/A	
81	Tanzania*	No	N/A	Yes	N/A	
82	Thailand	No	N/A	Yes	N/A	
83	Trinidad and Tobago	No	N/A	Yes	N/A	
84	Tunisia	No	N/A	Yes	N/A	
85	Turkey	No	N/A	Yes	N/A	
86	Ukraine	Yes	PPT alone	N/A	N/A	
87	United Arab Emirates	Yes	PPT alone	N/A	N/A	
88	United Kingdom	Yes	PPT alone	N/A	N/A	
89	United States	No	N/A	No	N/A	
90	Uzbekistan*	No	N/A	No	N/A	
91	Venezuela*	No	N/A	No	N/A	
92	Viet Nam	No	N/A	Yes	N/A	
93	Zambia	No	N/A	Yes	N/A	
94	Zimbabwe*	No	N/A	Yes	N/A	

Cayman Islands

A. Progress in the implementation of the minimum standard

The Cayman Islands has no tax agreements, as reported in its response to the Peer Review questionnaire.

B. Implementation issues

No jurisdiction has raised any concerns about the Cayman Islands.

Chile

A. Progress in the implementation of the minimum standard

Chile has 33 tax agreements in force, as reported in its response to the Peer Review questionnaire. Five of those agreements, the agreements with Argentina, China, Italy, Japan and Uruguay, comply with the minimum standard.

Chile signed the MLI in 2017 and deposited its instrument of ratification on 26 November 2020. The MLI will enter into force for Chile on 1 March 2021.

Chile is implementing the minimum standard through the inclusion of the preamble statement and the PPT combined with the LOB. For its compliant agreements with Italy and Japan, the minimum standard is implemented through the inclusion of the preamble statement and the PPT.[31] Chile notes that all of its agreements that do not contain a PPT provision include a main purpose test in the dividends, interest and royalties articles.

The agreements that will be modified by the MLI will come into compliance with the minimum standard once the provisions of the MLI take effect.

B. Implementation issues

No jurisdiction has raised any concerns about their agreements with Chile.

Summary of the jurisdiction response - Chile

	Treaty partners	Compliance with the standard	If compliant, the alternative implemented	Signature of a complying instrument	The alternative implemented through the complying instrument (if not the MLI)	Comments
1	Argentina	Yes	PPT and LOB	N/A	N/A	
2	Australia	No	N/A	Yes	N/A	
3	Austria	No	N/A	Yes	N/A	
4	Belgium	No	N/A	Yes	N/A	
5	Brazil	No	N/A	Yes	N/A	
6	Canada	No	N/A	Yes	N/A	
7	China (People's Republic of)	Yes	PPT and LOB	N/A	N/A	
8	Colombia	No	N/A	Yes	N/A	
9	Croatia	No	N/A	Yes	N/A	
10	Czech Republic	No	N/A	Yes	N/A	

[31] For 28 of its agreements listed under the MLI, Chile is implementing the preamble statement (Article 6 of the MLI) and the PPT (Article 7 of the MLI). Chile also opted for the simplified LOB under Article 7(6) of the MLI and expressed a statement that while Chile accepts the application of the PPT under the MLI, it intends where possible to adopt an LOB provision through bilateral negotiation. Chile made a reservation pursuant to Article 6(4) of the MLI not to apply Article 6(1) of the MLI with respect to agreements, which already contain the relevant preamble language. Chile also made a reservation pursuant to Article 7(15)(b) of the MLI not to apply Article 7(1) of the MLI with respect to agreements which already contain a PPT. Four of Chile's agreements are within the scope of these reservations.

11	Denmark	No	N/A	Yes	N/A	
12	Ecuador*	No	N/A	Yes	N/A	
13	France	No	N/A	Yes	N/A	
14	Ireland	No	N/A	Yes	N/A	
15	Italy	Yes	PPT alone	N/A	N/A	
16	Japan	Yes	PPT alone	N/A	N/A	
17	Korea	No	N/A	Yes	N/A	
18	Malaysia	No	N/A	Yes	N/A	
19	Mexico	No	N/A	Yes	N/A	
20	New Zealand	No	N/A	Yes	N/A	
21	Norway	No	N/A	Yes	N/A	
22	Paraguay	No	N/A	Yes	N/A	
23	Peru	No	N/A	Yes	N/A	
24	Poland	No	N/A	Yes	N/A	
25	Portugal	No	N/A	Yes	N/A	
26	Russia	No	N/A	Yes	N/A	
27	South Africa	No	N/A	Yes	N/A	
28	Spain	No	N/A	Yes	N/A	
29	Sweden	No	N/A	Yes	N/A	
30	Switzerland	No	N/A	Yes	N/A	
31	Thailand	No	N/A	Yes	N/A	
32	United Kingdom	No	N/A	Yes	N/A	
33	Uruguay	Yes	PPT and LOB	N/A	N/A	

China (People's Republic of)

A. Progress in the implementation of the minimum standard

China has 102 tax agreements in force, as reported in its response to the Peer Review questionnaire. Three of those agreements, the agreements with Chile, India and New Zealand, comply with the minimum standard.

China signed the MLI in 2017, listing its non-compliant agreements.

China is generally implementing the minimum standard through the inclusion of the preamble statement and the PPT.[32]

The agreements that will be modified by the MLI will come into compliance with the minimum standard once the provisions of the MLI take effect.

B. Implementation issues

China's listed agreements under the MLI will start to be compliant after China's ratification of the MLI. China is encouraged to ratify the MLI as soon as possible.

Summary of the jurisdiction response – China (People's Republic of)

	Treaty partners	Compliance with the standard	If compliant, the alternative implemented	Signature of a complying instrument	The alternative implemented through the complying instrument (if not the MLI)	Comments
1	Albania	No	N/A	Yes	N/A	
2	Algeria*	No	N/A	Yes	N/A	
3	Armenia	No	N/A	Yes	N/A	
4	Australia	No	N/A	Yes	N/A	
5	Austria	No	N/A	Yes	N/A	
6	Azerbaijan*	No	N/A	Yes	N/A	
7	Bahrain	No	N/A	Yes	N/A	
8	Bangladesh*	No	N/A	Yes	N/A	
9	Barbados	No	N/A	Yes	N/A	
10	Belarus*	No	N/A	Yes	N/A	
11	Belgium	No	N/A	Yes	N/A	
12	Bosnia-Herzegovina	No	N/A	Yes	N/A	
13	Botswana	No	N/A	Yes	N/A	
14	Brazil	No	N/A	Yes	N/A	
15	Brunei Darussalam	No	N/A	Yes	N/A	
16	Bulgaria	No	N/A	Yes	N/A	
17	Cambodia*	No	N/A	Yes	N/A	
18	Canada	No	N/A	Yes	N/A	
19	Chile	Yes	PPT and LOB	N/A	N/A	

[32] For its agreements listed under the MLI, China is implementing the preamble statement (Article 6 of the MLI) and the PPT (Article 7 of the MLI).

20	Croatia	No	N/A	Yes	N/A	
21	Cuba*	No	N/A	Yes	N/A	
22	Cyprus*	No	N/A	Yes	N/A	
23	Czech Republic	No	N/A	Yes	N/A	
24	Denmark	No	N/A	Yes	N/A	
25	Ecuador*	No	N/A	Yes	N/A	
26	Egypt	No	N/A	Yes	N/A	
27	Estonia	No	N/A	Yes	N/A	
28	Ethiopia*	No	N/A	Yes	N/A	
29	Finland	No	N/A	Yes	N/A	
30	France	No	N/A	Yes	N/A	
31	Georgia	No	N/A	Yes	N/A	
32	Germany	No	N/A	Yes	N/A	
33	Greece	No	N/A	Yes	N/A	
34	Hungary	No	N/A	Yes	N/A	
35	Iceland	No	N/A	Yes	N/A	
36	India	Yes	PPT alone	N/A	N/A	
37	Indonesia	No	N/A	Yes	N/A	
38	Iran*	No	N/A	Yes	N/A	
39	Ireland	No	N/A	Yes	N/A	
40	Israel	No	N/A	Yes	N/A	
41	Italy	No	N/A	Yes	PPT alone	
42	Jamaica	No	N/A	Yes	N/A	
43	Japan	No	N/A	Yes	N/A	
44	Kazakhstan	No	N/A	Yes	N/A	
45	Korea	No	N/A	Yes	N/A	
46	Kuwait*	No	N/A	Yes	N/A	
47	Kyrgyzstan*	No	N/A	Yes	N/A	
48	Lao People's Democratic Republic*	No	N/A	Yes	N/A	
49	Latvia	No	N/A	Yes	N/A	
50	Lithuania	No	N/A	Yes	N/A	
51	Luxembourg	No	N/A	Yes	N/A	
52	Malaysia	No	N/A	Yes	N/A	
53	Malta	No	N/A	Yes	N/A	
54	Mauritius	No	N/A	Yes	N/A	
55	Mexico	No	N/A	Yes	N/A	
56	Moldova*	No	N/A	Yes	N/A	
57	Mongolia	No	N/A	Yes	N/A	
58	Montenegro	No	N/A	Yes	N/A	
59	Morocco	No	N/A	Yes	N/A	
60	Nepal*	No	N/A	Yes	N/A	
61	Netherlands	No	N/A	Yes	N/A	
62	New Zealand	Yes	PPT alone	N/A	N/A	
63	Nigeria	No	N/A	Yes	N/A	
64	North Macedonia	No	N/A	Yes	N/A	
65	Norway	No	N/A	Yes	N/A	
66	Oman	No	N/A	Yes	N/A	
67	Pakistan	No	N/A	Yes	N/A	
68	Papua New Guinea	No	N/A	Yes	N/A	
69	Philippines*	No	N/A	Yes	N/A	
70	Poland	No	N/A	Yes	N/A	
71	Portugal	No	N/A	Yes	N/A	

72	Qatar	No	N/A	Yes	N/A
73	Romania	No	N/A	Yes	N/A
74	Russia	No	N/A	Yes	N/A
75	Saudi Arabia	No	N/A	Yes	N/A
76	Serbia	No	N/A	Yes	N/A
77	Seychelles	No	N/A	Yes	N/A
78	Singapore	No	N/A	Yes	N/A
79	Slovak Republic	No	N/A	Yes	N/A
80	Slovenia	No	N/A	Yes	N/A
81	South Africa	No	N/A	Yes	N/A
82	Spain	No	N/A	Yes	PPT alone
83	Sri Lanka	No	N/A	Yes	N/A
84	Sudan*	No	N/A	Yes	N/A
85	Sweden	No	N/A	Yes	N/A
86	Switzerland	No	N/A	Yes	N/A
87	Syrian Arab Republic*	No	N/A	Yes	N/A
88	Tajikistan*	No	N/A	Yes	N/A
89	Thailand	No	N/A	Yes	N/A
90	Trinidad and Tobago	No	N/A	Yes	N/A
91	Tunisia	No	N/A	Yes	N/A
92	Turkey	No	N/A	Yes	N/A
93	Turkmenistan*	No	N/A	Yes	N/A
94	Ukraine	No	N/A	Yes	N/A
95	United Arab Emirates	No	N/A	Yes	N/A
96	United Kingdom	No	N/A	Yes	N/A
97	United States	No	N/A	Yes	N/A
98	Uzbekistan*	No	N/A	Yes	N/A
99	Venezuela*	No	N/A	Yes	N/A
100	Viet Nam	No	N/A	Yes	N/A
101	Zambia	No	N/A	Yes	N/A
102	Zimbabwe*	No	N/A	Yes	N/A

Colombia

A. Progress in the implementation of the minimum standard

Colombia has eleven tax agreements in force, as reported in its response to the Peer Review questionnaire, including the Decision 578 of the Andean Community Commission (Decision 578) for the members of the Andean Community (the Andean Community Agreement).[33] One of those agreements, the agreement with the United Kingdom, complies with the minimum standard.

Colombia signed the MLI in 2017, listing its non-compliant bilateral agreements.

Colombia indicated in its response to the Peer Review questionnaire that the Andean Community Agreement has not been listed under the MLI as it is a decision of the Andean Community Commission.[34] However, in order to bring the Andean Community Agreement into compliance with the Action 6 minimum standard, Colombia has entered into negotiations with its treaty partners and reported that good process had been made.

Colombia further indicated that bilateral negotiations would be pursued with respect to its agreement with Switzerland.

Colombia is implementing the minimum standard through the inclusion of the preamble statement and the PPT combined with the LOB.[35]

The agreements that will be modified by the MLI will come into compliance with the minimum standard once the provisions of the MLI take effect.

B. Implementation issues

Colombia's listed agreements under the MLI will start to be compliant after Colombia's ratification of the MLI. Colombia indicated that it had presented a draft bill for the approval of the MLI to the Congress of the Republic in January 2021. Colombia is encouraged to ratify the MLI as soon as possible.

Summary of the jurisdiction response - Colombia

	Treaty partners	Compliance with the standard	If compliant, the alternative implemented	Signature of a complying instrument	The alternative implemented through the complying instrument (if not the MLI)	Comments
1	Bolivia*	No	N/A	No	N/A	Currently renegotiating Decision 578
2	Canada	No	N/A	Yes	N/A	
3	Chile	No	N/A	Yes	N/A	
4	Czech Republic	No	N/A	Yes	N/A	

33 The Decision of the Commission of the Andean Community 578 on the regime for the avoidance of double taxation and the prevention of fiscal evasion, adopted on 4 May 2004. The current members of the Andean Community are Bolivia*, Colombia, Ecuador* and Peru. In total, Colombia identified thirteen "agreements" in its List of Tax agreements: ten bilateral agreements and the Andean Community Agreement.

34 Bolivia* and Ecuador* are not members of the BEPS Inclusive Framework.

35 For its agreements listed under the MLI, Colombia is implementing the preamble statement (Article 6 of the MLI) and the PPT (Article 7 of the MLI). Colombia also opted for the simplified LOB under Article 7(6) of the MLI.

5	Ecuador*	No	N/A	No	N/A	Currently renegotiating Decision 578
6	India	No	N/A	Yes	N/A	
7	Korea	No	N/A	Yes	N/A	
8	Mexico	No	N/A	Yes	N/A	
9	Peru	No	N/A	No	N/A	Currently renegotiating Decision 578
10	Portugal	No	N/A	Yes	N/A	
11	Spain	No	N/A	Yes	N/A	
12	Switzerland[36]	No	N/A	Yes	N/A	
13	United Kingdom	Yes	PPT alone	N/A	N/A	

[36] Colombia and Switzerland are finalising an Amending Protocol expected for signature during 2020. The Protocol adopts the preamble statement and the PPT and LOB.

Congo

A. Progress in the implementation of the minimum standard

Congo has three tax agreements in force, as reported in its response to the Peer Review questionnaire.

None of Congo's agreements comply with the minimum standard or are subject to a complying instrument.

Congo has not signed the MLI.

B. Implementation issues

As Congo has not signed the MLI or implemented anti-treaty-shopping measures in its agreements, the Secretariat will offer its support to design a plan for the implementation of the minimum standard to strengthen its network of agreements.

Summary of the jurisdiction response - Congo

	Treaty partners	Compliance with the standard	If compliant, the alternative implemented	Signature of a complying instrument	The alternative implemented through the complying instrument (if not the MLI)	Comments
1	France	No	N/A	No	N/A	
2	Italy	No	N/A	No	N/A	
3	Mauritius	No	N/A	No	N/A	

Cook Islands

A. Progress in the implementation of the minimum standard

The Cook Islands has no tax agreements, as reported in its response to the Peer Review questionnaire.

B. Implementation issues

No jurisdiction has raised any concerns about the Cook Islands.

Costa Rica

A. Progress in the implementation of the minimum standard

Costa Rica has three tax agreements in force, as reported in its response to the Peer Review questionnaire.

Costa Rica signed the MLI in 2017 and deposited its instrument of ratification on 22 September 2020. The MLI will enter into force for Costa Rica on 1 January 2021.

Costa Rica indicated in its response to the Peer Review questionnaire that bilateral negotiations would be used with respect to its agreement with Germany.

Costa Rica is implementing the minimum standard through the inclusion of the preamble statement and the PPT.[37]

The agreements that will be modified by the MLI will come into compliance with the minimum standard once the provisions of the MLI take effect.

B. Implementation issues

No jurisdiction has raised any concerns about the Costa Rica.

Summary of the jurisdiction response – Costa Rica

	Treaty partners	Compliance with the standard	If compliant, the alternative implemented	Signature of a complying instrument	The alternative implemented through the complying instrument (if not the MLI)	Comments
1	Germany	No	N/A	No	N/A	
2	Mexico	No	N/A	Yes	N/A	
3	Spain	No	N/A	Yes	N/A	

37 For its agreements listed under the MLI, Costa Rica is implementing the preamble statement (Article 6 of the MLI) and the PPT (Article 7 of the MLI).

Côte d'Ivoire

A. Progress in the implementation of the minimum standard

Côte d'Ivoire has 12 tax agreements in force, as reported in its response to the Peer Review questionnaire, including the multilateral Regulation 08/2008/COM adopting the rules for the avoidance of double taxation within the West African Economic and Monetary Union and the rule for assistance in tax matters (the UEMOA) concluded with seven partners.[38]

Côte d'Ivoire signed the MLI in 2018 and has not listed its agreement with Switzerland.

Côte d'Ivoire is implementing the minimum standard through the inclusion of the preamble statement and the PPT.[39]

The agreements that will be modified by the MLI will come into compliance with the minimum standard once the provisions of the MLI take effect.

B. Implementation issues

Côte d'Ivoire's listed agreements under the MLI will start to be compliant after Côte d'Ivoire's ratification of the MLI. Côte d'Ivoire is encouraged to ratify the MLI as soon as possible.

Côte d'Ivoire is encouraged to consider entering into negotiations with respect to the UEMOA.

Summary of the jurisdiction response – Côte d'Ivoire

	Treaty partners	Compliance with the standard	If compliant, the alternative implemented	Signature of a complying instrument	The alternative implemented through the complying instrument (if not the MLI)	Comments
1	Belgium	No	N/A	Yes	N/A	
2	Benin	No	N/A	No	N/A	UEMOA
3	Burkina Faso	No	N/A	No	N/A	UEMOA
4	Canada	No	N/A	Yes	N/A	
5	France	No	N/A	Yes	N/A	
6	Germany	No	N/A	Yes	N/A	
7	Guinea-Bissau*	No	N/A	No	N/A	UEMOA
8	Italy	No	N/A	Yes	N/A	
9	Mali*	No	N/A	No	N/A	UEMOA
10	Morocco	No	N/A	Yes	N/A	
11	Niger*	No	N/A	No	N/A	UEMOA
12	Norway	No	N/A	Yes	N/A	

[38] Règlement n°08/2008/CM des pays de l'Union économique et monétaire Ouest Africaine (UEMOA) du 26 septembre 2008 portant adoption des règles visant à éviter la double imposition au sein de l'UEMOA et des règles d'assistance en matière fiscale. In total, Côte d'Ivoire identified 18 "agreements" in its List of Tax agreements: eleven bilateral agreements and the UEMOA.

[39] For its agreements listed under the MLI, Côte d'Ivoire is implementing the preamble statement (Article 6 of the MLI) and the PPT (Article 7 of the MLI). Côte d'Ivoire also opted for the asymmetrical application of the simplified LOB under Article 7(7)(b) of the MLI.

13	Portugal	No	N/A	Yes	N/A	
14	Senegal	No	N/A	No	N/A	UEMOA
15	Switzerland	No	N/A	No	N/A	
16	Togo*	No	N/A	No	N/A	UEMOA
17	Tunisia	No	N/A	Yes	N/A	
18	United Kingdom	No	N/A	Yes	N/A	

Croatia

A. Progress in the implementation of the minimum standard

Croatia has 66 tax agreements in force, as reported in its response to the Peer Review questionnaire. One of those agreements, the agreement with Japan, complies with the minimum standard.

Croatia signed the MLI in 2017. It did not list its agreements with Kazakhstan, the United Arab Emirates and Viet Nam. These agreements will therefore not, at this stage, be modified by the MLI. Croatia indicated in its response to the Peer Review questionnaire that it will add these agreements under the MLI when it will ratify the MLI.

Croatia is implementing the minimum standard through the inclusion of the preamble statement and the PPT.[40]

The agreements that will be modified by the MLI will come into compliance with the minimum standard once the provisions of the MLI take effect.

B. Implementation issues

Croatia's listed agreements under the MLI will start to be compliant after Croatia's ratification of the MLI. Croatia indicated that its Parliament had approved a draft bill for the ratification of the MLI on 26 November 2020 that would soon be promulgated by the Croatian President. Croatia further indicated that it expected to deposit its instrument of ratification of the MLI by the end of 2020 or early in 2021.

Summary of the jurisdiction response - Croatia

	Treaty partners	Compliance with the standard	If compliant, the alternative implemented	Signature of a complying instrument	The alternative implemented through the complying instrument (if not the MLI)	Comments
1	Albania	No	N/A	Yes	N/A	
2	Armenia	No	N/A	Yes	N/A	
3	Austria	No	N/A	Yes	N/A	
4	Azerbaijan*	No	N/A	Yes	N/A	
5	Belarus*	No	N/A	Yes	N/A	
6	Belgium	No	N/A	Yes	N/A	
7	Bosnia-Herzegovina	No	N/A	Yes	N/A	
8	Bulgaria	No	N/A	Yes	N/A	
9	Canada	No	N/A	Yes	N/A	
10	Chile	No	N/A	Yes	N/A	
11	China (People's Republic of)	No	N/A	Yes	N/A	
12	Czech Republic	No	N/A	Yes	N/A	
13	Denmark	No	N/A	Yes	N/A	
14	Estonia	No	N/A	Yes	N/A	
15	Finland	No	N/A	Yes	N/A	

[40] For its agreements listed under the MLI, Croatia is implementing the preamble statement (Article 6 of the MLI) and the PPT (Article 7 of the MLI).

16	France	No	N/A	Yes	N/A	
17	Georgia	No	N/A	Yes	N/A	
18	Germany	No	N/A	Yes	N/A	
19	Greece	No	N/A	Yes	N/A	
20	Hungary	No	N/A	Yes	N/A	
21	Iceland	No	N/A	Yes	N/A	
22	India	No	N/A	Yes	N/A	
23	Indonesia	No	N/A	Yes	N/A	
24	Iran*	No	N/A	Yes	N/A	
25	Ireland	No	N/A	Yes	N/A	
26	Israel	No	N/A	Yes	N/A	
27	Italy	No	N/A	Yes	N/A	
28	Jordan	No	N/A	Yes	N/A	
29	Japan	Yes	PPT and LOB	N/A	N/A	
30	Kazakhstan	No	N/A	No	N/A	
31	Korea	No	N/A	Yes	N/A	
32	Kosovo*	No	N/A	Yes	N/A	
33	Kuwait*	No	N/A	Yes	N/A	
34	Latvia	No	N/A	Yes	N/A	
35	Lithuania	No	N/A	Yes	N/A	
36	Luxembourg	No	N/A	Yes	N/A	
37	Malaysia	No	N/A	Yes	N/A	
38	Malta	No	N/A	Yes	N/A	
39	Mauritius	No	N/A	Yes	N/A	
40	Moldova*	No	N/A	Yes	N/A	
41	Montenegro	No	N/A	Yes	N/A	
42	Morocco	No	N/A	Yes	N/A	
43	Netherlands	No	N/A	Yes	N/A	
44	North Macedonia	No	N/A	Yes	N/A	
45	Norway	No	N/A	Yes	N/A	
46	Oman	No	N/A	Yes	N/A	
47	Poland	No	N/A	Yes	N/A	
48	Portugal	No	N/A	Yes	N/A	
49	Qatar	No	N/A	Yes	N/A	
50	Romania	No	N/A	Yes	N/A	
51	Russia	No	N/A	Yes	N/A	
52	San Marino	No	N/A	Yes	N/A	
53	Serbia	No	N/A	Yes	N/A	
54	Slovak Republic	No	N/A	Yes	N/A	
55	Slovenia	No	N/A	Yes	N/A	
56	South Africa	No	N/A	Yes	N/A	
57	Spain	No	N/A	Yes	N/A	
58	Sweden	No	N/A	Yes	N/A	
59	Switzerland	No	N/A	Yes	N/A	
60	Syrian Arab Republic*	No	N/A	Yes	N/A	
61	Turkey	No	N/A	Yes	N/A	
62	Turkmenistan*	No	N/A	Yes	N/A	
63	Ukraine	No	N/A	Yes	N/A	
64	United Arab Emirates	No	N/A	No	N/A	
65	United Kingdom	No	N/A	Yes	N/A	
66	Viet Nam	No	N/A	No	N/A	

Curaçao

A. Progress in the implementation of the minimum standard

Curaçao has three tax agreements in force, as reported in its response to the Peer Review questionnaire. One of those agreements, the agreement with Malta, complies with the minimum standard.

Curaçao joined the MLI in 2017 and the Kingdom of the Netherlands deposited its instrument of acceptance on 29 March 2019, listing its non-compliant agreements. The MLI entered into force for Curaçao on 1 July 2019.

Curaçao indicated in its response to the Peer Review questionnaire that its agreement with the Netherlands has not been listed under the MLI as it is an arrangement governed by the domestic law of the Kingdom of the Netherlands.

Curaçao is implementing the minimum standard through the inclusion of the preamble statement and the PPT.[41]

The agreements modified by the MLI come into compliance with the minimum standard once the provisions of the MLI take effect.

B. Implementation issues

Curaçao is encouraged to consider entering into bilateral renegotiations with respect to its agreement with the Netherlands to implement the minimum standard.

Summary of the jurisdiction response – Curaçao

	Treaty partners	Compliance with the standard	If compliant, the alternative implemented	Signature of a complying instrument	The alternative implemented through the complying instrument (if not the MLI)	Comments
1	Malta	Yes	PPT alone	N/A	N/A	
2	Netherlands	No	N/A	No	N/A	
3	Norway	No	N/A	Yes	N/A	

[41] For its agreements listed under the MLI, Curaçao is implementing the preamble statement (Article 6 of the MLI) and the PPT (Article 7 of the MLI).

Czech Republic

A. Progress in the implementation of the minimum standard

The Czech Republic has 88 tax agreements in force, as reported in its response to the Peer Review questionnaire.[42] One of those agreements, the agreement with Korea, complies with the minimum standard.

The Czech Republic signed the MLI in 2017 and deposited its instrument of ratification on 13 May 2020. The MLI will enter into force for the Czech Republic on 1 September 2020. The Czech Republic has not listed its agreements with Albania, Bahrain, Barbados, Bosnia-Herzegovina, Brazil, Estonia, Indonesia, Jordan, Kazakhstan, Malaysia, Mongolia, Montenegro, Morocco, North Macedonia, Panama, Saudi Arabia, Sri Lanka, Thailand, Tunisia, Ukraine, the United Arab Emirates and Viet Nam. These agreements will therefore not, at this stage, be modified by the MLI. Albania, Barbados, Bosnia-Herzegovina, Estonia, Indonesia, Jordan, Kazakhstan, Malaysia, Morocco, North Macedonia, Panama, Saudi Arabia, Tunisia, Ukraine and the United Arab Emirates have listed their agreements with the Czech Republic under the MLI.

The Czech Republic is implementing the minimum standard through the inclusion of the preamble statement and the PPT.[43]

The agreements that will be modified by the MLI will come into compliance with the minimum standard once the provisions of the MLI take effect.

B. Implementation issues

As mentioned above, the Czech Republic has not listed its agreements with Albania, Bahrain, Barbados, Bosnia-Herzegovina, Brazil, Estonia, Indonesia, Jordan, Kazakhstan, Malaysia, Mongolia, Montenegro, Morocco, North Macedonia, Panama, Saudi Arabia, Sri Lanka, Thailand, Tunisia, Ukraine, the United Arab Emirates and Viet Nam under the MLI. Listing the agreements under the MLI or entering into bilateral renegotiations to implement the minimum standard would ensure that the minimum standard could be implemented in those non-covered agreements.

Summary of the jurisdiction response – Czech Republic

	Treaty partners	Compliance with the standard	If compliant, the alternative implemented	Signature of a complying instrument	The alternative implemented through the complying instrument (if not the MLI)	Comments
1	Albania	No	N/A	No	N/A	
2	Armenia	No	N/A	Yes	N/A	
3	Australia	No	N/A	Yes	N/A	
4	Austria	No	N/A	Yes	N/A	
5	Azerbaijan*	No	N/A	No	N/A	

42 The Czech Republic continues to apply the treaty with former Serbia & Montenegro to both Serbia and Montenegro.

43 For its agreements listed under the MLI, the Czech Republic is implementing the preamble statement (Article 6 of the MLI) and the PPT (Article 7 of the MLI).

6	Bahrain	No	N/A	No	N/A
7	Barbados	No	N/A	No	N/A
8	Belarus*	No	N/A	No	N/A
9	Belgium	No	N/A	Yes	N/A
10	Bosnia-Herzegovina	No	N/A	No	N/A
11	Brazil	No	N/A	No	N/A
12	Bulgaria	No	N/A	Yes	N/A
13	Canada	No	N/A	Yes	N/A
14	Chile	No	N/A	Yes	N/A
15	China (People's Republic of)	No	N/A	Yes	N/A
16	Colombia	No	N/A	Yes	N/A
17	Croatia	No	N/A	Yes	N/A
18	Cyprus*	No	N/A	Yes	N/A
19	Democratic People's Republic of Korea*	No	N/A	No	N/A
20	Denmark	No	N/A	Yes	N/A
21	Egypt	No	N/A	Yes	N/A
22	Estonia	No	N/A	No	N/A
23	Ethiopia*	No	N/A	No	N/A
24	Finland	No	N/A	Yes	N/A
25	France	No	N/A	Yes	N/A
26	Georgia	No	N/A	Yes	N/A
27	Germany	No	N/A	Yes	N/A
28	Greece	No	N/A	Yes	N/A
29	Hong Kong (China)	No	N/A	Yes	N/A
30	Hungary	No	N/A	Yes	N/A
31	Iceland	No	N/A	Yes	N/A
32	India	No	N/A	Yes	N/A
33	Indonesia	No	N/A	No	N/A
34	Iran*	No	N/A	No	N/A
35	Ireland	No	N/A	Yes	N/A
36	Israel	No	N/A	Yes	N/A
37	Italy	No	N/A	Yes	N/A
38	Japan	No	N/A	Yes	N/A
39	Jordan	No	N/A	No	N/A
40	Kazakhstan	No	N/A	No	N/A
41	Korea	Yes	PPT alone	N/A	N/A
42	Kuwait*	No	N/A	Yes	N/A
43	Latvia	No	N/A	Yes	N/A
44	Lebanon*	No	N/A	No	N/A
45	Liechtenstein	No	N/A	Yes	N/A
46	Lithuania	No	N/A	Yes	N/A
47	Luxembourg	No	N/A	Yes	N/A
48	Malaysia	No	N/A	No	N/A
49	Malta	No	N/A	Yes	N/A
50	Mexico	No	N/A	Yes	N/A
51	Moldova*	No	N/A	No	N/A
52	Mongolia	No	N/A	No	N/A
53	Montenegro	No	N/A	No	N/A
54	Morocco	No	N/A	No	N/A
55	Netherlands	No	N/A	Yes	N/A

56	New Zealand	No	N/A	Yes	N/A	
57	Nigeria	No	N/A	Yes	N/A	
58	North Macedonia	No	N/A	No	N/A	
59	Norway	No	N/A	Yes	N/A	
60	Pakistan	No	N/A	Yes	N/A	
61	Panama	No	N/A	No	N/A	
62	Philippines*	No	N/A	No	N/A	
63	Poland	No	N/A	Yes	N/A	
64	Portugal	No	N/A	Yes	N/A	
65	Romania	No	N/A	Yes	N/A	
66	Russia	No	N/A	Yes	N/A	
67	Saudi Arabia	No	N/A	No	N/A	
68	Serbia	No	N/A	Yes	N/A	
69	Singapore	No	N/A	Yes	N/A	
70	Slovak Republic	No	N/A	Yes	N/A	
71	Slovenia	No	N/A	Yes	N/A	
72	South Africa	No	N/A	Yes	N/A	
73	Spain	No	N/A	Yes	N/A	
74	Sri Lanka	No	N/A	No	N/A	
75	Sweden	No	N/A	Yes	N/A	
76	Switzerland	No	N/A	Yes	N/A	
77	Syrian Arab Republic*	No	N/A	No	N/A	
78	Tajikistan*	No	N/A	No	N/A	
79	Thailand	No	N/A	No	N/A	
80	Tunisia	No	N/A	No	N/A	
81	Turkey	No	N/A	Yes	N/A	
82	Turkmenistan*	No	N/A	No	N/A	
83	Ukraine	No	N/A	No	N/A	
84	United Arab Emirates	No	N/A	No	N/A	
85	United Kingdom	No	N/A	Yes	N/A	
86	United States	No	N/A	No	N/A	
87	Uzbekistan*	No	N/A	No	N/A	
88	Venezuela*	No	N/A	No	N/A	
89	Viet Nam	No	N/A	No	N/A	

Democratic Republic of the Congo

A. Progress in the implementation of the minimum standard

The Democratic Republic of the Congo has two tax agreements in force, as reported in its response to the Peer Review questionnaire.

Neither of the Democratic Republic of the Congo's agreements comply with the minimum standard or are subject to a complying instrument.

The Democratic Republic of the Congo has not signed the MLI.

B. Implementation issues

As the Democratic Republic of the Congo has not signed the MLI or implemented anti-treaty-shopping measures in its agreements, the Secretariat will offer its support to design a plan for the implementation of the minimum standard to strengthen its network of agreements.

Summary of the jurisdiction response – Democratic Republic of the Congo

	Treaty partners	Compliance with the standard	If compliant, the alternative implemented	Signature of a complying instrument	The alternative implemented through the complying instrument (if not the MLI)	Comments
1	Belgium	No	N/A	No	N/A	
2	South Africa	No	N/A	No	N/A	

Denmark

A. Progress in the implementation of the minimum standard

Denmark has 71 tax agreements in force, as reported in its response to the Peer Review questionnaire, including the multilateral Nordic Convention concluded with Finland, Iceland, Norway and Sweden (the "Nordic Convention").[44] 19 of those agreements, the agreements with Australia, Belgium, Canada, India, Ireland, Israel, Japan, Lithuania, Luxembourg, Malta, the Netherlands, New Zealand, Poland, Serbia, the Slovak Republic, Slovenia, Ukraine, the United Kingdom and the Nordic Convention, comply with the minimum standard.

Denmark signed the MLI in 2017 and deposited its instrument of ratification on 30 September 2019. The MLI entered into force for Denmark on 1 January 2020. Denmark has not listed its agreements with Armenia, Germany, and Switzerland, but has indicated its intention to notify its agreement with Armenia under the MLI. These agreements will therefore not, at this stage, be modified by the MLI.

The Parties to the Nordic Convention signed a complying instrument in 2018. The protocol entered into force on 28 November 2019 and its provisions took effect on 1 January 2020.

Denmark is implementing the minimum standard through the inclusion of the preamble statement and the PPT.[45]

The agreements modified by the MLI come into compliance with the minimum standard once the provisions of the MLI take effect.

B. Implementation issues

As mentioned above, Denmark has not listed its agreements with Armenia, Germany and Switzerland under the MLI. Listing the agreements under the MLI or entering into bilateral renegotiations to implement the minimum standard would ensure that the minimum standard could be implemented in those non-covered agreements.

Summary of the jurisdiction response - Denmark

	Treaty partners	Compliance with the standard	If compliant, the alternative implemented	Signature of a complying instrument	The alternative implemented through the complying instrument (if not the MLI)	Comments
1	Argentina	No	N/A	Yes	N/A	
2	Armenia	No	N/A	No	N/A	The treaty will be notified as a CTA under the MLI.
3	Australia	Yes	PPT alone	N/A	N/A	

[44] See the Multilateral convention concluded by Denmark, Finland, the Faroe Islands, Iceland, Norway and Sweden: for the avoidance of double taxation with respect to taxes on income and on capital (1996, 1997, 2008 and 2018). In total, Denmark identified 74 "agreements" in its List of Tax agreements: 70 bilateral agreements and the Nordic Convention concluded with four of its treaty partners.

[45] For its agreements listed under the MLI, Denmark is implementing the preamble statement (Article 6 of the MLI) and the PPT (Article 7 of the MLI). Denmark has also accepted to implement a simplified LOB in agreements concluded with partners that opted in for the simplified LOB (Article 7(7)(a) of the MLI).

4	Austria	No	N/A	Yes	N/A	
5	Azerbaijan*	No	N/A	Yes	N/A	
6	Bangladesh*	No	N/A	Yes	N/A	
7	Belarus*	No	N/A	No	N/A	
8	Belgium	Yes	PPT alone	N/A	N/A	
9	Brazil	No	N/A	Yes	N/A	
10	Bulgaria	No	N/A	Yes	N/A	
11	Canada	Yes	PPT alone	N/A	N/A	
12	Chile	No	N/A	Yes	N/A	
13	China (People's Republic of)	No	N/A	Yes	N/A	
14	Chinese Taipei*	No	N/A	Yes	N/A	
15	Croatia	No	N/A	Yes	N/A	
16	Cyprus*	No	N/A	Yes	N/A	
17	Czech Republic	No	N/A	Yes	N/A	
18	Egypt	No	N/A	Yes	N/A	
19	Estonia	No	N/A	Yes	N/A	
20	Finland	Yes	PPT alone	N/A	N/A	Nordic Convention
21	Georgia	No	N/A	Yes	N/A	
22	Germany	No	N/A	No	N/A	
23	Ghana*	No	N/A	Yes	N/A	
24	Greece	No	N/A	Yes	N/A	
25	Hungary	No	N/A	Yes	N/A	
26	Iceland	Yes	PPT alone	N/A	N/A	Nordic Convention
27	India	Yes	PPT and LOB	N/A	N/A	
28	Indonesia	No	N/A	Yes	N/A	
29	Ireland	Yes	PPT alone	N/A	N/A	
30	Israel	Yes	PPT alone	N/A	N/A	
31	Italy	No	N/A	Yes	N/A	
32	Jamaica	No	N/A	Yes	N/A	
33	Japan	Yes	PPT and LOB	N/A	N/A	
34	Kenya	No	N/A	Yes	N/A	
35	Korea	No	N/A	Yes	N/A	
36	Kuwait*	No	N/A	Yes	N/A	
37	Latvia	No	N/A	Yes	N/A	
38	Lithuania	Yes	PPT alone	N/A	N/A	
39	Luxembourg	Yes	PPT alone	N/A	N/A	
40	Malaysia	No	N/A	Yes	N/A	
41	Malta	Yes	PPT alone	N/A	N/A	
42	Mexico	No	N/A	Yes	N/A	
43	Montenegro	No	N/A	Yes	N/A	
44	Morocco	No	N/A	Yes	N/A	
45	Netherlands	Yes	PPT alone	N/A	N/A	
46	New Zealand	Yes	PPT alone	N/A	N/A	
47	North Macedonia	No	N/A	Yes	N/A	
48	Norway	Yes	PPT alone	N/A	N/A	Nordic Convention
49	Pakistan	No	N/A	Yes	N/A	
50	Philippines*	No	N/A	Yes	N/A	
51	Poland	Yes	PPT alone	N/A	N/A	
52	Portugal	No	N/A	Yes	N/A	
53	Romania	No	N/A	Yes	N/A	
54	Russia	No	N/A	Yes	N/A	
55	Serbia	Yes	PPT alone	N/A	N/A	
56	Singapore	No	N/A	Yes	N/A	

57	Slovak Republic	Yes	PPT alone	N/A	N/A	
58	Slovenia	Yes	PPT alone	N/A	N/A	
59	South Africa	No	N/A	Yes	N/A	
60	Sri Lanka	No	N/A	Yes	N/A	
61	Sweden	Yes	PPT alone	N/A	N/A	Nordic Convention
62	Switzerland	No	N/A	No	N/A	
63	Tanzania*	No	N/A	Yes	N/A	
64	Thailand	No	N/A	Yes	N/A	
65	Trinidad and Tobago	No	N/A	Yes	N/A	
66	Tunisia	No	N/A	Yes	N/A	
67	Turkey	No	N/A	Yes	N/A	
68	Uganda*	No	N/A	Yes	N/A	
69	Ukraine	Yes	PPT alone	N/A	N/A	
70	United Kingdom	Yes	PPT alone	N/A	N/A	
71	United States	No	N/A	Yes	N/A	
72	Venezuela*	No	N/A	Yes	N/A	
73	Viet Nam	No	N/A	Yes	N/A	
74	Zambia	No	N/A	Yes	N/A	

Djibouti

A. Progress in the implementation of the minimum standard

Djibouti has no tax agreements, as reported in its response to the Peer Review questionnaire.

B. Implementation issues

No jurisdiction has raised any concerns about Djibouti.

Dominica

A. Progress in the implementation of the minimum standard

Dominica has three tax agreements in force, as reported in its response to the Peer Review questionnaire, including the multilateral agreement among the members of the CARICOM concluded with ten treaty partners (the CARICOM Agreement).[46]

None of Dominica's agreements comply with the minimum standard or are subject to a complying instrument.

Dominica has not signed the MLI.

B. Implementation issues

As Dominica has not signed the MLI or implemented anti-treaty-shopping measures in its agreements, the Secretariat will offer its support to design a plan for the implementation of the minimum standard to strengthen its network of agreements.

Dominica is encouraged to bring the CARICOM Agreement up to date by commencing talks among all the treaty partners.[47]

Summary of the jurisdiction response - Dominica

	Treaty partners	Compliance with the standard	If compliant, the alternative implemented	Signature of a complying instrument	The alternative implemented through the complying instrument (if not the MLI)	Comments
1	Antigua and Barbuda	No	N/A	No	N/A	CARICOM
2	Barbados	No	N/A	No	N/A	CARICOM
3	Belize	No	N/A	No	N/A	CARICOM
4	Grenada	No	N/A	No	N/A	CARICOM
5	Guyana*	No	N/A	No	N/A	CARICOM
6	Jamaica	No	N/A	No	N/A	CARICOM
7	Saint Kitts and Nevis	No	N/A	No	N/A	CARICOM
8	Saint Lucia	No	N/A	No	N/A	CARICOM
9	Saint Vincent and the Grenadines	No	N/A	No	N/A	CARICOM
10	Switzerland	No	N/A	No	N/A	
11	Trinidad and Tobago	No	N/A	No	N/A	CARICOM
12	United Kingdom	No	N/A	No	N/A	

46 In total, Dominica identified twelve "agreements" in its List of Tax agreements: two bilateral agreements and the CARICOM Agreement.

47 Revisions to the CARICOM Agreement require an agreement from its eleven treaty partners.

Dominican Republic

A. Progress in the implementation of the minimum standard

The Dominican Republic has two tax agreements in force, as reported in its response to the Peer Review questionnaire.

Neither of the Dominican Republic's agreements comply with the minimum standard or are subject to a complying instrument.

The Dominican Republic has not signed the MLI.

The Dominican Republic indicated in its response to the Peer Review questionnaire that bilateral negotiations would be used with respect to its agreement with Canada and Spain.

B. Implementation issues

As the Dominican Republic has not signed the MLI or implemented anti-treaty-shopping measures in its agreements, the Secretariat will offer its support to design a plan for the implementation of the minimum standard to strengthen its network of agreements.

Summary of the jurisdiction response – Dominican Republic

	Treaty partners	Compliance with the standard	If compliant, the alternative implemented	Signature of a complying instrument	The alternative implemented through the complying instrument (if not the MLI)	Comments
1	Canada	No	N/A	No	N/A	
2	Spain	No	N/A	No	N/A	Partial compliance. Treaty has a PPT, but no new preamble

Egypt

A. Progress in the implementation of the minimum standard

Egypt has 58 tax agreements in force, as reported in its response to the Peer Review questionnaire. One of those agreements, the agreement with Cyprus*, complies with the minimum standard.

Egypt signed the MLI in 2017 and deposited its instrument of ratification on 30 September 2020. The MLI will enter into force for Egypt on 1 January 2021.

Egypt is implementing the minimum standard through the inclusion of the preamble statement and the PPT.[48]

The agreements that will be modified by the MLI will come into compliance with the minimum standard once the provisions of the MLI take effect.

B. Implementation issues

No jurisdiction has raised any concerns about their agreements with Egypt.

Summary of the jurisdiction response - Egypt

	Treaty partners	Compliance with the standard	If compliant, the alternative implemented	Signature of a complying instrument	The alternative implemented through the complying instrument (if not the MLI)	Comments
1	Albania	No	N/A	Yes	N/A	
2	Algeria*	No	N/A	Yes	N/A	
3	Austria	No	N/A	Yes	N/A	
4	Bahrain	No	N/A	Yes	N/A	
5	Belarus*	No	N/A	Yes	N/A	
6	Belgium	No	N/A	Yes	N/A	
7	Bulgaria	No	N/A	Yes	N/A	
8	Canada	No	N/A	Yes	N/A	
9	China (People's Republic of)	No	N/A	Yes	N/A	
10	Cyprus*	Yes	PPT alone	No	N/A	
11	Czech Republic	No	N/A	Yes	N/A	
12	Denmark	No	N/A	Yes	N/A	
13	Ethiopia*	No	N/A	Yes	N/A	
14	Finland	No	N/A	Yes	N/A	
15	France	No	N/A	Yes	N/A	
16	Georgia	No	N/A	Yes	N/A	
17	Germany	No	N/A	Yes	N/A	
18	Greece	No	N/A	Yes	N/A	
19	Hungary	No	N/A	Yes	N/A	
20	India	No	N/A	Yes	N/A	

48 For its agreements listed under the MLI, Egypt is implementing the preamble statement (Article 6 of the MLI) and the PPT (Article 7 of the MLI).

21	Indonesia	No	N/A	Yes	N/A	
22	Iraq*	No	N/A	Yes	N/A	
23	Ireland	No	N/A	Yes	N/A	
24	Italy	No	N/A	Yes	N/A	
25	Japan	No	N/A	Yes	N/A	
26	Jordan	No	N/A	Yes	N/A	
27	Korea	No	N/A	Yes	N/A	
28	Kuwait*	No	N/A	Yes	N/A	
29	Lebanon*	No	N/A	Yes	N/A	
30	Libya*	No	N/A	Yes	N/A	
31	Malaysia	No	N/A	Yes	N/A	
32	Malta	No	N/A	Yes	N/A	
33	Mauritius	No	N/A	Yes	N/A	
34	Morocco	No	N/A	Yes	N/A	
35	Netherlands	No	N/A	Yes	N/A	
36	Norway	No	N/A	Yes	N/A	
37	Pakistan	No	N/A	Yes	N/A	
38	Palestine*	No	N/A	Yes	N/A	
39	Poland	No	N/A	Yes	N/A	
40	Romania	No	N/A	Yes	N/A	
41	Russia	No	N/A	Yes	N/A	
42	Saudi Arabia	No	N/A	No	N/A	
43	Serbia	No	N/A	Yes	N/A	
44	Singapore	No	N/A	Yes	N/A	
45	South Africa	No	N/A	Yes	N/A	
46	Spain	No	N/A	Yes	N/A	
47	Sudan*	No	N/A	Yes	N/A	
48	Sweden	No	N/A	Yes	N/A	
49	Switzerland	No	N/A	Yes	N/A	
50	Syrian Arab Republic*	No	N/A	Yes	N/A	
51	Tunisia	No	N/A	Yes	N/A	
52	Turkey	No	N/A	Yes	N/A	
53	Ukraine	No	N/A	Yes	N/A	
54	United Arab Emirates	No	N/A	Yes	PPT alone	
55	United Kingdom	No	N/A	Yes	N/A	
56	United States	No	N/A	No	N/A	
57	Uzbekistan*	No	N/A	No	N/A	
58	Yemen*	No	N/A	Yes	N/A	

Estonia

A. Progress in the implementation of the minimum standard

Estonia has 60 tax agreements in force, as reported in its response to the Peer Review questionnaire. Two of those agreements, the agreements with Hong Kong (China) and Japan, comply with the minimum standard.

Estonia signed the MLI in 2018 and has not listed its agreements with Germany and Switzerland. It indicated in its response to the Peer Review questionnaire that bilateral negotiations would be pursued with respect to those agreements.

Estonia is generally implementing the minimum standard through the inclusion of the preamble statement and the PPT.[49]

The agreements that will be modified by the MLI will come into compliance with the minimum standard once the provisions of the MLI take effect.

B. Implementation issues

Estonia's listed agreements under the MLI will start to be compliant after Estonia's ratification of the MLI. Estonia indicated that the amended ratification bill was submitted to its Parliament. Estonia further indicated that it expected to deposit its instrument of ratification of the MLI early in 2021.

Summary of the jurisdiction response - Estonia

	Treaty partners	Compliance with the standard	If compliant, the alternative implemented	Signature of a complying instrument	The alternative implemented through the complying instrument (if not the MLI)	Comments
1	Albania	No	N/A	Yes	N/A	
2	Armenia	No	N/A	Yes	N/A	
3	Austria	No	N/A	Yes	N/A	
4	Azerbaijan*	No	N/A	Yes	N/A	
5	Bahrain	No	N/A	Yes	N/A	
6	Belarus*	No	N/A	Yes	N/A	
7	Belgium	No	N/A	Yes	N/A	
8	Bulgaria	No	N/A	Yes	N/A	
9	Canada	No	N/A	Yes	N/A	
10	China (People's Republic of)	No	N/A	Yes	N/A	
11	Croatia	No	N/A	Yes	N/A	
12	Cyprus*	No	N/A	Yes	N/A	
13	Czech Republic	No	N/A	Yes	N/A	
14	Denmark	No	N/A	Yes	N/A	
15	Finland	No	N/A	Yes	N/A	

49 For its agreements listed under the MLI, Estonia is implementing the preamble statement (Article 6 of the MLI) and the PPT (Article 7 of the MLI).

16	France	No	N/A	Yes	N/A	
17	Georgia	No	N/A	Yes	N/A	
18	Germany	No	N/A	Yes	PPT alone	
19	Greece	No	N/A	Yes	N/A	
20	Hong Kong (China)	Yes	PPT alone	N/A	N/A	
21	Hungary	No	N/A	Yes	N/A	
22	Iceland	No	N/A	Yes	N/A	
23	India	No	N/A	Yes	N/A	
24	Ireland	No	N/A	Yes	N/A	
25	Isle of Man	No	N/A	Yes	N/A	
26	Israel	No	N/A	Yes	N/A	
27	Italy	No	N/A	Yes	N/A	
28	Japan	Yes	PPT and LOB	N/A	N/A	
29	Jersey	No	N/A	Yes	N/A	
30	Kazakhstan	No	N/A	Yes	N/A	
31	Korea	No	N/A	Yes	N/A	
32	Kyrgyzstan*	No	N/A	Yes	N/A	
33	Latvia	No	N/A	Yes	N/A	
34	Lithuania	No	N/A	Yes	N/A	
35	Luxembourg	No	N/A	Yes	N/A	
36	Malta	No	N/A	Yes	N/A	
37	Mexico	No	N/A	Yes	N/A	
38	Moldova*	No	N/A	Yes	N/A	
39	Netherlands	No	N/A	Yes	N/A	
40	North Macedonia	No	N/A	Yes	N/A	
41	Norway	No	N/A	Yes	N/A	
42	Poland	No	N/A	Yes	N/A	
43	Portugal	No	N/A	Yes	N/A	
44	Romania	No	N/A	Yes	N/A	
45	Serbia	No	N/A	Yes	N/A	
46	Singapore	No	N/A	Yes	N/A	
47	Slovak Republic	No	N/A	Yes	N/A	
48	Slovenia	No	N/A	Yes	N/A	
49	Spain	No	N/A	Yes	N/A	
50	Sweden	No	N/A	Yes	N/A	
51	Switzerland	No	N/A	No	N/A	
52	Thailand	No	N/A	Yes	N/A	
53	Turkey	No	N/A	Yes	N/A	
54	Turkmenistan*	No	N/A	Yes	N/A	
55	Ukraine	No	N/A	Yes	N/A	
56	United Arab Emirates	No	N/A	Yes	N/A	
57	United Kingdom	No	N/A	Yes	N/A	
58	United States	No	N/A	Yes	N/A	
59	Uzbekistan*	No	N/A	Yes	N/A	
60	Viet Nam	No	N/A	Yes	N/A	

Eswatini

A. Progress in the implementation of the minimum standard

Eswatini has five tax agreements in force, as reported in its peer review questionnaire.

None of Eswatini's agreements comply with the minimum standard or are subject to a complying instrument.

Eswatini has not signed the MLI.

B. Implementation issues

As Eswatini has not signed the MLI or implemented anti-treaty-shopping measures in its agreements, the Secretariat will offer its support to design a plan for the implementation of the minimum standard to strengthen its network of agreements.

Summary of the jurisdiction response - Eswatini

	Treaty partners	Compliance with the standard	If compliant, the alternative implemented	Signature of a complying instrument	The alternative implemented through the complying instrument (if not the MLI)	Comments
1	Chinese Taipei*	No	N/A	No	N/A	
2	Mauritius	No	N/A	No	N/A	
3	Seychelles	No	N/A	No	N/A	
4	South Africa	No	N/A	No	N/A	
5	United Kingdom	No	N/A	No	N/A	

Faroe Islands

A. Progress in the implementation of the minimum standard

The Faroe Islands has five tax agreements in force, as reported in its response to the Peer Review questionnaire, including the multilateral Nordic Convention concluded with Denmark, Finland, Iceland, Norway and Sweden (the "Nordic Convention").[50] Three of those agreements, the agreements with Greenland and India as well as the Nordic Convention, comply with the minimum standard.

The Faroe Islands has not joined the MLI.

The Faroe Islands is implementing the minimum standard through the inclusion of the preamble statement and the PPT.

The Faroe Islands signed a complying instrument with respect to its agreement with Greenland.

The Faroe Islands indicated in its response to the Peer Review questionnaire that the agreements with India and Switzerland are agreements concluded by Denmark that apply to its territory.

The Parties to the Nordic Convention signed a complying instrument in 2018. The protocol entered into force on 28 November 2019 and its provisions took effect 1 January 2020.

B. Implementation issues

No jurisdiction has raised any concerns about their agreements with the Faroe Islands.

Summary of the jurisdiction response – Faroe Islands

	Treaty partners	Compliance with the standard	If compliant, the alternative implemented	Signature of a complying instrument	The alternative implemented through the complying instrument (if not the MLI)	Comments
1	Denmark	Yes	PPT alone	N/A	N/A	Nordic Convention
2	Finland	Yes	PPT alone	N/A	N/A	Nordic Convention
3	Greenland	Yes	PPT alone	N/A	N/A	
4	India	Yes	PPT and LOB	N/A	N/A	DK MLI
5	Iceland	Yes	PPT alone	N/A	N/A	Nordic Convention
6	Norway	Yes	PPT alone	N/A	N/A	Nordic Convention
7	Sweden	Yes	PPT alone	N/A	N/A	Nordic Convention
8	Switzerland	No	N/A	No	N/A	DK Protocol
9	United Kingdom	No	N/A	No	N/A	

[50] See the Multilateral convention concluded by Denmark, Finland, the Faroe Islands, Iceland, Norway and Sweden: for the avoidance of double taxation with respect to taxes on income and on capital (1996, 1997, 2008 and 2018). In total, the Faroe Islands identified eight "agreements" in its List of Tax agreements: three bilateral agreements and the Nordic Convention.

Finland

A. Progress in the implementation of the minimum standard

Finland has 73 tax agreements in force, as reported in its response to the Peer Review questionnaire, including the multilateral Nordic Convention concluded with Denmark, the Faroe Islands, Iceland, Norway and Sweden ("Nordic Convention").[51] Twenty-five of those agreements, the agreements with Australia, Austria, Belgium, Canada, France, Georgia, Hong Kong (China), India, Ireland, Israel, Japan, Lithuania, Luxembourg, Malta, Netherlands, New Zealand, Poland, Serbia, Singapore, the Slovak Republic, Slovenia, Ukraine, the United Arab Emirates and the United Kingdom as well as the Nordic Convention, comply with the minimum standard.

Finland signed the MLI in 2017 and deposited its instrument of acceptance on 25 February 2019. The MLI entered into force for Finland on 1 June 2019. Finland has not listed its agreements with Bulgaria and Germany but indicated in its response to the Peer Review questionnaire that bilateral negotiations would be pursued with respect to those agreements and that a complying instrument was signed with Germany in November 2019.

The Parties to the Nordic Convention signed a complying instrument in 2018. The protocol entered into force on 28 November 2019 and its provisions took effect 1 January 2020.

Finland is implementing the minimum standard through the inclusion of the preamble statement and the PPT.[52]

The agreements that will be modified by the MLI will come into compliance with the minimum standard once the provisions of the MLI take effect.

B. Implementation issues

No jurisdiction has raised any concerns about their agreements with Finland.

Summary of the jurisdiction response - Finland

	Treaty partners	Compliance with the standard	If compliant, the alternative implemented	Signature of a complying instrument	The alternative implemented through the complying instrument (if not the MLI)	Comments
1	Argentina	No	N/A	Yes	N/A	
2	Armenia	No	N/A	Yes	N/A	
3	Australia	Yes	PPT alone	N/A	N/A	
4	Austria	Yes	PPT alone	N/A	N/A	
5	Azerbaijan*	No	N/A	Yes	N/A	

[51] See the Multilateral convention concluded by Denmark, Finland, the Faroe Islands, Iceland, Norway and Sweden: for the avoidance of double taxation with respect to taxes on income and on capital (1996, 1997, 2008 and 2018). In total, Finland identified 77 "agreements" in its List of Tax agreements: 72 bilateral agreements and the Nordic Convention concluded with five of its treaty partners.

[52] For its agreements listed under the MLI, Finland is implementing the preamble statement (Article 6 of the MLI) and the PPT (Article 7 of the MLI).

6	Barbados	No	N/A	Yes	N/A	
7	Belarus*	No	N/A	Yes	N/A	
8	Belgium	Yes	PPT alone	N/A	N/A	
9	Bosnia-Herzegovina	No	N/A	Yes	N/A	
10	Brazil	No	N/A	Yes	N/A	
11	Bulgaria	No	N/A	No	N/A	
12	Canada	Yes	PPT alone	N/A	N/A	
13	China (People's Republic of)	No	N/A	Yes	N/A	
14	Croatia	No	N/A	Yes	N/A	
15	Cyprus*	No	N/A	Yes	N/A	
16	Czech Republic	No	N/A	Yes	N/A	
17	Denmark	Yes	PPT alone	N/A	N/A	Nordic Convention
18	Egypt	No	N/A	Yes	N/A	
19	Estonia	No	N/A	Yes	N/A	
20	Faroe Islands	Yes	PPT alone	N/A	N/A	Nordic Convention
21	France	Yes	PPT alone	N/A	N/A	
22	Georgia	Yes	PPT alone	N/A	N/A	
23	Germany	No	N/A	Yes	PPT alone	
24	Greece	No	N/A	Yes	N/A	
25	Hong Kong (China)	Yes	PPT alone	N/A	N/A	
26	Hungary	No	N/A	Yes	N/A	
27	Iceland	Yes	PPT alone	N/A	N/A	Nordic Convention
28	India	Yes	PPT alone	N/A	N/A	
29	Indonesia	No	N/A	Yes	N/A	
30	Ireland	Yes	PPT alone	N/A	N/A	
31	Israel	Yes	PPT alone	N/A	N/A	
32	Italy	No	N/A	Yes	N/A	
33	Japan	Yes	PPT alone	N/A	N/A	
34	Kazakhstan	No	N/A	Yes	N/A	
35	Korea	No	N/A	Yes	N/A	
36	Kosovo*	No	N/A	Yes	N/A	
37	Kyrgyzstan*	No	N/A	Yes	N/A	
38	Latvia	No	N/A	Yes	N/A	
39	Lithuania	Yes	PPT alone	N/A	N/A	
40	Luxembourg	Yes	PPT alone	N/A	N/A	
41	Malaysia	No	N/A	Yes	N/A	
42	Malta	Yes	PPT alone	N/A	N/A	
43	Mexico	No	N/A	Yes	N/A	
44	Moldova*	No	N/A	Yes	N/A	
45	Montenegro	No	N/A	Yes	N/A	
46	Morocco	No	N/A	Yes	N/A	
47	Netherlands	Yes	PPT alone	N/A	N/A	
48	New Zealand	Yes	PPT alone	N/A	N/A	
49	North Macedonia	No	N/A	Yes	N/A	
50	Norway	Yes	PPT alone	N/A	N/A	Nordic Convention
51	Pakistan	No	N/A	Yes	N/A	
52	Philippines*	No	N/A	Yes	N/A	
53	Poland	Yes	PPT alone	N/A	N/A	
54	Romania	No	N/A	Yes	N/A	
55	Russia	No	N/A	Yes	N/A	
56	Serbia	Yes	PPT alone	N/A	N/A	
57	Singapore	Yes	PPT alone	N/A	N/A	

58	Slovak Republic	Yes	PPT alone	N/A	N/A	
59	Slovenia	Yes	PPT alone	N/A	N/A	
60	South Africa	No	N/A	Yes	N/A	
61	Spain	No	N/A	Yes	N/A	
62	Sri Lanka	No	N/A	Yes	N/A	
63	Sweden	Yes	PPT alone	N/A	N/A	Nordic Convention
64	Switzerland	No	N/A	Yes	N/A	The treaty partner has not listed this agreement in its MLI position.
65	Tajikistan*	No	N/A	Yes	N/A	
66	Tanzania*	No	N/A	Yes	N/A	
67	Thailand	No	N/A	Yes	N/A	
68	Turkey	No	N/A	Yes	N/A	
69	Turkmenistan*	No	N/A	Yes	N/A	
70	Ukraine	Yes	PPT alone	N/A	N/A	
71	United Arab Emirates	Yes	PPT alone	N/A	N/A	
72	United Kingdom	Yes	PPT alone	N/A	N/A	
73	United States	No	N/A	Yes	N/A	
74	Uruguay	No	N/A	Yes	N/A	
75	Uzbekistan*	No	N/A	Yes	N/A	
76	Viet Nam	No	N/A	Yes	N/A	
77	Zambia	No	N/A	Yes	N/A	

France

A. Progress in the implementation of the minimum standard

France has 119 tax agreements in force, as reported in its response to the Peer Review questionnaire. Twenty-five of those agreements, the agreements with Australia, Austria, Belgium, Canada, Finland, Georgia, Iceland, India, Ireland, Israel, Japan, Lithuania, Luxembourg, Malta, Monaco, the Netherlands, New Zealand, Poland, Serbia, the Slovak Republic, Singapore, Slovenia, Ukraine, the United Arab Emirates and the United Kingdom, comply with the minimum standard.

France signed the MLI in 2017 and deposited its instrument of ratification on 26 September 2018. The MLI entered into force for France on 1 January 2019. Further, France deposited additional notifications under the MLI on 22 September 2020 to list its agreements that were initially not listed in its definitive MLI Position.

France is implementing the minimum standard through the inclusion of the preamble statement and the PPT.[53]

The agreements modified by the MLI come into compliance with the minimum standard once the provisions of the MLI take effect.

B. Implementation issues

No jurisdiction has raised any concerns about their agreements with France.

France indicated that it had contacted its treaty partners and encouraged them to join the MLI. France also contacted some of its treaty partners that are Signatories to the MLI and encouraged them to list those agreements under the MLI.

Summary of the jurisdiction response - France

	Treaty partners	Compliance with the standard	If compliant, the alternative implemented	Signature of a complying instrument	The alternative implemented through the complying instrument (if not the MLI)	Comments
1	Albania	No	N/A	Yes	N/A	
2	Algeria*	No	N/A	Yes	N/A	
3	Andorra	No	N/A	Yes	N/A	
4	Argentina	No	N/A	Yes	N/A	
5	Armenia	No	N/A	Yes	N/A	
6	Australia	Yes	PPT alone	N/A	N/A	
7	Austria	Yes	PPT alone	N/A	N/A	
8	Azerbaijan*	No	N/A	Yes	N/A	
9	Bahrain	No	N/A	Yes	N/A	
10	Bangladesh*	No	N/A	Yes	N/A	
11	Belarus*	No	N/A	Yes	N/A	
12	Belgium	Yes	PPT alone	N/A	N/A	
13	Benin	No	N/A	Yes	N/A	
14	Bolivia*	No	N/A	Yes	N/A	
15	Bosnia-Herzegovina	No	N/A	Yes	N/A	
16	Botswana	No	N/A	Yes	N/A	
17	Brazil	No	N/A	Yes	N/A	
18	Bulgaria	No	N/A	Yes	N/A	

[53] For its agreements listed under the MLI, France is implementing the preamble statement (Article 6 of the MLI) and the PPT (Article 7 of the MLI).

19	Burkina Faso	No	N/A	Yes	N/A	
20	Cameroon	No	N/A	Yes	N/A	
21	Canada	Yes	PPT alone	N/A	N/A	
22	Central African Republic*	No	N/A	Yes	N/A	
23	Chile	No	N/A	Yes	N/A	
24	China (People's Republic of)	No	N/A	Yes	N/A	
25	Congo	No	N/A	Yes	N/A	
26	Côte d'Ivoire	No	N/A	Yes	N/A	
27	Croatia	No	N/A	Yes	N/A	
28	Cyprus*	No	N/A	Yes	N/A	
29	Czech Republic	No	N/A	Yes	N/A	
30	Ecuador*	No	N/A	Yes	N/A	
31	Egypt	No	N/A	Yes	N/A	
32	Estonia	No	N/A	Yes	N/A	
33	Ethiopia*	No	N/A	Yes	N/A	
34	Finland	Yes	PPT alone	N/A	N/A	
35	Gabon	No	N/A	Yes	N/A	
36	Georgia	Yes	PPT alone	N/A	N/A	
37	Germany	No	N/A	Yes	N/A	
38	Ghana*	No	N/A	Yes	N/A	
39	Greece	No	N/A	Yes	N/A	
40	Guinea*	No	N/A	Yes	N/A	
41	Hong Kong (China)	No	N/A	Yes	N/A	
42	Hungary	No	N/A	Yes	N/A	
43	Iceland	Yes	PPT alone	N/A	N/A	
44	India	Yes	PPT alone	N/A	N/A	
45	Indonesia	No	N/A	Yes	N/A	
46	Iran*	No	N/A	Yes	N/A	
47	Ireland	Yes	PPT alone	N/A	N/A	
48	Israel	Yes	PPT alone	N/A	N/A	
49	Italy	No	N/A	Yes	N/A	
50	Jamaica	No	N/A	Yes	N/A	
51	Japan	Yes	PPT and LOB	N/A	N/A	
52	Jordan	No	N/A	Yes	N/A	
53	Kazakhstan	No	N/A	Yes	N/A	
54	Kenya	No	N/A	Yes	N/A	
55	Korea	No	N/A	Yes	N/A	
56	Kosovo*	No	N/A	Yes	N/A	
57	Kuwait*	No	N/A	Yes	N/A	
58	Kyrgyzstan*	No	N/A	Yes	N/A	
59	Latvia	No	N/A	Yes	N/A	
60	Lebanon*	No	N/A	Yes	N/A	
61	Libya*	No	N/A	Yes	N/A	
62	Lithuania	Yes	PPT alone	N/A	N/A	
63	Luxembourg	Yes	PPT alone	N/A	N/A	New treaty in force on 19 August 2019
64	Madagascar*	No	N/A	Yes	N/A	
65	Malawi*	No	N/A	Yes	N/A	
66	Malaysia	No	N/A	Yes	N/A	
67	Mali*	No	N/A	Yes	N/A	
68	Malta	Yes	PPT alone	N/A	N/A	
69	Mauritania*	No	N/A	Yes	N/A	

70	Mauritius	No	N/A	Yes	N/A	
71	Mexico	No	N/A	Yes	N/A	
72	Monaco	Yes	PPT alone	N/A	N/A	
73	Mongolia	No	N/A	Yes	N/A	
74	Montenegro	No	N/A	Yes	N/A	
75	Morocco	No	N/A	Yes	N/A	
76	Namibia	No	N/A	Yes	N/A	
77	Netherlands	Yes	PPT alone	N/A	N/A	
78	New Zealand	Yes	PPT alone	N/A	N/A	
79	Niger*	No	N/A	Yes	N/A	
80	Nigeria	No	N/A	Yes	N/A	
81	North Macedonia	No	N/A	Yes	N/A	
82	Norway	No	N/A	Yes	N/A	
83	Oman	No	N/A	Yes	N/A	
84	Pakistan	No	N/A	Yes	N/A	
85	Panama	No	N/A	Yes	N/A	
86	Philippines*	No	N/A	Yes	N/A	
87	Poland	Yes	PPT alone	N/A	N/A	
88	Portugal	No	N/A	Yes	N/A	
89	Qatar	No	N/A	Yes	N/A	
90	Quebec*	No	N/A	Yes	N/A	
91	Romania	No	N/A	Yes	N/A	
92	Russia	No	N/A	Yes	N/A	
93	Saudi Arabia	No	N/A	Yes	N/A	
94	Senegal	No	N/A	Yes	N/A	
95	Serbia	Yes	PPT alone	N/A	N/A	
96	Singapore	Yes	PPT alone	N/A	N/A	
97	Slovak Republic	Yes	PPT alone	N/A	N/A	
98	Slovenia	Yes	PPT alone	N/A	N/A	
99	South Africa	No	N/A	Yes	N/A	
100	Spain	No	N/A	Yes	N/A	
101	Sri Lanka	No	N/A	Yes	N/A	
102	Sweden	No	N/A	Yes	N/A	
103	Switzerland	No	N/A	Yes	N/A	
104	Syrian Arab Republic*	No	N/A	Yes	N/A	
105	Thailand	No	N/A	Yes	N/A	
106	Togo*	No	N/A	Yes	N/A	
107	Trinidad and Tobago	No	N/A	Yes	N/A	
108	Tunisia	No	N/A	Yes	N/A	
109	Turkey	No	N/A	Yes	N/A	
110	Turkmenistan*	No	N/A	Yes	N/A	
111	Ukraine	Yes	PPT alone	N/A	N/A	
112	United Arab Emirates	Yes	PPT alone	N/A	N/A	
113	United Kingdom	Yes	PPT alone	N/A	N/A	
114	United States	No	N/A	Yes	N/A	
115	Uzbekistan*	No	N/A	Yes	N/A	
116	Venezuela*	No	N/A	Yes	N/A	
117	Viet Nam	No	N/A	Yes	N/A	
118	Zambia	No	N/A	Yes	N/A	
119	Zimbabwe*	No	N/A	Yes	N/A	

Gabon

A. Progress in the implementation of the minimum standard

Gabon has five tax agreements in force, as reported in its response to the Peer Review questionnaire.

Gabon signed the MLI in 2017 and has not listed its agreement with Korea .This agreement will not, at this stage, be modified by the MLI. Korea has listed its agreement with Gabon under the MLI.

Gabon is implementing the minimum standard through the inclusion of the preamble statement and the PPT.[54]

The agreements that will be modified by the MLI will come into compliance with the minimum standard once the provisions of the MLI take effect.

B. Implementation issues

Gabon's listed agreements under the MLI will start to be compliant after Gabon's ratification of the MLI. Gabon is encouraged to ratify the MLI as soon as possible.

Summary of the jurisdiction response - Gabon

	Treaty partners	Compliance with the standard	If compliant, the alternative implemented	Signature of a complying instrument	The alternative implemented through the complying instrument (if not the MLI)	Comments
1	Belgium	No	N/A	Yes	N/A	
2	Canada	No	N/A	Yes	N/A	
3	France	No	N/A	Yes	N/A	
4	Korea	No	N/A	No	N/A	
5	Morocco	No	N/A	Yes	N/A	

[54] For its agreements listed under the MLI, Gabon is implementing the preamble statement (Article 6 of the MLI) and the PPT (Article 7 of the MLI).

Georgia

A. Progress in the implementation of the minimum standard

Georgia has 56 tax agreements in force, as reported in its response to the Peer Review questionnaire. 16 of those agreements, the agreements with Belgium, Finland, France, Iceland, India, Ireland, Israel, Lithuania, Luxembourg, the Netherlands, Norway, Serbia, Singapore, the Slovak Republic, Slovenia, and the United Kingdom, comply with the minimum standard.

Georgia signed the MLI in 2017 and deposited its instrument of ratification on 29 March 2019. The MLI entered into force for Georgia on 1 July 2019. Georgia has not listed its agreements with Armenia, Austria, Bahrain, Denmark, Egypt, Germany, Japan, Kazakhstan, Malta, Poland, Qatar, Saudi Arabia, Switzerland, Ukraine, and the United Arab Emirates. These agreements will therefore not, at this stage, be modified by the MLI. Armenia, Denmark, Egypt, Kazakhstan, Malta, Saudi Arabia, Ukraine and the United Arab Emirates have listed their agreements with Georgia under the MLI.

Georgia indicated in its response to the Peer Review questionnaire that bilateral negotiations would be used for its agreements with Malta and Poland.

Georgia is implementing the minimum standard through the inclusion of the preamble statement and the PPT.[55]

The agreements modified by the MLI come into compliance with the minimum standard once the provisions of the MLI take effect.

B. Implementation issues

As mentioned above, Georgia has not listed its agreements with Armenia, Austria, Bahrain, Denmark, Egypt, Germany, Japan, Kazakhstan, Qatar, Saudi Arabia, Switzerland, Ukraine and the United Arab Emirates under the MLI. Listing the agreements under the MLI or entering into bilateral renegotiations to implement the minimum standard would ensure that the minimum standard could be implemented in those non-covered agreements.

Georgia indicated that it would provide a revised list of agreements under the MLI in 2021 and would list all its agreements in force.

Summary of the jurisdiction response - Georgia

	Treaty partners	Compliance with the standard	If compliant, the alternative implemented	Signature of a complying instrument	The alternative implemented through the complying instrument (if not the MLI)	Comments
1	Armenia	No	N/A	No	N/A	
2	Austria	No	N/A	No	N/A	
3	Azerbaijan*	No	N/A	No	N/A	
4	Bahrain	No	N/A	No	N/A	
5	Belarus*	No	N/A	No	N/A	

55 For its agreements listed under the MLI, Georgia is implementing the preamble statement (Article 6 of the MLI) and the PPT (Article 7 of the MLI).

6	Belgium	Yes	PPT alone	N/A	N/A	
7	Bulgaria	No	N/A	Yes	N/A	
8	China (People's Republic of)	No	N/A	Yes	N/A	
9	Croatia	No	N/A	Yes	N/A	
10	Cyprus*	No	N/A	Yes	N/A	
11	Czech Republic	No	N/A	Yes	N/A	
12	Denmark	No	N/A	No	N/A	
13	Egypt	No	N/A	No	N/A	
14	Estonia	No	N/A	Yes	N/A	
15	Finland	Yes	PPT alone	N/A	N/A	
16	France	Yes	PPT alone	N/A	N/A	
17	Germany	No	N/A	No	N/A	
18	Greece	No	N/A	Yes	N/A	
19	Hungary	No	N/A	Yes	N/A	
20	Iceland	Yes	PPT alone	N/A	N/A	
21	India	Yes	PPT alone	N/A	N/A	
22	Iran*	No	N/A	No	N/A	
23	Ireland	Yes	PPT alone	N/A	N/A	
24	Israel	Yes	PPT alone	N/A	N/A	
25	Italy	No	N/A	Yes	N/A	
26	Japan	No	N/A	No	N/A	
27	Kazakhstan	No	N/A	No	N/A	
28	Korea	No	N/A	Yes	N/A	
29	Kuwait*	No	N/A	No	N/A	
30	Latvia	No	N/A	Yes	N/A	
31	Liechtenstein	No	N/A	Yes	N/A	
32	Lithuania	Yes	PPT alone	N/A	N/A	
33	Luxembourg	Yes	PPT alone	N/A	N/A	
34	Malta	No	N/A	No	N/A	
35	Moldova*	No	N/A	No	N/A	
36	Netherlands	Yes	PPT alone	N/A	N/A	
37	Norway	Yes	PPT alone	N/A	N/A	
38	Poland	No	N/A	No	N/A	
39	Portugal	No	N/A	Yes	N/A	
40	Qatar	No	N/A	No	N/A	
41	Romania	No	N/A	Yes	N/A	
42	San Marino	No	N/A	Yes	N/A	
43	Saudi Arabia	No	N/A	No	N/A	
44	Serbia	Yes	PPT alone	N/A	N/A	
45	Singapore	Yes	PPT alone	N/A	N/A	
46	Slovak Republic	Yes	PPT alone	N/A	N/A	
47	Slovenia	Yes	PPT alone	N/A	N/A	
48	Spain	No	N/A	Yes	N/A	
49	Sweden	No	N/A	Yes	N/A	
50	Switzerland	No	N/A	No	N/A	
51	Turkey	No	N/A	Yes	N/A	
52	Turkmenistan*	No	N/A	No	N/A	
53	Ukraine	No	N/A	No	N/A	
54	United Arab Emirates	No	N/A	No	N/A	
55	United Kingdom	Yes	PPT alone	N/A	N/A	
56	Uzbekistan*	No	N/A	No	N/A	

Germany

A. Progress in the implementation of the minimum standard

Germany has 96 tax agreements in force, as reported in its response to the Peer Review questionnaire. Two of those agreements, the agreements with Australia and Japan, comply with the minimum standard.

Germany signed the MLI in 2017 and deposited its instrument of ratification on 18 December 2020. The MLI will enter into force for Germany on 1 April 2021. Germany has listed its agreements with Austria, Croatia, the Czech Republic, France, Greece, Hungary, Italy, Japan, Luxembourg, Malta, Romania, the Slovak Republic, Spain and Turkey. After consultation with its treaty partners Germany prefers to implement the minimum standards and treaty-related recommendations of the BEPS action plan by bilateral negotiations wherever this appears to be an easier, faster or more adequate approach. Albania, Armenia, Bosnia-Herzegovina, Côte d'Ivoire, Egypt, India, Jamaica, Kazakhstan, Malaysia, Morocco, North Macedonia, Pakistan, Portugal, Serbia, Singapore, Tunisia, Ukraine and Uruguay have listed their agreements with Germany under the MLI.

Germany indicated that bilateral negotiations will be used to adjust agreements not covered by the MLI and are currently ongoing with Argentina, Belgium, Bulgaria, Canada, China (People's Republic of), Costa Rica, Cyprus*, Ecuador*, Egypt, Iceland, India, Indonesia, Iran*, Israel, Ireland, Korea, Kyrgyzstan*, Latvia, Liberia, Lithuania, Morocco, Mauritius, Mexico, New Zealand, the Netherlands, Norway, Poland, Portugal, Russia, Serbia, Slovenia, South Africa, Sri Lanka, Sweden, Switzerland, Tajikistan*, Thailand, Trinidad and Tobago, Ukraine and the United Kingdom. Revised agreements have been already signed with Denmark, Estonia, Finland, Liechtenstein and Singapore. With Kazakhstan there is agreement to take up bilateral negotiations soon.

Germany further indicated that steps had been undertaken with respect to the agreements with Kazakhstan, Kenya, Mongolia, Namibia, Pakistan, Uruguay, Viet Nam and that it planned to initiate negotiations with: Albania, Armenia Bosnia-Herzegovina, Côte d'Ivoire, Georgia, Jamaica, Malaysia, Montenegro, North Macedonia, Tunisia and Zambia.

Germany indicated in its response to the Peer Review questionnaire that most of its agreements contain a provision based on paragraph 1 of Article 28 of the German Treaty Negotiation Basis which enables Contracting States to apply domestic anti-abuse provisions such as Section 50d of the German Income Tax Act (Anti Conduit Rule) or Section 42 of the German Fiscal Code (GAAR).

Germany is implementing the minimum standard through the inclusion of the preamble statement and the PPT.[56]

The agreements that will be modified by the MLI will come into compliance with the minimum standard once the provisions of the MLI take effect.

B. Implementation issues

No jurisdiction has raised any concerns about their agreements with Germany.

---

[56] For its 14 agreements listed under the MLI, Germany is implementing the preamble statement (Article 6 of the MLI). For 13 of its agreements listed under the MLI, Germany is implementing the PPT (Paragraph 1 of Article 7 of the MLI). Germany made a reservation pursuant to Article 7(15)(b) of the MLI not to apply Article 7(1) of the MLI with respect to agreements which already contain a PPT. The listed agreement with Japan is within the scope of this reservation.

Summary of the jurisdiction response - Germany

	Treaty partners	Compliance with the standard	If compliant, the alternative implemented	Signature of a complying instrument	The alternative implemented through the complying instrument (if not the MLI)	Comments
1	Albania	No	N/A	No	N/A	
2	Algeria*	No	N/A	No	N/A	
3	Argentina	No	N/A	No	N/A	
4	Armenia	No	N/A	No	N/A	
5	Australia	Yes	PPT alone	N/A	N/A	
6	Austria	No	N/A	Yes	N/A	
7	Azerbaijan*	No	N/A	No	N/A	
8	Bangladesh*	No	N/A	No	N/A	
9	Belarus*	No	N/A	No	N/A	
10	Belgium	No	N/A	No	N/A	
11	Bolivia*	No	N/A	No	N/A	
12	Bosnia-Herzegovina	No	N/A	No	N/A	
13	Bulgaria	No	N/A	No	N/A	
14	Canada	No	N/A	No	N/A	
15	China (People's Republic of)	No	N/A	No	N/A	
16	Chinese Taipei*	No	N/A	No	N/A	
17	Costa Rica	No	N/A	No	N/A	
18	Côte d'Ivoire	No	N/A	No	N/A	
19	Croatia	No	N/A	Yes	N/A	
20	Cyprus*	No	N/A	No	N/A	
21	Czech Republic	No	N/A	Yes	N/A	
22	Denmark	No	N/A	Yes	PPT alone	
23	Ecuador*	No	N/A	No	N/A	
24	Egypt	No	N/A	No	N/A	
25	Estonia	No	N/A	Yes	PPT alone	
26	Finland	No	N/A	Yes	PPT alone	
27	France	No	N/A	Yes	N/A	
28	Georgia	No	N/A	No	N/A	
29	Ghana*	No	N/A	No	N/A	
30	Greece	No	N/A	Yes	N/A	
31	Hungary	No	N/A	Yes	N/A	
32	Iceland	No	N/A	No	N/A	
33	India	No	N/A	No	N/A	
34	Indonesia	No	N/A	No	N/A	
35	Iran*	No	N/A	No	N/A	
36	Ireland	No	N/A	No	N/A	
37	Israel	No	N/A	No	N/A	
38	Italy	No	N/A	Yes	N/A	
39	Jamaica	No	N/A	No	N/A	
40	Japan	Yes	PPT and LOB	N/A	N/A	
41	Kazakhstan	No	N/A	No	N/A	
42	Kenya	No	N/A	No	N/A	
43	Korea	No	N/A	No	N/A	
44	Kosovo*	No	N/A	No	N/A	
45	Kuwait*	No	N/A	No	N/A	
46	Kyrgyzstan*	No	N/A	No	N/A	
47	Latvia	No	N/A	No	N/A	

48	Liberia	No	N/A	No	N/A	
49	Liechtenstein	No	N/A	Yes	PPT alone	
50	Lithuania	No	N/A	No	N/A	
51	Luxembourg	No	N/A	Yes	N/A	
52	Malaysia	No	N/A	No	N/A	
53	Malta	No	N/A	Yes	N/A	
54	Mauritius	No	N/A	No	N/A	
55	Mexico	No	N/A	No	N/A	
56	Moldova*	No	N/A	No	N/A	
57	Mongolia	No	N/A	No	N/A	
58	Montenegro	No	N/A	No	N/A	
59	Morocco	No	N/A	No	N/A	
60	Namibia	No	N/A	No	N/A	
61	Netherlands	No	N/A	No	N/A	
62	New Zealand	No	N/A	No	N/A	
63	North Macedonia	No	N/A	No	N/A	
64	Norway	No	N/A	No	N/A	
65	Pakistan	No	N/A	No	N/A	
66	Philippines*	No	N/A	No	N/A	
67	Poland	No	N/A	No	N/A	
68	Portugal	No	N/A	No	N/A	
69	Romania	No	N/A	Yes	N/A	
70	Russia	No	N/A	No	N/A	
71	Serbia	No	N/A	No	N/A	
72	Singapore	No	N/A	Yes	PPT alone	
73	Slovak Republic	No	N/A	Yes	N/A	
74	Slovenia	No	N/A	No	N/A	
75	South Africa	No	N/A	No	N/A	
76	Spain	No	N/A	Yes	N/A	
77	Sri Lanka	No	N/A	No	N/A	
78	Sweden	No	N/A	No	N/A	
79	Switzerland	No	N/A	No	N/A	
80	Syrian Arab Republic*	No	N/A	No	N/A	
81	Tajikistan*	No	N/A	No	N/A	
82	Thailand	No	N/A	No	N/A	
83	Trinidad and Tobago	No	N/A	No	N/A	
84	Tunisia	No	N/A	No	N/A	
85	Turkey	No	N/A	No	N/A	
86	Turkmenistan*	No	N/A	No	N/A	
87	Ukraine	No	N/A	No	N/A	
88	United Arab Emirates	No	N/A	No	N/A	
89	United Kingdom	No	N/A	No	N/A	
90	United States	No	N/A	No	N/A	
91	Uruguay	No	N/A	No	N/A	
92	Uzbekistan*	No	N/A	No	N/A	
93	Venezuela*	No	N/A	No	N/A	
94	Viet Nam	No	N/A	No	N/A	
95	Zambia	No	N/A	No	N/A	
96	Zimbabwe*	No	N/A	No	N/A	

Gibraltar

A. Progress in the implementation of the minimum standard

Gibraltar has one tax agreement in force with the United Kingdom, as reported in its response to the Peer Review questionnaire. Gibraltar's agreement complies with the minimum standard.

Gibraltar is implementing the minimum standard through the inclusion of the preamble statement and the PPT.

B. Implementation issues

No jurisdiction has raised any concerns about their agreements with Gibraltar.

Summary of the jurisdiction response - Gibraltar

	Treaty partners	Compliance with the standard	If compliant, the alternative implemented	Signature of a complying instrument	The alternative implemented through the complying instrument (if not the MLI)	Comments
1	United Kingdom	Yes	PPT alone	N/A	N/A	

Greece

A. Progress in the implementation of the minimum standard

Greece has 57 tax agreements in force, as reported in its response to the Peer Review questionnaire.

Greece signed the MLI in 2017, listing its non-compliant agreements.

Greece is implementing the minimum standard in its tax agreements through the inclusion of the preamble statement and the PPT.[57]

The agreements that will be modified by the MLI will come into compliance with the minimum standard once the provisions of the MLI take effect.

B. Implementation issues

Greece's listed agreements under the MLI will start to be compliant after Greece's ratification of the MLI. Greece is encouraged to ratify the MLI as soon as possible.

Summary of the jurisdiction response - Greece

	Treaty partners	Compliance with the standard	If compliant, the alternative implemented	Signature of a complying instrument	The alternative implemented through the complying instrument (if not the MLI)	Comments
1	Albania	No	N/A	Yes	N/A	
2	Armenia	No	N/A	Yes	N/A	
3	Austria	No	N/A	Yes	N/A	
4	Azerbaijan*	No	N/A	Yes	N/A	
5	Belgium	No	N/A	Yes	N/A	
6	Bosnia-Herzegovina	No	N/A	Yes	N/A	
7	Bulgaria	No	N/A	Yes	N/A	
8	Canada	No	N/A	Yes	N/A	
9	China (People's Republic of)	No	N/A	Yes	N/A	
10	Croatia	No	N/A	Yes	N/A	
11	Cyprus*	No	N/A	Yes	N/A	
12	Czech Republic	No	N/A	Yes	N/A	
13	Denmark	No	N/A	Yes	N/A	
14	Egypt	No	N/A	Yes	N/A	
15	Estonia	No	N/A	Yes	N/A	
16	Finland	No	N/A	Yes	N/A	
17	France	No	N/A	Yes	N/A	
18	Georgia	No	N/A	Yes	N/A	
19	Germany	No	N/A	Yes	N/A	

57 For its agreements listed under the MLI, Greece is implementing the preamble statement (Article 6 of the MLI) and the PPT (Article 7 of the MLI). Greece also opted for asymmetrical application of the simplified LOB under Article 7(7)(b) of the MLI.

20	Hungary	No	N/A	Yes	N/A	
21	Iceland	No	N/A	Yes	N/A	
22	India	No	N/A	Yes	N/A	
23	Ireland	No	N/A	Yes	N/A	
24	Israel	No	N/A	Yes	N/A	
25	Italy	No	N/A	Yes	N/A	
26	Korea	No	N/A	Yes	N/A	
27	Kuwait*	No	N/A	Yes	N/A	
28	Latvia	No	N/A	Yes	N/A	
29	Lithuania	No	N/A	Yes	N/A	
30	Luxembourg	No	N/A	Yes	N/A	
31	Malta	No	N/A	Yes	N/A	
32	Mexico	No	N/A	Yes	N/A	
33	Moldova*	No	N/A	Yes	N/A	
34	Morocco	No	N/A	Yes	N/A	
35	Netherlands	No	N/A	Yes	N/A	
36	Norway	No	N/A	Yes	N/A	
37	Poland	No	N/A	Yes	N/A	
38	Portugal	No	N/A	Yes	N/A	
39	Qatar	No	N/A	Yes	N/A	
40	Romania	No	N/A	Yes	N/A	
41	Russia	No	N/A	Yes	N/A	
42	San Marino	No	N/A	Yes	N/A	
43	Saudi Arabia	No	N/A	Yes	N/A	
44	Serbia	No	N/A	Yes	N/A	
45	Slovak Republic	No	N/A	Yes	N/A	
46	Slovenia	No	N/A	Yes	N/A	
47	South Africa	No	N/A	Yes	N/A	
48	Spain	No	N/A	Yes	N/A	
49	Sweden	No	N/A	Yes	N/A	
50	Switzerland	No	N/A	Yes	N/A	
51	Tunisia	No	N/A	Yes	N/A	
52	Turkey	No	N/A	Yes	N/A	
53	Ukraine	No	N/A	Yes	N/A	
54	United Arab Emirates	No	N/A	Yes	N/A	
55	United Kingdom	No	N/A	Yes	N/A	
56	United States	No	N/A	Yes	N/A	
57	Uzbekistan*	No	N/A	Yes	N/A	

Greenland

A. Progress in the implementation of the minimum standard

Greenland has four tax agreements in force, as reported in its response to the Peer Review questionnaire. One of those agreements, the agreement with the Faroe Islands, complies with the minimum standard.

Greenland has not signed the MLI.

Greenland indicated in its response to the Peer Review questionnaire that bilateral negotiations would be pursued with respect to its other agreements.

B. Implementation issues

No jurisdiction has raised any concerns about their agreements with Greenland.

Summary of the jurisdiction response - Greenland

	Treaty partners	Compliance with the standard	If compliant, the alternative implemented	Signature of a complying instrument	The alternative implemented through the complying instrument (if not the MLI)	Comments
1	Denmark	No	N/A	No	N/A	Greenland and Denmark are currently in negotiations about their tax agreement.
2	Faroe Islands	Yes	PPT alone	No	N/A	The tax agreement between Greenland and The Faroe Islands has been amended. The amendment entered into force on 24 February 2020.
3	Iceland	No	N/A	No	N/A	Greenland and Iceland have agreed to start the negotiation of amendments to the tax agreement. The negotiations are expected to begin in the autumn of 2019, and will be aimed at securing compliance with the minimum standards. Greenland and Iceland are awaiting the amendment resulting from the negotiations between Greenland and Denmark.

4	Norway	No	N/A	No	N/A	Greenland and Iceland have agreed to start the negotiation of amendments to the tax agreement. The negotiations are expected to begin in the autumn of 2019, and will be aimed at securing compliance with the minimum standards. Greenland and Iceland are awaiting the amendment resulting from the negotiations between Greenland and Denmark.

Grenada

A. Progress in the implementation of the minimum standard

Grenada has four tax agreements in force, as reported in its response to the Peer Review questionnaire, including the multilateral agreement among the members of the CARICOM concluded with ten treaty partners (the CARICOM Agreement).[58]

None of Grenada's agreements comply with the minimum standard or are subject to a complying instrument.

Grenada has not signed the MLI.

B. Implementation issues

As Grenada has not signed the MLI or implemented anti-treaty-shopping measures in its treaties, the Secretariat will offer its support to design a plan for the implementation of the minimum standard to strengthen its network of agreements.

Grenada is encouraged to bring the CARICOM Agreement up to date by commencing talks among all the treaty partners.[59]

Summary of the jurisdiction response - Grenada

	Treaty partners	Compliance with the standard	If compliant, the alternative implemented	Signature of a complying instrument	The alternative implemented through the complying instrument (if not the MLI)	Comments
1	Antigua and Barbuda	No	N/A	No	N/A	CARICOM
2	Barbados	No	N/A	No	N/A	CARICOM
3	Belize	No	N/A	No	N/A	CARICOM
4	Dominica	No	N/A	No	N/A	CARICOM
5	Guyana*	No	N/A	No	N/A	CARICOM
6	Jamaica	No	N/A	No	N/A	CARICOM
7	Saint Kitts and Nevis	No	N/A	No	N/A	CARICOM
8	Saint Lucia	No	N/A	No	N/A	CARICOM
9	Saint Vincent and the Grenadines	No	N/A	No	N/A	CARICOM
10	South Africa	No	N/A	No	N/A	
11	Switzerland	No	N/A	No	N/A	
12	Trinidad and Tobago	No	N/A	No	N/A	CARICOM
13	United Kingdom	No	N/A	No	N/A	

[58] In total, Grenada identified thirteen "agreements" in its List of Tax agreements: three bilateral agreements and the CARICOM Agreement.

[59] Revisions to the CARICOM Agreement require an agreement from its eleven treaty partners.

Guernsey

A. Progress in the implementation of the minimum standard

Guernsey has thirteen tax agreements in force, as reported in its response to the Peer Review questionnaire. Five of those agreements, the agreements with Isle of Man, Luxembourg, Malta, Monaco, Singapore and the United Kingdom, comply with the minimum standard.

Guernsey signed the MLI in 2017 and deposited its instrument of ratification on 12 February 2019. The MLI entered into force for Guernsey on 1 June 2019.

Guernsey indicated in its response to the Peer Review questionnaire that bilateral negotiations would be used with respect to its agreements with Jersey and Qatar.

Guernsey is implementing the minimum standard through the inclusion of the preamble statement and the PPT.[60]

The agreements modified by the MLI come into compliance with the minimum standard once the provisions of the MLI take effect.

B. Implementation issues

No jurisdiction has raised any concerns about their agreements with Guernsey.

Summary of the jurisdiction response - Guernsey

	Treaty partners	Compliance with the standard	If compliant, the alternative implemented	Signature of a complying instrument	The alternative implemented through the complying instrument (if not the MLI)	Comments
1	Cyprus*	No	N/A	Yes	N/A	Entry into force for Cyprus* 1 May 2020; for Guernsey 1 June 2019
2	Hong Kong (China)	No	N/A	Yes	N/A	
3	Isle of Man	Yes	N/A	Yes	PPT alone	An amending Protocol was signed with the Isle of Man on 18 October (by the Isle of Man) + 12 November 2019 (by Guernsey). It is anticipated that the Protocol will be ratified by Guernsey on 15 July 2020. The text of the Protocol is available at https://www.gov.gg/CHttpHandler.ashx?id=122034&p=0
4	Jersey	No	N/A	No	N/A	Under bilateral renegotiation

[60] For its agreements listed under the MLI, Guernsey is implementing the preamble statement (Article 6 of the MLI) and the PPT (Article 7 of the MLI).

5	Liechtenstein	No	N/A	Yes	N/A	Entry into force for Liechtenstein 1 April 2020; for Guernsey 1 June 2019
6	Luxembourg	Yes	PPT alone	N/A	N/A	Entry into force for Luxembourg was 1 August 2019; for Guernsey 1 June 2019
7	Malta	Yes	PPT alone	N/A	N/A	Entry into force for Malta was 1 April 2019; for Guernsey 1 June 2019.
8	Mauritius	No	N/A	Yes	N/A	Entry into force for Mauritius 1 February 2020; for Guernsey 1 June 2019
9	Monaco	Yes	PPT alone	N/A	N/A	Entry into force for Monaco was 1 May 2019; for Guernsey 1 June 2019.
10	Qatar	No	N/A	No	N/A	Under bilateral renegotiation; arrangements for signature being made.
11	Seychelles	No	N/A	Yes	N/A	
12	Singapore	Yes	PPT alone	N/A	N/A	Entry into force for Singapore was 1 April 2019; for Guernsey 1 June 2019.
13	United Kingdom	Yes	PPT alone	N/A	N/A	New agreement in force from 7 January 2019, replacing earlier agreement. The express statement in the preamble and the PPT alone (text equivalent to paragraph 9 of Article 29 of the 2017 OECD Model Tax Convention).

Haiti

A. Progress in the implementation of the minimum standard

Haiti has no tax agreements, as reported in its response to the Peer Review questionnaire.

B. Implementation issues

No jurisdiction has raised any concerns about Haiti.

Honduras

A. Progress in the implementation of the minimum standard

Honduras has no tax agreements, as reported in its response to the Peer Review questionnaire.

B. Implementation issues

No jurisdiction has raised any concerns about Honduras.

Hong Kong (China)

A. Progress in the implementation of the minimum standard

Hong Kong (China) has 41 tax agreements in force, as reported in its response to the Peer Review questionnaire. Three of those agreements, the agreements with Belarus*, Estonia and Finland, comply with the minimum standard.

Hong Kong (China) joined the MLI in 2017 and has not listed its agreements with India and Saudi Arabia. It indicated in its response to the Peer Review questionnaire that it would list those agreements under the MLI. India and Saudi Arabia have listed their agreements with Hong Kong (China) under the MLI.

Hong Kong (China) is implementing the minimum standard through the inclusion of the preamble statement and the PPT.[61]

The agreements that will be modified by the MLI will come into compliance with the minimum standard once the provisions of the MLI take effect.

B. Implementation issues

Hong Kong (China)'s listed agreements under the MLI will start to be compliant after the ratification of the MLI. It is encouraged that the MLI be ratified as soon as possible.

Summary of the jurisdiction response – Hong Kong (China)

	Treaty partners	Compliance with the standard	If compliant, the alternative implemented	Signature of a complying instrument	The alternative implemented through the complying instrument (if not the MLI)	Comments
1	Austria	No	N/A	Yes	N/A	
2	Belarus*	Yes	PPT alone	N/A	N/A	
3	Belgium	No	N/A	Yes	N/A	
4	Brunei Darussalam	No	N/A	Yes	N/A	
5	Cambodia*	No	N/A	No	N/A	To be added to the list of agreements that Hong Kong wishes to cover under the MLI or through bilateral negotiations of an amending protocol
6	Canada	No	N/A	Yes	N/A	
7	Czech Republic	No	N/A	Yes	N/A	
8	Estonia	Yes	PPT alone	N/A	N/A	
9	Finland	Yes	PPT alone	N/A	N/A	

[61] For 35 of its agreements listed under the MLI, Hong Kong is implementing the preamble statement (Article 6 of the MLI). For 34 of its agreements listed under the MLI, Hong Kong is implementing the PPT (Article 7 of the MLI). Hong Kong made a reservation pursuant to Article 6(4) of the MLI not to apply Article 6(1) of the MLI with respect to agreements, which already contain the relevant preamble language. One of Hong Kong's agreements is within the scope of this reservation. Hong Kong made a reservation pursuant to Article 7(15)(b) of the MLI not to apply Article 7(1) of the MLI with respect to agreements, which already contain a PPT.

Two of Hong Kong's agreements are within the scope of this reservation.

10	France	No	N/A	Yes	N/A	
11	Guernsey	No	N/A	Yes	N/A	
12	Hungary	No	N/A	Yes	N/A	
13	India	No	N/A	No	N/A	To be added to the list of agreements that Hong Kong wishes to cover under the MLI or through bilateral negotiations of an amending protocol
14	Indonesia	No	N/A	Yes	N/A	
15	Ireland	No	N/A	Yes	N/A	
16	Italy	No	N/A	Yes	N/A	
17	Japan	No	N/A	Yes	N/A	
18	Jersey	No	N/A	Yes	N/A	
19	Korea	No	N/A	Yes	N/A	
20	Kuwait*	No	N/A	Yes	N/A	
21	Latvia	No	N/A	Yes	N/A	
22	Liechtenstein	No	N/A	Yes	N/A	
23	Luxembourg	No	N/A	Yes	N/A	
24	Malaysia	No	N/A	Yes	N/A	
25	Malta	No	N/A	Yes	N/A	
26	Mexico	No	N/A	Yes	N/A	
27	Netherlands	No	N/A	Yes	N/A	
28	New Zealand	No	N/A	Yes	N/A	
29	Pakistan	No	N/A	Yes	N/A	Partial compliance (just lacks the new preamble)
30	Portugal	No	N/A	Yes	N/A	
31	Qatar	No	N/A	Yes	N/A	
32	Romania	No	N/A	Yes	N/A	
33	Russia	No	N/A	Yes	N/A	
34	Saudi Arabia	No	N/A	No	N/A	To be added to the list of agreements that Hong Kong wishes to cover under the MLI or through bilateral negotiations of an amending protocol
35	South Africa	No	N/A	Yes	N/A	
36	Spain	No	N/A	Yes	N/A	
37	Switzerland	No	N/A	Yes	N/A	Switzerland has not listed this agreement in its MLI position and has proposed bilateral negotiations of an amending protocol instead.
38	Thailand	No	N/A	Yes	N/A	
39	United Arab Emirates	No	N/A	Yes	N/A	
40	United Kingdom	No	N/A	Yes	N/A	
41	Viet Nam	No	N/A	Yes	N/A	

Hungary

A. Progress in the implementation of the minimum standard

Hungary has 81 tax agreements, as reported in its response to the Peer Review questionnaire.

Hungary signed the MLI in 2017 and has not listed its agreements with Albania, Armenia, Bahrain, Bosnia-Herzegovina, Montenegro, North Macedonia, Oman and the United Arab Emirates. These agreements will therefore not, at this stage, be modified by the MLI. Albania, Armenia, Bosnia-Herzegovina, North Macedonia, Oman and the United Arab Emirates have listed their agreements with Hungary under the MLI.

Hungary indicated in its response to the Peer Review questionnaire that the agreements not listed under the MLI were concluded with treaty partners that were not Ad Hoc Group members at the time of Hungary's signature. Hungary further indicated that it is not concerned by treaty shopping with respect to those agreements.

Hungary is implementing the minimum standard through the inclusion of the preamble statement and the PPT.[62]

The agreements that will be modified by the MLI will come into compliance with the minimum standard once the provisions of the MLI take effect.

B. Implementation issues

Hungary's listed agreements under the MLI will start to be compliant after Hungary's ratification of the MLI. Hungary indicated that it expected to deposit its instrument of ratification of the MLI early in 2021.

As mentioned above, Hungary has not listed its agreements with Albania, Armenia, Bahrain, Bosnia Herzegovina, Montenegro, North Macedonia, Oman and the United Arab Emirates under the MLI. Listing the agreements under the MLI or entering into bilateral renegotiations to implement the minimum standard would ensure that the minimum standard could be implemented in those non-covered agreements.

Summary of the jurisdiction response - Hungary

	Treaty partners	Compliance with the standard	If compliant, the alternative implemented	Signature of a complying instrument	The alternative implemented through the complying instrument (if not the MLI)	Comments
1	Albania	No	N/A	No	N/A	
2	Armenia	No	N/A	No	N/A	
3	Australia	No	N/A	Yes	N/A	
4	Austria	No	N/A	Yes	N/A	
5	Azerbaijan*	No	N/A	Yes	N/A	
6	Bahrain	No	N/A	No	N/A	
7	Belarus*	No	N/A	No	N/A	
8	Belgium	No	N/A	Yes	N/A	
9	Bosnia	No	N/A	No	N/A	

[62] For its agreements listed under the MLI, Hungary is implementing the preamble statement (Article 6 of the MLI) and the PPT (Article 7 of the MLI).

	Herzegovina				
10	Brazil	No	N/A	Yes	N/A
11	Bulgaria	No	N/A	Yes	N/A
12	Canada	No	N/A	Yes	N/A
13	China (People's Republic of)	No	N/A	Yes	N/A
14	Chinese Taipei*	No	N/A	No	N/A
15	Croatia	No	N/A	Yes	N/A
16	Cyprus*	No	N/A	Yes	N/A
17	Czech Republic	No	N/A	Yes	N/A
18	Denmark	No	N/A	Yes	N/A
19	Egypt	No	N/A	Yes	N/A
20	Estonia	No	N/A	Yes	N/A
21	Finland	No	N/A	Yes	N/A
22	France	No	N/A	Yes	N/A
23	Georgia	No	N/A	Yes	N/A
24	Germany	No	N/A	Yes	N/A
25	Greece	No	N/A	Yes	N/A
26	Hong Kong	No	N/A	Yes	N/A
27	Iceland	No	N/A	Yes	N/A
28	India	No	N/A	Yes	N/A
29	Indonesia	No	N/A	Yes	N/A
30	Iran*	No	N/A	No	N/A
31	Ireland	No	N/A	Yes	N/A
32	Israel	No	N/A	Yes	N/A
33	Italy	No	N/A	Yes	N/A
34	Japan	No	N/A	Yes	N/A
35	Kazakhstan	No	N/A	Yes	N/A
36	Korea	No	N/A	Yes	N/A
37	Kosovo*	No	N/A	No	N/A
38	Kuwait*	No	N/A	No	N/A
39	Latvia	No	N/A	Yes	N/A
40	Liechtenstein	No	N/A	Yes	N/A
41	Lithuania	No	N/A	Yes	N/A
42	Luxembourg	No	N/A	Yes	N/A
43	Malaysia	No	N/A	Yes	N/A
44	Malta	No	N/A	Yes	N/A
45	Mexico	No	N/A	Yes	N/A
46	Moldova*	No	N/A	Yes	N/A
47	Mongolia	No	N/A	Yes	N/A
48	Montenegro	No	N/A	No	N/A
49	Morocco	No	N/A	Yes	N/A
50	Netherlands	No	N/A	Yes	N/A
51	North Macedonia	No	N/A	No	N/A
52	Norway	No	N/A	Yes	N/A
53	Oman	No	N/A	No	N/A
54	Pakistan	No	N/A	Yes	N/A
55	Philippines*	No	N/A	Yes	N/A
56	Poland	No	N/A	Yes	N/A
57	Portugal	No	N/A	Yes	N/A
58	Qatar	No	N/A	Yes	N/A
59	Romania	No	N/A	Yes	N/A
60	Russia	No	N/A	Yes	N/A
61	San Marino	No	N/A	Yes	N/A

62	Saudi Arabia	No	N/A	Yes	N/A	
63	Serbia	No	N/A	Yes	N/A	
64	Singapore	No	N/A	Yes	N/A	
65	Slovak republic	No	N/A	Yes	N/A	
66	Slovenia	No	N/A	Yes	N/A	
67	South Africa	No	N/A	Yes	N/A	
68	Spain	No	N/A	Yes	N/A	
69	Sweden	No	N/A	Yes	N/A	
70	Switzerland	No	N/A	Yes	N/A	
71	Thailand	No	N/A	Yes	N/A	
72	Tunisia	No	N/A	Yes	N/A	
73	Turkey	No	N/A	Yes	N/A	
74	Turkmenistan*	No	N/A	No	N/A	
75	Ukraine	No	N/A	Yes	N/A	
76	United Arab Emirates	No	N/A	No	N/A	
77	United Kingdom	No	N/A	Yes	N/A	
78	United States	No	N/A	Yes	N/A	
79	Uruguay	No	N/A	Yes	N/A	
80	Uzbekistan*	No	N/A	No	N/A	
81	Viet Nam	No	N/A	Yes	N/A	

Iceland

A. Progress in the implementation of the minimum standard

Iceland has 41 tax agreements in force, as reported in its response to the Peer Review questionnaire, including the multilateral Nordic Convention concluded with Denmark, the Faroe Islands, Finland, Norway and Sweden (the "Nordic Convention").[63] Nineteen of those agreements, the agreements with Belgium, Canada, France, Georgia, India, Ireland, Japan, Liechtenstein, Lithuania, Luxembourg, Malta, the Netherlands, Poland, the Slovak Republic, Slovenia, Switzerland, Ukraine and the United Kingdom as well as the Nordic Convention, comply with the minimum standard.

Iceland signed the MLI in 2017 and deposited its instrument of ratification on 26 September 2019. The MLI entered into force for Iceland on 1 January 2020. Iceland has not listed its agreements with Austria, Germany and Greenland but indicated in its response to the Peer Review questionnaire that bilateral negotiations would be pursued with respect to those agreements.

The Parties to the Nordic Convention signed a complying instrument in 2018. The protocol entered into force on 28 November 2019 and its provisions took effect on 1 January 2020.

Iceland is generally implementing the minimum standard through the inclusion of the preamble statement and the PPT.[64]

The agreements modified by the MLI come into compliance with the minimum standard once the provisions of the MLI take effect.

B. Implementation issues

No jurisdiction has raised any concerns about their agreements with Iceland.

Summary of the jurisdiction response - Iceland

	Treaty partners	Compliance with the standard	If compliant, the alternative implemented	Signature of a complying instrument	The alternative implemented through the complying instrument (if not the MLI)	Comments
1	Albania	No	N/A	Yes	N/A	
2	Austria	No	N/A	No	N/A	Bilateral
3	Barbados	No	N/A	Yes	N/A	
4	Belgium	Yes	PPT alone	N/A	N/A	
5	Canada	Yes	PPT alone	N/A	N/A	
6	China (People's Republic of)	No	N/A	Yes	N/A	

[63] See the Multilateral convention concluded by Denmark, Finland, the Faroe Islands, Iceland, Norway and Sweden: for the avoidance of double taxation with respect to taxes on income and on capital (1996, 1997, 2008 and 2018). In total, Iceland identified 45 "agreements" in its List of Tax agreements: 40 bilateral agreements and the Nordic Convention concluded with five of its treaty partners.

[64] For its agreements listed under the MLI, Iceland is implementing the preamble statement (Article 6 of the MLI) and the PPT (Article 7 of the MLI). Iceland has also accepted to implement a simplified LOB in agreements concluded with partners that opted in for the simplified LOB under Article 7(7)(a) of the MLI.

7	Croatia	No	N/A	Yes	N/A	
8	Cyprus*	No	N/A	Yes	N/A	MLI entered into force on 1.5.2020 – Not in effect
9	Czech Republic	No	N/A	Yes	N/A	
10	Denmark	Yes	PPT alone	N/A	N/A	Nordic Convention
11	Estonia	No	N/A	Yes	N/A	
12	Faroe Islands	Yes	PPT alone	N/A	N/A	Nordic Convention
13	Finland	Yes	PPT alone	N/A	N/A	Nordic Convention
14	France	Yes	PPT alone	N/A	N/A	
15	Georgia	Yes	PPT alone	N/A	N/A	
16	Germany	No	N/A	No	N/A	Bilateral
17	Greece	No	N/A	Yes	N/A	
18	Greenland	No	N/A	No	N/A	Bilateral
19	Hungary	No	N/A	Yes	N/A	
20	India	Yes	PPT and LOB	N/A	N/A	
21	Ireland	Yes	PPT alone	N/A	N/A	
22	Italy	No	N/A	Yes	N/A	
23	Japan	Yes	PPT and LOB	N/A	N/A	Bilateral
24	Korea	No	N/A	Yes	N/A	
25	Latvia	No	N/A	Yes	N/A	MLI entered into force on 1.2.2020 – Not in effect
26	Liechtenstein	Yes	PPT alone	N/A	N/A	Bilateral
27	Lithuania	Yes	PPT alone	N/A	N/A	
28	Luxembourg	Yes	PPT alone	N/A	N/A	
29	Malta	Yes	PPT alone	N/A	N/A	
30	Mexico	No	N/A	Yes	N/A	
31	Netherlands	Yes	PPT alone	N/A	N/A	
32	Norway	Yes	PPT alone	N/A	N/A	Nordic Convention
33	Poland	Yes	PPT alone	N/A	N/A	
34	Portugal	No	N/A	Yes	N/A	MLI entered into force on 1.6.2020 – Not in effect
35	Romania	No	N/A	Yes	N/A	
36	Russia	No	N/A	Yes	N/A	MLI entered into force on 1.10.2019 but notification made pursuant to Article 35(7)(b) of the MLI was made on 30.4.2020 – Not in effect
37	Slovak Republic	Yes	PPT alone	N/A	N/A	
38	Slovenia	Yes	PPT alone	N/A	N/A	
39	Spain	No	N/A	Yes	N/A	
40	Sweden	Yes	PPT alone	N/A	N/A	Nordic Convention
41	Switzerland	Yes	PPT alone	N/A	N/A	
42	Ukraine	Yes	PPT alone	N/A	N/A	
43	United Kingdom	Yes	PPT and LOB	N/A	N/A	
44	United States	No	N/A	Yes	N/A	Preamble in place but detailed LOB to be implemented bilaterally
45	Viet Nam	No	N/A	Yes	N/A	

India

A. Progress in the implementation of the minimum standard

India has 95 tax agreements in force, as reported in its response to the Peer Review questionnaire. 36 of those agreements, the agreements with Australia, Austria, Belgium, Canada, China, Cyprus*, Denmark, Finland, France, Georgia, Iceland, Iran*[65], Ireland, Israel, Japan, Latvia, Lithuania, Luxembourg, Malta, the Netherlands, New Zealand, Norway, Poland, Portugal, Qatar, Russia, Saudi Arabia, Serbia, Singapore, the Slovak Republic, Slovenia, Ukraine, United Arab Emirates, the United Kingdom and Uruguay comply with the minimum standard.

India signed the MLI in 2017 and deposited its instrument of ratification on 25 June 2019. The MLI entered into force for India on 1 October 2019.

India is implementing the minimum standard through the inclusion of the preamble statement and the PPT combined with the LOB.[66] India has also given a statement of acceptance of the PPT as an interim measure.

The agreements modified by the MLI come into compliance with the minimum standard once the provisions of the MLI take effect.

B. Implementation issues

No jurisdiction has raised any concerns about their agreements with India.

Summary of the jurisdiction response - India

	Treaty partners	Compliance with the standard	If compliant, the alternative implemented	Signature of a complying instrument	The alternative implemented through the complying instrument (if not the MLI)	Comments
1	Albania	No	N/A	Yes	N/A	
2	Armenia	No	N/A	Yes	N/A	
3	Australia	Yes	PPT alone	N/A	N/A	
4	Austria	Yes	PPT alone	N/A	N/A	
5	Bangladesh*	No	N/A	Yes	N/A	Not a signatory to the MLI
6	Belarus*	No	N/A	Yes	N/A	Not a signatory to the MLI
7	Belgium	Yes	PPT alone	N/A	N/A	
8	Bhutan*	No	N/A	Yes	N/A	Not a signatory to the MLI
9	Botswana	No	N/A	Yes	N/A	Not a signatory to the MLI
10	Brazil	No	N/A	Yes	N/A	Not a signatory to the MLI
11	Bulgaria	No	N/A	Yes	N/A	
12	Canada	Yes	PPT alone	N/A	N/A	
13	China (People's	Yes	PPT alone	N/A	N/A	

[65] Internal procedures have been completed for India, whereas, in respect of Iran*, internal procedures for the ratification of the agreement are underway.

[66] For its agreements listed under the MLI, India is implementing the preamble statement (Article 6 of the MLI), the PPT (Article 7 of the MLI) and the simplified LOB (Article 7(6) of the MLI).

	Republic of)					
14	Colombia	No	N/A	Yes	N/A	
15	Croatia	No	N/A	Yes	N/A	
16	Cyprus*	Yes	PPT alone	N/A	N/A	
17	Czech Republic	No	N/A	Yes	N/A	
18	Denmark	Yes	PPT and LOB	N/A	N/A	
19	Egypt	No	N/A	Yes	N/A	
20	Estonia	No	N/A	Yes	N/A	
21	Ethiopia*	No	N/A	Yes	N/A	Not a signatory to the MLI
22	Fiji*	No	N/A	Yes	N/A	
23	Finland	Yes	PPT alone	N/A	N/A	
24	France	Yes	PPT alone	N/A	N/A	
25	Georgia	Yes	PPT alone	N/A	N/A	
26	Germany	No	N/A	Yes	N/A	India not included as a CTA
27	Greece	No	N/A	Yes	N/A	
28	Hong Kong (China)	No	N/A	Yes	N/A	India not included as a CTA
29	Hungary	No	N/A	Yes	N/A	
30	Iceland	Yes	PPT alone	N/A	N/A	
31	Indonesia	No	N/A	Yes	N/A	
32	Iran*	Yes	PPT alone	N/A	N/A	
33	Ireland	Yes	PPT alone	N/A	N/A	
34	Israel	Yes	PPT alone	N/A	N/A	
35	Italy	No	N/A	Yes	N/A	
36	Japan	Yes	PPT alone	N/A	N/A	
37	Jordan	No	N/A	Yes	N/A	
38	Kazakhstan	No	N/A	Yes	N/A	
39	Kenya	No	N/A	Yes	N/A	
40	Korea	No	N/A	Yes	N/A	
41	Kuwait*	No	N/A	Yes	N/A	
42	Kyrgyzstan*	No	N/A	Yes	N/A	Not a signatory to the MLI
43	Latvia	Yes	PPT alone	N/A	N/A	
44	Libya*	No	N/A	Yes	N/A	Not a signatory to the MLI
45	Lithuania	Yes	PPT alone	N/A	N/A	
46	Luxembourg	Yes	PPT alone	N/A	N/A	
47	Malaysia	No	N/A	Yes	N/A	
48	Malta	Yes	PPT alone	N/A	N/A	
49	Mauritius	No	N/A	Yes	N/A	India not included as a CTA
50	Mexico	No	N/A	Yes	N/A	
51	Mongolia	No	N/A	Yes	N/A	Not a signatory to the MLI
52	Montenegro	No	N/A	Yes	N/A	Not a signatory to the MLI
53	Morocco	No	N/A	Yes	N/A	
54	Mozambique*	No	N/A	Yes	N/A	Not a signatory to the MLI
55	Myanmar*	No	N/A	Yes	N/A	Not a signatory to the MLI
56	Namibia	No	N/A	Yes	N/A	Not a signatory to the MLI
57	Nepal*	No	N/A	Yes	N/A	Not a signatory to the MLI
58	Netherlands	Yes	PPT alone	Yes	N/A	
59	New Zealand	Yes	PPT alone	Yes	N/A	
60	North Macedonia	No	N/A	Yes	N/A	
61	Norway	Yes	PPT and LOB	Yes	N/A	
62	Oman	No	N/A	Yes	N/A	India not included as a CTA

63	Philippines*	No	N/A	Yes	N/A	Not a signatory to the MLI
64	Poland	Yes	PPT alone	N/A	N/A	
65	Portugal	Yes	PPT alone	N/A	N/A	
66	Qatar	Yes	PPT alone	N/A	N/A	
67	Romania	No	N/A	Yes	N/A	
68	Russia	Yes	PPT and LOB	N/A	N/A	
69	Saudi Arabia	Yes	PPT alone	N/A	N/A	
70	Serbia	Yes	PPT alone	N/A	N/A	
71	Singapore	Yes	PPT alone	N/A	N/A	
72	Slovak Republic	Yes	PPT and LOB	N/A	N/A	
73	Slovenia	Yes	PPT alone	N/A	N/A	
74	South Africa	No	N/A	Yes	N/A	
75	Spain	No	N/A	Yes	N/A	
76	Sri Lanka	No	N/A	Yes	N/A	Not a signatory to the MLI
77	Sudan*	No	N/A	Yes	N/A	Not a signatory to the MLI
78	Sweden	No	N/A	Yes	N/A	
79	Switzerland	No	N/A	Yes	N/A	India not included as a CTA
80	Syrian Arab Republic*	No	N/A	Yes	N/A	Not a signatory to the MLI
81	Tajikistan*	No	N/A	Yes	N/A	Not a signatory to the MLI
82	Tanzania*	No	N/A	Yes	N/A	Not a signatory to the MLI
83	Thailand	No	N/A	Yes	N/A	Not a signatory to the MLI
84	Trinidad and Tobago	No	N/A	Yes	N/A	Not a signatory to the MLI
85	Turkey	No	N/A	Yes	N/A	
86	Turkmenistan*	No	N/A	Yes	N/A	Not a signatory to the MLI
87	Uganda*	No	N/A	Yes	N/A	Not a signatory to the MLI
88	Ukraine	Yes	PPT alone	N/A	N/A	
89	United Arab Emirates	Yes	PPT alone	N/A	N/A	
90	United Kingdom	Yes	PPT alone	N/A	N/A	
91	United States	No	N/A	Yes	N/A	Not a signatory to the MLI
92	Uruguay	Yes	PPT and LOB	N/A	N/A	
93	Uzbekistan*	No	N/A	Yes	N/A	Not a signatory to the MLI
94	Viet Nam	No	N/A	Yes	N/A	
95	Zambia	No	N/A	Yes	N/A	Not a signatory to the MLI

Indonesia

A. Progress in the implementation of the minimum standard

Indonesia has 69 tax agreements in force, as reported in its response to the Peer Review questionnaire.

Indonesia signed the MLI in 2017 and deposited its instrument of ratification on 28 April 2020. The MLI will enter into force for Indonesia on 1 August 2020. Indonesia has not listed its agreements with Austria, Germany, Jordan, Mongolia, Morocco, Papua New Guinea, Sri Lanka, Tunisia and Ukraine. These agreements will therefore not, at this stage, be modified by the MLI. Jordan, Morocco, Tunisia, Papua New Guinea and Ukraine have listed their agreements with Indonesia under the MLI.

Indonesia has made a reservation under the MLI that delays its entry into effect after completing its internal procedures for this purpose for each of its listed agreements.[67] Indonesia had notified that it completed its internal procedures for the entry into effect of the MLI with respect to its agreements with Australia, Belgium, Canada, Denmark, Finland, France, India, Japan, Korea, Luxembourg, the Netherlands, New Zealand, Poland, Portugal, Qatar, the Russian Federation, Serbia, Singapore, the Slovak Republic, Sweden, the United Arab Emirates and the United Kingdom on 26 November 2020.

Indonesia is implementing the minimum standard through the inclusion of the preamble statement and the PPT.[68]

The agreements that will be modified by the MLI will come into compliance with the minimum standard once the provisions of the MLI take effect.

B. Implementation issues

As mentioned above, Indonesia has not listed its agreements with Austria, Germany, Jordan, Mongolia, Morocco, Papua New Guinea, Sri Lanka, Tunisia and Ukraine under the MLI. Listing the agreements under the MLI or entering into bilateral renegotiations to implement the minimum standard would ensure that the minimum standard could be implemented in those non-covered agreements.

Summary of the jurisdiction response - Indonesia

	Treaty partners	Compliance with the standard	If compliant, the alternative implemented	Signature of a complying instrument	The alternative implemented through the complying instrument (if not the MLI)	Comments
1	Algeria*	No	N/A	No	N/A	
2	Armenia	No	N/A	Yes	N/A	
3	Australia	No	N/A	Yes	N/A	
4	Austria	No	N/A	No	N/A	
5	Bangladesh*	No	N/A	No	N/A	
6	Belarus*	No	N/A	No	N/A	
7	Belgium	No	N/A	Yes	N/A	

[67] The reservation was made under Article 35(7)(a) of the MLI.

[68] For its agreements listed under the MLI, Indonesia is implementing the preamble statement (Article 6 of the MLI) and the PPT (Article 7 of the MLI).

8	Brunei Darussalam	No	N/A	Yes	N/A	Brunei Darussalam is not signatory to the MLI
9	Bulgaria	No	N/A	Yes	N/A	
10	Canada	No	N/A	Yes	N/A	
11	China (People's Republic of)	No	N/A	Yes	N/A	
12	Chinese Taipei*	No	N/A	No	N/A	
13	Croatia	No	N/A	Yes	N/A	
14	Czech Republic	No	N/A	Yes	N/A	Czech Republic has not listed Indonesia
15	Democratic People's Republic of Korea*	No	N/A	No	N/A	
16	Denmark	No	N/A	Yes	N/A	
17	Egypt	No	N/A	Yes	N/A	
18	Finland	No	N/A	Yes	N/A	
19	France	No	N/A	Yes	N/A	
20	Germany	No	N/A	No	N/A	
21	Hong Kong (China)	No	N/A	Yes	N/A	
22	Hungary	No	N/A	Yes	N/A	
23	India	No	N/A	Yes	N/A	
24	Iran*	No	N/A	No	N/A	
25	Italy	No	N/A	Yes	N/A	
26	Japan	No	N/A	Yes	N/A	
27	Jordan	No	N/A	No	N/A	
28	Korea	No	N/A	Yes	N/A	
29	Kuwait*	No	N/A	No	N/A	
30	Lao People's Democratic Republic*	No	N/A	Yes	N/A	Lao People's Democratic Republic* is not signatory to the MLI
31	Luxembourg	No	N/A	Yes	N/A	
32	Malaysia	No	N/A	Yes	N/A	
33	Mexico	No	N/A	Yes	N/A	
34	Mongolia	No	N/A	No	N/A	
35	Morocco	No	N/A	No	N/A	
36	Netherlands	No	N/A	Yes	N/A	
37	New Zealand	No	N/A	Yes	N/A	
38	Norway	No	N/A	Yes	N/A	Norway has not listed Indonesia
39	Pakistan	No	N/A	Yes	N/A	
40	Papua New Guinea	No	N/A	No	N/A	
41	Philippines*	No	N/A	Yes	N/A	Philippines* is not signatory to the MLI
42	Poland	No	N/A	Yes	N/A	
43	Portugal	No	N/A	Yes	N/A	
44	Qatar	No	N/A	Yes	N/A	
45	Romania	No	N/A	Yes	N/A	
46	Russia	No	N/A	Yes	N/A	
47	Serbia	No	N/A	Yes	N/A	
48	Seychelles	No	N/A	Yes	N/A	
49	Singapore	No	N/A	Yes	N/A	
50	Slovak Republic	No	N/A	Yes	N/A	
51	South Africa	No	N/A	Yes	N/A	
52	Spain	No	N/A	Yes	N/A	
53	Sri Lanka	No	N/A	No	N/A	
54	Sudan*	No	N/A	No	N/A	

55	Suriname*	No	N/A	No	N/A	
56	Sweden	No	N/A	Yes	N/A	
57	Switzerland	No	N/A	Yes	N/A	Switzerland has not listed Indonesia
58	Syrian Arab Republic*	No	N/A	No	N/A	
59	Tajikistan*	No	N/A	No	N/A	
60	Thailand	No	N/A	Yes	N/A	Thailand is not signatory to the MLI
61	Tunisia	No	N/A	No	N/A	
62	Turkey	No	N/A	Yes	N/A	
63	Ukraine	No	N/A	No	N/A	
64	United Arab Emirates	No	N/A	Yes	N/A	
65	United Kingdom	No	N/A	Yes	N/A	
66	United States	No	N/A	Yes	N/A	United States is not signatory to the MLI
67	Uzbekistan*	No	N/A	No	N/A	
68	Venezuela*	No	N/A	No	N/A	
69	Viet Nam	No	N/A	Yes	N/A	Viet Nam is not signatory to the MLI

Ireland

A. Progress in the implementation of the minimum standard

Ireland has 73 tax agreements in force, as reported in its response to the Peer Review questionnaire. Twenty-six of those agreements, the agreements with Australia, Austria, Belgium, Canada, Denmark, Finland, France, Georgia, Iceland, India, Israel, Japan, Lithuania, Luxembourg, Malta, the Netherlands, New Zealand, Norway, Poland, Serbia, Singapore, the Slovak Republic, Slovenia, Ukraine, the United Arab Emirates and the United Kingdom, comply with the minimum standard.

Ireland signed the MLI in 2017 and deposited its instrument of ratification on 29 January 2019. The MLI entered into force for Ireland on 1 May 2019. Ireland has not listed its agreements with Germany, the Netherlands and Switzerland but indicated in its response to the Peer Review questionnaire that bilateral negotiations were being pursued with respect to those agreements.

Ireland is implementing the minimum standard through the inclusion of the preamble statement and the PPT.[69]

The agreements modified by the MLI come into compliance with the minimum standard once the provisions of the MLI take effect.

B. Implementation issues

No jurisdiction has raised any concerns about their agreements with Ireland.

Summary of the jurisdiction response - Ireland

	Treaty partners	Compliance with the standard	If compliant, the alternative implemented	Signature of a complying instrument	The alternative implemented through the complying instrument (if not the MLI)	Comments
1	Albania	No	N/A	Yes	N/A	
2	Armenia	No	N/A	Yes	N/A	
3	Australia	Yes	PPT alone	N/A	N/A	
4	Austria	Yes	PPT alone	N/A	N/A	
5	Bahrain	No	N/A	Yes	N/A	
6	Belarus*	No	N/A	Yes	N/A	
7	Belgium	Yes	PPT alone	N/A	N/A	
8	Bosnia-Herzegovina	No	N/A	Yes	N/A	
9	Botswana	No	N/A	Yes	N/A	
10	Bulgaria	No	N/A	Yes	N/A	
11	Canada	Yes	PPT alone	N/A	N/A	Effective for all other taxes from 1 June 2020
12	Chile	No	N/A	Yes	N/A	
13	China (People's Republic of)	No	N/A	Yes	N/A	

[69] For its agreements listed under the MLI, Ireland is implementing the preamble statement (Article 6 of the MLI) and the PPT (Article 7 of the MLI).

14	Croatia	No	N/A	Yes	N/A	
15	Cyprus*	No	N/A	Yes	N/A	
16	Czech Republic	No	N/A	Yes	N/A	
17	Denmark	Yes	PPT alone	N/A	N/A	Effective for all other taxes from 1 July 2020
18	Egypt	No	N/A	Yes	N/A	
19	Estonia	No	N/A	Yes	N/A	
20	Ethiopia*	No	N/A	Yes	N/A	
21	Finland	Yes	PPT alone	N/A	N/A	
22	France	Yes	PPT alone	N/A	N/A	
23	Georgia	Yes	PPT alone	N/A	N/A	
24	Germany	No	N/A	No	N/A	Protocol implementing the minimum standard is finalised and procedures are underway for permission to sign.
25	Greece	No	N/A	Yes	N/A	
26	Hong Kong (China)	No	N/A	Yes	N/A	
27	Hungary	No	N/A	Yes	N/A	
28	Iceland	Yes	PPT alone	N/A	N/A	Effective for all other taxes from 1 July 2020
29	India	Yes	PPT alone	N/A	N/A	
30	Israel	Yes	PPT alone	N/A	N/A	
31	Italy	No	N/A	Yes	N/A	
32	Japan	Yes	PPT alone	N/A	N/A	
33	Kazakhstan	No	N/A	Yes	N/A	Partial compliance with minimum standard. PPT included; preamble missing.
34	Korea	No	N/A	Yes	N/A	
35	Kuwait*	No	N/A	Yes	N/A	
36	Latvia	No	N/A	Yes	N/A	
37	Lithuania	Yes	PPT alone	N/A	N/A	
38	Luxembourg	Yes	PPT alone	N/A	N/A	
39	Malaysia	No	N/A	Yes	N/A	
40	Malta	Yes	PPT alone	N/A	N/A	
41	Mexico	No	N/A	Yes	N/A	
42	Moldova*	No	N/A	Yes	N/A	
43	Montenegro	No	N/A	Yes	N/A	
44	Morocco	No	N/A	Yes	N/A	
45	Netherlands	Yes	PPT alone	N/A	PPT alone	New treaty was signed on 13 June 2019 and came into force on 29 February 2020. Its provisions will enter into effect from 2021.
46	New Zealand	Yes	PPT alone	N/A	N/A	
47	North Macedonia	No	N/A	Yes	N/A	
48	Norway	Yes	PPT alone	N/A	N/A	
49	Pakistan	No	N/A	Yes	N/A	
50	Panama	No	N/A	Yes	N/A	
51	Poland	Yes	PPT alone	N/A	N/A	
52	Portugal	No	N/A	Yes	N/A	
53	Qatar	No	N/A	Yes	N/A	
54	Romania	No	N/A	Yes	N/A	
55	Russia	No	N/A	Yes	N/A	
56	Saudi Arabia	No	N/A	Yes	N/A	

57	Serbia	Yes	PPT alone	N/A	N/A	
58	Singapore	Yes	PPT alone	N/A	N/A	
59	Slovak Republic	Yes	PPT alone	N/A	N/A	
60	Slovenia	Yes	PPT alone	N/A	N/A	
61	South Africa	No	N/A	Yes	N/A	
62	Spain	No	N/A	Yes	N/A	
63	Sweden	No	N/A	Yes	N/A	
64	Switzerland	No	N/A	Yes	PPT alone	Protocol incorporating the minimum standard was signed on 13 June 2019 and was ratified by Ireland via Finance Act 2019 but is not yet in force.
65	Thailand	No	N/A	Yes	N/A	
66	Turkey	No	N/A	Yes	N/A	
67	Ukraine	Yes	PPT alone	N/A	N/A	
68	United Arab Emirates	Yes	PPT alone	N/A	N/A	
69	United Kingdom	Yes	PPT alone	N/A	N/A	
70	United States	No	N/A	Yes	N/A	
71	Uzbekistan*	No	N/A	Yes	N/A	
72	Viet Nam	No	N/A	Yes	N/A	
73	Zambia	No	N/A	Yes	N/A	

Isle of Man

A. Progress in the implementation of the minimum standard

The Isle of Man has ten tax agreements in force, as reported in its response to the Peer Review questionnaire. Five of those agreements, the agreements with Guernsey, Luxembourg, Malta, Singapore and the United Kingdom comply with the minimum standard.

The Isle of Man signed the MLI in 2017 and deposited its instrument of ratification on 25 October 2017. The MLI entered into force for the Isle of Man on 1 July 2018.

The Isle of Man indicated in its response to the Peer Review questionnaire that bilateral negotiations would be used with respect to its arrangements with other Crown Dependencies.

The Isle of Man is implementing the minimum standard through the inclusion of the preamble statement and the PPT.[70]

The agreements modified by the MLI come into compliance with the minimum standard once the provisions of the MLI take effect.

B. Implementation issues

No jurisdiction has raised any concerns about their agreements with the Isle of Man.

Summary of the jurisdiction response – Isle of Man

	Treaty partners	Compliance with the standard	If compliant, the alternative implemented	Signature of a complying instrument	The alternative implemented through the complying instrument (if not the MLI)	Comments
1	Bahrain	No	N/A	Yes	N/A	
2	Estonia	No	N/A	Yes	N/A	
3	Guernsey	Yes	N/A	N/A	PPT alone	
4	Jersey	No	N/A	No	N/A	Bilateral negotiations ongoing
5	Luxembourg	Yes	PPT alone	N/A	N/A	Synthesised text agreed and published
6	Malta	Yes	PPT alone	N/A	N/A	Synthesised text agreed and published
7	Qatar	No	N/A	Yes	N/A	Synthesised text being prepared
8	Seychelles	No	N/A	Yes	N/A	
9	Singapore	Yes	PPT alone	N/A	N/A	Synthesised text agreed and published
10	United Kingdom	Yes	PPT alone	N/A	N/A	

70 For its agreements listed under the MLI, the Isle of Man is implementing the preamble statement (Article 6 of the MLI) and the PPT (Article 7 of the MLI).

Israel

A. Progress in the implementation of the minimum standard

Israel has 58 tax agreements in force, as reported in its response to the Peer Review questionnaire. Twenty-five of those agreements, the agreements with Australia, Austria, Belgium, Canada, Denmark, Finland, France, Georgia, India, Ireland, Japan, Latvia, Lithuania, Luxembourg, Malta, the Netherlands, Poland, Portugal, Russia, Serbia, Singapore, the Slovak Republic, Slovenia, Ukraine, and the United Kingdom comply with the minimum standard.

Israel signed the MLI in 2017 and deposited its instrument of ratification on 13 September 2018. The MLI entered into force for Israel on 1 January 2019. Israel has not listed its agreements with Germany and Switzerland but indicated in its response to the Peer Review questionnaire that bilateral negotiations would be used with respect to those agreements.

Israel is implementing the minimum standard through the inclusion of the preamble statement and the PPT.[71]

The agreements modified by the MLI come into compliance with the minimum standard once the provisions of the MLI take effect.

B. Implementation issues

No jurisdiction has raised any concerns about their agreements with Israel.

Summary of the jurisdiction response - Israel

	Treaty partners	Compliance with the standard	If compliant, the alternative implemented	Signature of a complying instrument	The alternative implemented through the complying instrument (if not the MLI)	Comments
1	Armenia	No	N/A	Yes	N/A	
2	Australia	Yes	PPT alone	N/A	N/A	
3	Austria	Yes	PPT alone	N/A	N/A	
4	Azerbaijan*	No	N/A	Yes	N/A	
5	Belarus*	No	N/A	Yes	N/A	
6	Belgium	Yes	PPT alone	N/A	N/A	
7	Brazil	No	N/A	Yes	N/A	
8	Bulgaria	No	N/A	Yes	N/A	
9	Canada	Yes	PPT alone	N/A	N/A	
10	China (People's Republic of)	No	N/A	Yes	N/A	
11	Chinese Taipei*	No	N/A	Yes	N/A	
12	Croatia	No	N/A	Yes	N/A	
13	Czech Republic	No	N/A	Yes	N/A	
14	Denmark	Yes	PPT alone	N/A	N/A	

71 For its agreements listed under the MLI, Israel is implementing the preamble statement (Article 6 of the MLI) and the PPT (Article 7 of the MLI).

15	Estonia	No	N/A	Yes	N/A	
16	Ethiopia*	No	N/A	Yes	N/A	
17	Finland	Yes	PPT alone	N/A	N/A	
18	France	Yes	PPT alone	N/A	N/A	
19	Georgia	Yes	PPT alone	N/A	N/A	
20	Germany	No	N/A	No	N/A	An amending protocol was initiated. It is compliant with Action 6 minimum standard.
21	Greece	No	N/A	Yes	N/A	
22	Hungary	No	N/A	Yes	N/A	
23	India	Yes	PPT alone	N/A	N/A	
24	Ireland	Yes	PPT alone	N/A	N/A	
25	Italy	No	N/A	Yes	N/A	
26	Jamaica	No	N/A	Yes	N/A	
27	Japan	Yes	PPT alone	N/A	N/A	
28	Korea	No	N/A	Yes	N/A	
29	Latvia	Yes	PPT alone	N/A	N/A	
30	Lithuania	Yes	PPT alone	N/A	N/A	
31	Luxembourg	Yes	PPT alone	N/A	N/A	
32	Malta	Yes	PPT alone	N/A	N/A	
33	Mexico	No	N/A	Yes	N/A	
34	Moldova*	No	N/A	Yes	N/A	
35	Netherlands	Yes	PPT alone	N/A	N/A	
36	North Macedonia	No	N/A	Yes	N/A	
37	Norway	No	N/A	Yes	N/A	
38	Panama	No	N/A	Yes	N/A	
39	Philippines*	No	N/A	Yes	N/A	
40	Poland	Yes	PPT alone	N/A	N/A	
41	Portugal	Yes	PPT alone	N/A	N/A	
42	Romania	No	N/A	Yes	N/A	
43	Russia	Yes	PPT alone	N/A	N/A	
44	Serbia	Yes	PPT alone	N/A	N/A	
45	Singapore	Yes	PPT alone	N/A	N/A	
46	Slovak Republic	Yes	PPT alone	N/A	N/A	
47	Slovenia	Yes	PPT alone	N/A	N/A	
48	South Africa	No	N/A	Yes	N/A	
49	Spain	No	N/A	Yes	N/A	
50	Sweden	No	N/A	Yes	N/A	
51	Switzerland	No	N/A	No	N/A	An amending protocol was initiated. It is compliant with Action 6 minimum standard.
52	Thailand	No	N/A	Yes	N/A	
53	Turkey	No	N/A	Yes	N/A	
54	Ukraine	Yes	PPT alone	N/A	N/A	
55	United Kingdom	Yes	PPT alone	N/A	N/A	
56	United States	No	N/A	Yes	N/A	
57	Uzbekistan*	No	N/A	Yes	N/A	
58	Viet Nam	No	N/A	Yes	N/A	

Italy

A. Progress in the implementation of the minimum standard

Italy has 99 tax agreements in force, as reported in its response to the Peer Review questionnaire. One of those agreements, the agreement with Chile, complies with the minimum standard.

Italy signed the MLI in 2017 and has not listed its agreements with Albania, Congo, Montenegro, North Macedonia, Oman, Panama and Trinidad and Tobago. These agreements will therefore not, at this stage, be modified by the MLI. Albania, North Macedonia, Oman and Panama have listed their agreements with Italy under the MLI.

Italy indicated in its response to the Peer Review questionnaire that the agreements not listed under the MLI were concluded with treaty partners that were not Ad Hoc Group members at the time of Italy's signature of the MLI.

Italy is implementing the minimum standard through the inclusion of the preamble statement and the PPT.[72]

The agreements that will be modified by the MLI will come into compliance with the minimum standard once the provisions of the MLI take effect.

B. Implementation issues

Italy's listed agreements under the MLI will start to be compliant after Italy's ratification of the MLI. Italy is encouraged to ratify the MLI as soon as possible.

As mentioned above, Italy has not listed its agreements with Albania, Congo, Montenegro, North Macedonia, Oman, Panama and Trinidad and Tobago under the MLI. Listing the agreements under the MLI or entering into bilateral renegotiations to implement the minimum standard would ensure that the minimum standard could be implemented in those non-covered agreements.

Summary of the jurisdiction response - Italy

	Treaty partners	Compliance with the standard	If compliant, the alternative implemented	Signature of a complying instrument	The alternative implemented through the complying instrument (if not the MLI)	Comments
1	Albania	No	N/A	No	N/A	This agreement is likely to be included in the Italian CTA revised list which has not been updated at the current date.
2	Algeria*	No	N/A	No	N/A	This agreement is likely to be included in the Italian CTA

[72] For its 80 agreements listed under the MLI, Italy is implementing the preamble statement (Article 6 of the MLI). For 67 of its agreements listed under the MLI, Italy is implementing the PPT (Article 7 of the MLI). Thirteen of Italy's agreements, the agreements with Azerbaijan*, Estonia, Hong Kong, Iceland, Kazakhstan, Kuwait*, Latvia, Lebanon*, Lithuania, Mongolia, Qatar, San Marino and Saudi Arabia, are within the scope of a reservation made by Italy under Article 7(15)(b) of the MLI. Italy made a reservation pursuant to Article 7(15)(b) of the MLI not to apply Article 7(1) of the MLI with respect to agreements, which already contain a PPT.

						revised list which has not been updated at the current date.
3	Argentina	No	N/A	Yes	N/A	
4	Armenia	No	N/A	Yes	N/A	
5	Australia	No	N/A	Yes	N/A	
6	Austria	No	N/A	Yes	N/A	
7	Azerbaijan*	No	N/A	Yes	N/A	
8	Bangladesh*	No	N/A	Yes	N/A	
9	Barbados	No	N/A	Yes	N/A	
10	Belarus*	No	N/A	No	N/A	For the time being, Italy has included in the CTA list only Jurisdictions that were members of the Ad Hoc Group on MLI at the date of the signature of MLI by Italy.
11	Belgium	No	N/A	Yes	N/A	
12	Bosnia-Herzegovina	No	N/A	Yes	N/A	
13	Brazil	No	N/A	Yes	N/A	
14	Bulgaria	No	N/A	Yes	N/A	
15	Canada	No	N/A	Yes	N/A	
16	Chile	Yes	PPT alone	N/A	N/A	
17	China (People's Republic of)	No	N/A	Yes	PPT alone	
18	Congo	No	N/A	No	N/A	For the time being, Italy has included in the CTA list only Jurisdictions that were members of the Ad Hoc Group on MLI at the date of the signature of MLI by Italy.
19	Côte d'Ivoire	No	N/A	Yes	N/A	
20	Croatia	No	N/A	Yes	N/A	
21	Cyprus*	No	N/A	Yes	N/A	
22	Czech Republic	No	N/A	Yes	N/A	
23	Denmark	No	N/A	Yes	N/A	
24	Ecuador*	No	N/A	No	N/A	For the time being, Italy has included in the CTA list only Jurisdictions that were members of the Ad Hoc Group on MLI at the date of the signature of MLI by Italy.
25	Egypt	No	N/A	Yes	N/A	
26	Estonia	No	N/A	Yes	N/A	
27	Ethiopia*	No	N/A	No	N/A	For the time being, Italy has included in the CTA list only Jurisdictions that were members of the Ad Hoc Group on MLI at the date of the signature of MLI by Italy.
28	Finland	No	N/A	Yes	N/A	
29	France	No	N/A	Yes	N/A	
30	Georgia	No	N/A	Yes	N/A	
31	Germany	No	N/A	Yes	N/A	
32	Ghana*	No	N/A	No	N/A	For the time being, Italy has included in the CTA list only Jurisdictions that were members of the Ad Hoc Group on MLI at the date of

						the signature of MLI by Italy.
33	Greece	No	N/A	Yes	N/A	
34	Hong Kong (China)	No	N/A	Yes	N/A	
35	Hungary	No	N/A	Yes	N/A	
36	Iceland	No	N/A	Yes	N/A	
37	India	No	N/A	Yes	N/A	
38	Indonesia	No	N/A	Yes	N/A	
39	Ireland	No	N/A	Yes	N/A	
40	Israel	No	N/A	Yes	N/A	
41	Japan	No	N/A	Yes	N/A	
42	Jordan	No	N/A	Yes	N/A	
43	Kazakhstan	No	N/A	Yes	N/A	
44	Korea	No	N/A	Yes	N/A	
45	Kuwait*	No	N/A	Yes	N/A	The other Jurisdiction has not notified this Agreement as a CTA for the purpose of MLI,
46	Kyrgyzstan*	No	N/A	No	N/A	For the time being, Italy has included in the CTA list only Jurisdictions that were members of the Ad Hoc Group on MLI at the date of the signature of MLI by Italy.
47	Latvia	No	N/A	Yes	N/A	
48	Lebanon*	No	N/A	Yes	N/A	
49	Lithuania	No	N/A	Yes	N/A	
50	Luxembourg	No	N/A	Yes	N/A	
51	Malaysia	No	N/A	Yes	N/A	
52	Malta	No	N/A	Yes	N/A	
53	Mauritius	No	N/A	Yes	N/A	
54	Mexico	No	N/A	Yes	N/A	
55	Moldova*	No	N/A	Yes	N/A	
56	Montenegro	No	N/A	No	N/A	For the time being, Italy has included in the CTA list only Jurisdictions that were members of the Ad Hoc Group on MLI at the date of the signature of MLI by Italy.
57	Morocco	No	N/A	Yes	N/A	
58	Mozambique*	No	N/A	No	N/A	For the time being, Italy has included in the CTA list only Jurisdictions that were members of the Ad Hoc Group on MLI at the date of the signature of MLI by Italy.
59	Netherlands	No	N/A	Yes	N/A	
60	New Zealand	No	N/A	Yes	N/A	
62	North Macedonia	No	N/A	No	N/A	This Agreement is likely to be included in the Italian CTA revised list which has not been updated at the current date.
63	Norway	No	N/A	Yes	N/A	The other Jurisdiction has not notified this agreement as a Covered Tax Agreement for the purpose of MLI.
63	Oman	No	N/A	No	N/A	This agreement is likely to be included in the Italian CTA revised list which has not

						been updated at the current date.
64	Pakistan	No	N/A	Yes	N/A	
65	Panama	No	N/A	No	N/A	This agreement is likely to be included in the Italian CTA revised list which has not been updated at the current date.
66	Philippines*	No	N/A	Yes	N/A	
67	Poland	No	N/A	Yes	N/A	
68	Portugal	No	N/A	Yes	N/A	
69	Qatar	No	N/A	Yes	N/A	
70	Romania	No	N/A	Yes	N/A	
71	Russia	No	N/A	Yes	N/A	
72	San Marino	No	N/A	Yes	N/A	
73	Saudi Arabia	No	N/A	Yes	N/A	
74	Senegal	No	N/A	Yes	N/A	
75	Serbia	No	N/A	Yes	N/A	
76	Singapore	No	N/A	Yes	N/A	
77	Slovak Republic	No	N/A	Yes	N/A	
78	Slovenia	No	N/A	Yes	N/A	
79	South Africa	No	N/A	Yes	N/A	
80	Spain	No	N/A	Yes	N/A	
81	Sri Lanka	No	N/A	Yes	N/A	
82	Sweden	No	N/A	Yes	N/A	
83	Switzerland	No	N/A	Yes	N/A	
84	Syrian Arab Republic*	No	N/A	No	N/A	For the time being, Italy has included in the CTA list only Jurisdictions that were members of the Ad Hoc Group on MLI at the date of the signature of MLI by Italy.
85	Tajikistan*	No	N/A	No	N/A	For the time being, Italy has included in the CTA list only Jurisdictions that were members of the Ad Hoc Group on MLI at the date of the signature of MLI by Italy.
86	Tanzania*	No	N/A	Yes	N/A	
87	Thailand	No	N/A	Yes	N/A	
88	Trinidad and Tobago	No	N/A	No	N/A	For the time being, Italy has included in the CTA list only Jurisdictions that were members of the Ad Hoc Group on MLI at the date of the signature of MLI by Italy.
89	Tunisia	No	N/A	Yes	N/A	
90	Turkey	No	N/A	Yes	N/A	
91	Uganda*	No	N/A	Yes	N/A	
92	Ukraine	No	N/A	Yes	N/A	
93	United Arab Emirates	No	N/A	Yes	N/A	
94	United Kingdom	No	N/A	Yes	N/A	
95	United States	No	N/A	Yes	N/A	The Agreement already contains an LOB. However the preamble is missing but it could be included subject to the signature of the MLI by

						the other Jurisdiction.
96	Uzbekistan*	No	N/A	No	N/A	For the time being, Italy has included in the CTA list only Jurisdictions that were members of the Ad Hoc Group on MLI at the date of the signature of MLI by Italy.
97	Venezuela*	No	N/A	No	N/A	For the time being, Italy has included in the CTA list only Jurisdictions that were members of the Ad Hoc Group on MLI at the date of the signature of MLI by Italy.
98	Viet Nam	No	N/A	Yes	N/A	
99	Zambia	No	N/A	Yes	N/A	

Jamaica

A. Progress in the implementation of the minimum standard

Jamaica has 14 tax agreements in force, as reported in its response to the Peer Review questionnaire, including the multilateral agreement among the members of the CARICOM concluded with ten treaty partners (the CARICOM Agreement).[73]

Jamaica signed the MLI in 2018, listing its non-compliant bilateral agreements.

Jamaica is implementing the minimum standard through the inclusion of the preamble statement and the PPT combined with the LOB.[74]

The agreements that will be modified by the MLI will come into compliance with the minimum standard once the provisions of the MLI take effect.

B. Implementation issues

Jamaica's listed agreements under the MLI will start to be compliant after Jamaica's ratification of the MLI. Jamaica is encouraged to ratify the MLI as soon as possible. Jamaica indicated that it had started its legislative process for the ratification of the MLI and that it expected to ratify it in the first half of 2021.

Jamaica is encouraged to bring the CARICOM Agreement up to date by commencing talks among all the treaty partners.[75]

Summary of the jurisdiction response - Jamaica

	Treaty partners	Compliance with the standard	If compliant, the alternative implemented	Signature of a complying instrument	The alternative implemented through the complying instrument (if not the MLI)	Comments
1	Antigua and Barbuda	No	N/A	Yes	N/A	CARICOM
2	Barbados	No	N/A	Yes	N/A	CARICOM
3	Belize	No	N/A	Yes	N/A	CARICOM
4	Canada	No	N/A	Yes	N/A	
5	China (People's Republic of)	No	N/A	Yes	N/A	
6	Denmark	No	N/A	Yes	N/A	
7	Dominica	No	N/A	Yes	N/A	CARICOM
8	France	No	N/A	Yes	N/A	
9	Germany	No	N/A	Yes	N/A	
10	Grenada	No	N/A	Yes	N/A	CARICOM

[73] In total, Jamaica identified 23 "agreements" in its List of Tax agreements: thirteen bilateral agreements and the CARICOM Agreement.

[74] For its agreements listed under the MLI, Jamaica is implementing the preamble statement (Article 6 of the MLI) and the PPT (Article 7 of the MLI). Jamaica has opted for the simplified LOB under Article 7(7)(a) of the MLI.

[75] Revisions to the CARICOM Agreement require an agreement from its eleven treaty partners.

11	Guyana*	No	N/A	Yes	N/A	CARICOM
12	Israel	No	N/A	Yes	N/A	
13	Mexico	No	N/A	Yes	N/A	
14	Norway	No	N/A	Yes	N/A	
15	Saint Kitts and Nevis	No	N/A	Yes	N/A	CARICOM
16	Saint Lucia	No	N/A	Yes	N/A	CARICOM
17	Saint Vincent and the Grenadines	No	N/A	Yes	N/A	CARICOM
18	Spain	No	N/A	Yes	N/A	
19	Sweden	No	N/A	Yes	N/A	
20	Switzerland	No	N/A	Yes	N/A	
21	Trinidad and Tobago	No	N/A	Yes	N/A	CARICOM
22	United Kingdom	No	N/A	Yes	N/A	
23	United States	No	N/A	Yes	N/A	

Japan

A. Progress in the implementation of the minimum standard

Japan has 73 tax agreements in force, as reported in its response to the Peer Review questionnaire. Thirty of those agreements, the agreements with Australia, Austria, Belgium, Canada, Chile, Croatia, Denmark, Ecuador*, Estonia, Finland, France, Germany, Iceland, India, Ireland, Israel, Latvia, Lithuania, Luxembourg, the Netherlands, New Zealand, Norway, Poland, Russia, Singapore, the Slovak Republic, Slovenia, Ukraine, the United Arab Emirates and the United Kingdom, comply with the minimum standard.

Japan signed the MLI in 2017 and deposited its instrument of ratification on 26 September 2018. The MLI entered into force for Japan on 1 January 2019. Japan has not listed its agreements with Armenia, Brazil, Brunei Darussalam, Georgia, Spain, Sri Lanka, Switzerland, Thailand, the United States, Viet Nam and Zambia. These agreements with the Inclusive Framework members will therefore not, at this stage, be modified by the MLI.

Japan also signed a bilateral complying instrument with respect to one of its agreements, the agreement with Spain.

Japan indicated in its response to the Peer Review questionnaire that the agreements not listed under the MLI were concluded with treaty partners that had not ratified the MLI or that had joined the MLI but not listed the agreements with Japan. Japan indicated that it would list such agreements once the treaty partners ratify the MLI or list the agreements with Japan. For instance, Japan listed its agreements with Oman and Qatar upon their ratifications.

Japan is implementing the minimum standard through the inclusion of the preamble statement and the PPT for its compliant agreements with Canada, Chile, Ecuador, Finland, India, Ireland, Israel, Luxembourg, Norway, Poland, Singapore, the Slovak Republic, Slovenia, Ukraine and the United Arab Emirates. Japan is implementing the minimum standard through the inclusion of the preamble statement and the PPT combined with the LOB for its compliant agreements with Australia, Austria, Belgium, Croatia, Denmark, Estonia, France, Germany, Iceland, Latvia, Lithuania, the Netherlands, New Zealand, Russia and the United Kingdom.[76]

The agreements modified by the MLI come into compliance with the minimum standard once the provisions of the MLI take effect.

B. Implementation issues

No jurisdiction has raised any concerns about their agreements with Japan.

[76] For 39 of its agreements listed under the MLI, Japan is implementing the preamble statement (Article 6 of the MLI). For 39 of its agreements listed under the MLI, Japan is implementing the PPT (Article 7 of the MLI). Japan made a reservation pursuant to Article 6(4) of the MLI not to apply Article 6(1) of the MLI with respect to agreements, which already contain the relevant preamble language. One of Japan's agreements is within the scope of this reservation.

Summary of the jurisdiction response - Japan

	Treaty partners	Compliance with the standard	If compliant, the alternative implemented	Signature of a complying instrument	The alternative implemented through the complying instrument (if not the MLI)	Comments
1	Armenia	No	N/A	No	N/A	
2	Australia	Yes	PPT and LOB	N/A	N/A	
3	Austria	Yes	PPT and LOB	N/A	N/A	
4	Azerbaijan*	No	N/A	No	N/A	
5	Bangladesh*	No	N/A	No	N/A	
6	Belarus*	No	N/A	No	N/A	
7	Belgium	Yes	PPT and LOB	N/A	N/A	
8	Brazil	No	N/A	No	N/A	
9	Brunei Darussalam	No	N/A	No	N/A	
10	Bulgaria	No	N/A	Yes	N/A	
11	Canada	Yes	PPT alone	N/A	N/A	
12	Chile	Yes	PPT alone	N/A	N/A	
13	China (People's Republic of)	No	N/A	Yes	N/A	
14	Croatia	Yes	PPT and LOB	N/A	N/A	
15	Czech Republic	No	N/A	Yes	N/A	
16	Denmark	Yes	PPT and LOB	N/A	N/A	
17	Ecuador*	Yes	PPT alone	N/A	N/A	
18	Egypt	No	N/A	Yes	N/A	
19	Estonia	Yes	PPT and LOB	N/A	N/A	
20	Fiji*	No	N/A	Yes	N/A	
21	Finland	Yes	PPT alone	N/A	N/A	
22	France	Yes	PPT and LOB	N/A	N/A	
23	Georgia	No	N/A	No	N/A	
24	Germany	Yes	PPT and LOB	N/A	N/A	
25	Hong Kong (China)	No	N/A	Yes	N/A	
26	Hungary	No	N/A	Yes	N/A	
27	Iceland	Yes	PPT and LOB	N/A	N/A	
28	India	Yes	PPT alone	N/A	N/A	
29	Indonesia	No	N/A	Yes	N/A	
30	Ireland	Yes	PPT alone	N/A	N/A	
31	Israel	Yes	PPT alone	N/A	N/A	
32	Italy	No	N/A	Yes	N/A	
33	Kazakhstan	No	N/A	Yes	N/A	
34	Korea	No	N/A	Yes	N/A	
35	Kuwait*	No	N/A	Yes	N/A	
36	Kyrgyzstan*	No	N/A	No	N/A	
37	Latvia	Yes	PPT and LOB	N/A	N/A	
38	Lithuania	Yes	PPT and LOB	N/A	N/A	
39	Luxembourg	Yes	PPT alone	N/A	N/A	
40	Malaysia	No	N/A	Yes	N/A	
41	Mexico	No	N/A	Yes	N/A	
42	Moldova*	No	N/A	No	N/A	
43	Netherlands	Yes	PPT and LOB	N/A	N/A	
44	New Zealand	Yes	PPT and LOB	N/A	N/A	
45	Norway	Yes	PPT alone	N/A	N/A	

46	Oman	No	N/A	Yes	N/A	
47	Pakistan	No	N/A	Yes	N/A	
48	Philippines*	No	N/A	No	N/A	
49	Poland	Yes	PPT alone	N/A	N/A	
50	Portugal	No	N/A	Yes	N/A	
51	Qatar	No	N/A	Yes	N/A	
52	Romania	No	N/A	Yes	N/A	
53	Russia	Yes	PPT and LOB	N/A	N/A	
54	Saudi Arabia	No	N/A	Yes	N/A	
55	Singapore	Yes	PPT alone	N/A	N/A	
56	Slovak Republic	Yes	PPT alone	N/A	N/A	
57	Slovenia	Yes	PPT alone	N/A	N/A	
58	South Africa	No	N/A	Yes	N/A	
59	Spain	No	N/A	Yes	PPT and LOB	
60	Sri Lanka	No	N/A	No	N/A	
61	Sweden	No	N/A	Yes	N/A	
62	Switzerland	No	N/A	No	N/A	
63	Tajikistan*	No	N/A	No	N/A	
64	Thailand	No	N/A	No	N/A	
65	Turkey	No	N/A	Yes	N/A	
66	Turkmenistan*	No	N/A	No	N/A	
67	Ukraine	Yes	PPT alone	N/A	N/A	
68	United Arab Emirates	Yes	PPT alone	N/A	N/A	
69	United Kingdom	Yes	PPT and LOB	N/A	N/A	
70	United States	No	N/A	No	N/A	
71	Uzbekistan*	No	N/A	Yes	PPT and LOB	
72	Viet Nam	No	N/A	No	N/A	
73	Zambia	No	N/A	No	N/A	

Jersey

A. Progress in the implementation of the minimum standard

Jersey has 15 tax agreements in force, as reported in its response to the Peer Review questionnaire. Six of those agreements, the agreements with Liechtenstein, Luxembourg, Malta, Singapore, the United Arab Emirates and the United Kingdom, comply with the minimum standard.

Jersey signed the MLI in 2017 and deposited its instrument of ratification on 15 December 2018. The MLI entered into force for Jersey on 1 July 2018. Jersey has not listed its agreement with Mauritius. This agreement will therefore not, at this stage, be modified by the MLI. Mauritius has listed its agreement with Jersey under the MLI.

Jersey is implementing the minimum standard through the inclusion of the preamble statement and the PPT.[77]

The agreements modified by the MLI come into compliance with the minimum standard once the provisions of the MLI take effect.

B. Implementation issues

As mentioned above, Jersey has not listed its agreement with Mauritius under the MLI. Listing the agreement under the MLI or entering into bilateral renegotiations to implement the minimum standard would ensure that the minimum standard could be implemented in that non-covered agreement.

Summary of the jurisdiction response - Jersey

	Treaty partners	Compliance with the standard	If compliant, the alternative implemented	Signature of a complying instrument	The alternative implemented through the complying instrument (if not the MLI)	Comments
1	Cyprus*	No	N/A	Yes	N/A	
2	Estonia	No	N/A	Yes	N/A	
3	Guernsey	No	N/A	No	N/A	
4	Hong Kong (China)	No	N/A	Yes	N/A	
5	Isle of Man	No	N/A	No	N/A	
6	Liechtenstein	Yes	PPT alone	N/A	N/A	
7	Luxembourg	Yes	PPT alone	N/A	N/A	
8	Malta	Yes	PPT alone	N/A	N/A	
9	Mauritius	No	N/A	No	N/A	
10	Qatar	No	N/A	Yes	N/A	
11	Rwanda*	No	N/A	Yes	N/A	
12	Seychelles	No	N/A	Yes	N/A	
13	Singapore	Yes	PPT alone	N/A	N/A	
14	United Arab Emirates	Yes	PPT alone	N/A	N/A	
15	United Kingdom	Yes	PPT alone	N/A	N/A	

[77] For its agreements listed under the MLI, Jersey is implementing the preamble statement (Article 6 of the MLI) and the PPT (Article 7 of the MLI).

Jordan

A. Progress in the implementation of the minimum standard

Jordan has 36 tax agreements in force, as reported in its response to the Peer Review questionnaire.

Jordan signed the MLI in 2019 and deposited its instrument of ratification on 22 September 2020. The MLI will enter into force for Jordan on 1 January 2021.

Jordan is implementing the minimum standard through the inclusion of the preamble statement and the PPT.[78]

The agreements that will be modified by the MLI will come into compliance with the minimum standard once the provisions of the MLI take effect.

B. Implementation issues

No jurisdiction has raised any concerns about their agreements with Jordan.

Summary of the jurisdiction response - Jordan

	Treaty partners	Compliance with the standard	If compliant, the alternative implemented	Signature of a complying instrument	The alternative implemented through the complying instrument (if not the MLI)	Comments
1	Algeria*	No	N/A	Yes	N/A	
2	Azerbaijan*	No	N/A	Yes	N/A	
3	Bahrain	No	N/A	Yes	N/A	
4	Bosnia-Herzegovina	No	N/A	Yes	N/A	
5	Bulgaria	No	N/A	Yes	N/A	
6	Canada	No	N/A	Yes	N/A	
7	Croatia	No	N/A	Yes	N/A	
8	Czech Republic	No	N/A	Yes	N/A	
9	Egypt	No	N/A	Yes	N/A	
10	France	No	N/A	Yes	N/A	
11	India	No	N/A	Yes	N/A	
12	Indonesia	No	N/A	Yes	N/A	
13	Iran*	No	N/A	Yes	N/A	
14	Italy	No	N/A	Yes	N/A	
15	Korea	No	N/A	Yes	N/A	
16	Kuwait*	No	N/A	Yes	N/A	
17	Lebanon*	No	N/A	Yes	N/A	
18	Malaysia	No	N/A	Yes	N/A	
19	Malta	No	N/A	Yes	N/A	
20	Morocco	No	N/A	Yes	N/A	
21	Netherlands	No	N/A	Yes	N/A	

[78] For its agreements listed under the MLI, Jersey is implementing the preamble statement (Article 6 of the MLI) and the PPT (Article 7 of the MLI).

22	Palestine*	No	N/A	Yes	N/A	
23	Pakistan	No	N/A	Yes	N/A	
24	Poland	No	N/A	Yes	N/A	
25	Qatar	No	N/A	Yes	N/A	
26	Romania	No	N/A	Yes	N/A	
27	Saudi Arabia	No	N/A	Yes	N/A	
28	Sudan*	No	N/A	Yes	N/A	
29	Syria*	No	N/A	Yes	N/A	
30	Tunisia	No	N/A	Yes	N/A	
31	Turkey	No	N/A	Yes	N/A	
32	Ukraine	No	N/A	Yes	N/A	
33	United Arab Emirates	No	N/A	Yes	N/A	
34	United Kingdom	No	N/A	Yes	N/A	
35	Uzbekistan*	No	N/A	Yes	N/A	
36	Yemen*	No	N/A	Yes	N/A	

Kazakhstan

A. Progress in the implementation of the minimum standard

Kazakhstan has 55 tax agreements in force, as reported in its response to the Peer Review questionnaire.

Kazakhstan signed the MLI in 2018 and deposited its instrument of ratification on 24 June 2020. The MLI will enter into force for Kazakhstan on 1 October 2020.

Kazakhstan is implementing the minimum standard through the inclusion of the preamble statement and the PPT combined with the LOB.[79]

The agreements that will be modified by the MLI will come into compliance with the minimum standard once the provisions of the MLI take effect.

B. Implementation issues

No jurisdiction has raised any concerns about their agreements with Kazakhstan.

Summary of the jurisdiction response - Kazakhstan

	Treaty partners	Compliance with the standard	If compliant, the alternative implemented	Signature of a complying instrument	The alternative implemented through the complying instrument (if not the MLI)	Comments
1	Armenia	No	N/A	Yes	N/A	
2	Austria	No	N/A	Yes	N/A	
3	Azerbaijan*	No	N/A	Yes	N/A	
4	Belarus*	No	N/A	Yes	N/A	
5	Belgium	No	N/A	Yes	N/A	
6	Bulgaria	No	N/A	Yes	N/A	
7	Canada	No	N/A	Yes	N/A	
8	China (People's Republic of)	No	N/A	Yes	N/A	
9	Croatia	No	N/A	Yes	N/A	
10	Cyprus*	No	N/A	No	N/A	Partial compliance. The agreement has a PPT, but no compliant preamble
11	Czech Republic	No	N/A	Yes	N/A	
12	Estonia	No	N/A	Yes	N/A	
13	Finland	No	N/A	Yes	N/A	
14	France	No	N/A	Yes	N/A	
15	Georgia	No	N/A	Yes	N/A	
16	Germany	No	N/A	Yes	N/A	
17	Hungary	No	N/A	Yes	N/A	
18	India	No	N/A	Yes	N/A	

[79] For its agreements listed under the MLI, Kazakhstan is implementing the preamble statement (Article 6 of the MLI) and the PPT (Article 7 of the MLI). Kazakhstan also opted for the simplified LOB pursuant to Article 7(6) of the MLI.

19	Iran*	No	N/A	Yes	N/A	
20	Ireland	No	N/A	Yes	N/A	
21	Italy	No	N/A	Yes	N/A	
22	Japan	No	N/A	Yes	N/A	
23	Korea	No	N/A	Yes	N/A	
24	Kyrgyzstan*	No	N/A	Yes	N/A	
25	Latvia	No	N/A	Yes	N/A	
26	Lithuania	No	N/A	Yes	N/A	
27	Luxembourg	No	N/A	Yes	N/A	
28	Malaysia	No	N/A	Yes	N/A	
29	Moldova*	No	N/A	Yes	N/A	
30	Mongolia	No	N/A	Yes	N/A	
31	Netherlands	No	N/A	Yes	N/A	
32	North Macedonia	No	N/A	Yes	N/A	
33	Norway	No	N/A	Yes	N/A	
34	Pakistan	No	N/A	Yes	N/A	
35	Poland	No	N/A	Yes	N/A	
36	Qatar	No	N/A	Yes	N/A	
37	Romania	No	N/A	Yes	N/A	
38	Russia	No	N/A	Yes	N/A	
39	Saudi Arabia	No	N/A	Yes	N/A	
40	Serbia	No	N/A	Yes	N/A	
41	Singapore	No	N/A	Yes	N/A	
42	Slovak Republic	No	N/A	Yes	N/A	
43	Slovenia	No	N/A	Yes	N/A	
44	Spain	No	N/A	Yes	N/A	
45	Sweden	No	N/A	Yes	N/A	
46	Switzerland	No	N/A	Yes	N/A	
47	Tajikistan*	No	N/A	Yes	N/A	
48	Turkey	No	N/A	Yes	N/A	
49	Turkmenistan*	No	N/A	Yes	N/A	
50	Ukraine	No	N/A	Yes	N/A	
51	United Arab Emirates	No	N/A	Yes	N/A	
52	United Kingdom	No	N/A	Yes	N/A	
53	United States	No	N/A	Yes	N/A	
54	Uzbekistan*	No	N/A	Yes	N/A	
55	Viet Nam	No	N/A	Yes	N/A	

Kenya

A. Progress in the implementation of the minimum standard

Kenya has 15 tax agreements in force, as reported in its response to the Peer Review questionnaire.

Kenya signed the MLI in 2019 and has not listed its agreements with Germany, Korea and Zambia. These agreements will therefore not, at this stage, be modified by the MLI.

Kenya is implementing the minimum standard through the inclusion of the preamble statement and the PPT.[80]

The agreements that will be modified by the MLI will come into compliance with the minimum standard once the provisions of the MLI take effect.

B. Implementation issues

Kenya's listed agreements under the MLI will start to be compliant after Kenya's ratification of the MLI. Kenya is encouraged to ratify the MLI as soon as possible.

As mentioned above, Kenya has not listed its agreements with Germany, Korea and Zambia under the MLI. Listing the agreements under the MLI or entering into bilateral renegotiations to implement the minimum standard would ensure that the minimum standard could be implemented in those non-covered agreements.

Summary of the jurisdiction response - Kenya

	Treaty partners	Compliance with the standard	If compliant, the alternative implemented	Signature of a complying instrument	The alternative implemented through the complying instrument (if not the MLI)	Comments
1	Canada	No	N/A	Yes	N/A	
2	Denmark	No	N/A	Yes	N/A	
3	France	No	N/A	Yes	N/A	
4	Germany	No	N/A	No	N/A	
5	India	No	N/A	Yes	N/A	
6	Iran*	No	N/A	No	N/A	
7	Korea	No	N/A	No	N/A	
8	Norway	No	N/A	Yes	N/A	
9	Qatar	No	N/A	Yes	N/A	
10	Seychelles	No	N/A	Yes	N/A	
11	South Africa	No	N/A	Yes	N/A	
12	Sweden	No	N/A	Yes	N/A	
13	United Arab Emirates	No	N/A	Yes	N/A	
14	United Kingdom	No	N/A	Yes	N/A	
15	Zambia	No	N/A	No	N/A	

[80] For its agreements listed under the MLI, Kenya is implementing the preamble statement (Article 6 of the MLI) and the PPT (Article 7 of the MLI).

Korea

A. Progress in the implementation of the minimum standard

Korea has 93 tax agreements in force, as reported in its response to the Peer Review questionnaire. Four of those agreements, the agreements with the Czech Republic, Singapore, Turkmenistan*, and the United Arab Emirates comply with the minimum standard.

Korea signed the MLI in 2017 and deposited its instrument of ratification on 13 May 2020. The MLI will enter into force for Korea on 1 September 2020. Korea has not listed its agreements with Albania, Austria, Brazil, Germany, and Turkey. These agreements will therefore not, at this stage, be modified by the MLI.

Korea has also signed a bilateral complying instrument with Switzerland and Uzbekistan*.

Korea indicated in its response to the Peer Review questionnaire that bilateral negotiations would be used with respect to its agreements with Albania, Austria, Belarus*, Brazil, Ecuador*, Ethiopia*, Germany, Iran*, Kyrgyzstan*, Lao People's Democratic Republic*, Myanmar*, Nepal*, Norway, Tajikistan*, Turkey and Venezuela*.

Korea is implementing the minimum standard through the inclusion of the preamble statement and the PPT.[81]

The agreements that will be modified by the MLI will come into compliance with the minimum standard once the provisions of the MLI take effect.

B. Implementation issues

No jurisdiction has raised any concerns about their agreements with Korea.

Summary of the jurisdiction response - Korea

	Treaty partners	Compliance with the standard	If compliant, the alternative implemented	Signature of a complying instrument	The alternative implemented through the complying instrument (if not the MLI)	Comments
1	Albania	No	N/A	No	N/A	
2	Algeria*	No	N/A	Yes	N/A	
3	Australia	No	N/A	Yes	N/A	
4	Austria	No	N/A	No	N/A	
5	Azerbaijan*	No	N/A	Yes	N/A	
6	Bahrain	No	N/A	Yes	N/A	
7	Bangladesh*	No	N/A	Yes	N/A	
8	Belarus*	No	N/A	No	N/A	
9	Belgium	No	N/A	Yes	N/A	
10	Brazil	No	N/A	No	N/A	
11	Brunei	No	N/A	Yes	N/A	

[81] For its agreements listed under the MLI, Korea is implementing the preamble statement (Article 6 of the MLI) and the PPT (Article 7 of the MLI).

	Darussalam					
12	Bulgaria	No	N/A	Yes	N/A	
13	Canada	No	N/A	Yes	N/A	
14	Chile	No	N/A	Yes	N/A	
15	China (People's Republic of)	No	N/A	Yes	N/A	
16	Colombia	No	N/A	Yes	N/A	
17	Croatia	No	N/A	Yes	N/A	
18	Czech Republic	Yes	PPT alone	N/A	N/A	
19	Denmark	No	N/A	Yes	N/A	
20	Ecuador*	No	N/A	No	N/A	
21	Egypt	No	N/A	Yes	N/A	
22	Estonia	No	N/A	Yes	N/A	
23	Ethiopia*	No	N/A	No	N/A	
24	Fiji*	No	N/A	Yes	N/A	
25	Finland	No	N/A	Yes	N/A	
26	France	No	N/A	Yes	N/A	
27	Gabon	No	N/A	Yes	N/A	
28	Georgia	No	N/A	Yes	N/A	
29	Germany	No	N/A	No	N/A	
30	Greece	No	N/A	Yes	N/A	
31	Hong Kong (China)	No	N/A	Yes	N/A	
32	Hungary	No	N/A	Yes	N/A	
33	Iceland	No	N/A	Yes	N/A	
34	India	No	N/A	Yes	N/A	
35	Indonesia	No	N/A	Yes	N/A	
36	Iran*	No	N/A	No	N/A	
37	Ireland	No	N/A	Yes	N/A	
38	Israel	No	N/A	Yes	N/A	
39	Italy	No	N/A	Yes	N/A	
40	Japan	No	N/A	Yes	N/A	
41	Jordan	No	N/A	Yes	N/A	
42	Kazakhstan	No	N/A	Yes	N/A	
43	Kenya	No	N/A	Yes	N/A	
44	Kuwait*	No	N/A	Yes	N/A	
45	Kyrgyzstan*	No	N/A	No	N/A	
46	Lao People's Democratic Republic*	No	N/A	No	N/A	
47	Latvia	No	N/A	Yes	N/A	
48	Lithuania	No	N/A	Yes	N/A	
49	Luxembourg	No	N/A	Yes	N/A	
50	Malaysia	No	N/A	Yes	N/A	
51	Malta	No	N/A	Yes	N/A	
52	Mexico	No	N/A	Yes	N/A	
53	Mongolia	No	N/A	Yes	N/A	
54	Morocco	No	N/A	Yes	N/A	
55	Myanmar*	No	N/A	No	N/A	
56	Nepal*	No	N/A	No	N/A	
57	Netherlands	No	N/A	Yes	N/A	
58	New Zealand	No	N/A	Yes	N/A	
59	Norway	No	N/A	Yes	N/A	
60	Oman	No	N/A	Yes	N/A	

61	Pakistan	No	N/A	Yes	N/A	
62	Panama	No	N/A	Yes	N/A	
63	Papua New Guinea	No	N/A	Yes	N/A	
64	Peru	No	N/A	Yes	N/A	
65	Philippines*	No	N/A	Yes	N/A	
66	Poland	No	N/A	Yes	N/A	
67	Portugal	No	N/A	Yes	N/A	
68	Qatar	No	N/A	Yes	N/A	
69	Romania	No	N/A	Yes	N/A	
70	Russia	No	N/A	Yes	N/A	
71	Saudi Arabia	No	N/A	Yes	N/A	
72	Serbia	No	N/A	Yes	N/A	
73	Singapore	Yes	PPT alone	N/A	N/A	
74	Slovak Republic	No	N/A	Yes	N/A	
75	Slovenia	No	N/A	Yes	N/A	
76	South Africa	No	N/A	Yes	N/A	
77	Spain	No	N/A	Yes	N/A	
78	Sri Lanka	No	N/A	Yes	N/A	
79	Sweden	No	N/A	Yes	N/A	
80	Switzerland	No	N/A	Yes	PPT alone	
81	Tajikistan*	No	N/A	No	N/A	
82	Thailand	No	N/A	Yes	N/A	
83	Tunisia	No	N/A	Yes	N/A	
84	Turkey	No	N/A	No	N/A	
85	Turkmenistan*	Yes	PPT alone	N/A	N/A	
86	Ukraine	No	N/A	Yes	N/A	
87	United Arab Emirates	Yes	PPT alone	N/A	N/A	
88	United Kingdom	No	N/A	Yes	N/A	
89	United States	No	N/A	Yes	N/A	
90	Uruguay	No	N/A	Yes	N/A	
91	Uzbekistan*	No	N/A	Yes	PPT alone	
92	Venezuela*	No	N/A	No	N/A	
93	Viet Nam	No	N/A	Yes	N/A	

Latvia

A. Progress in the implementation of the minimum standard

Latvia has 62 tax agreements in force, as reported in its response to the Peer Review questionnaire. Two of those agreements, the agreements with Japan and Switzerland comply with the minimum standard.

Latvia signed the MLI in 2017 and deposited its instrument of ratification on 29 October 2019. The MLI entered into force for Latvia on 1 February 2020. Latvia has not listed its agreements with Germany and North Macedonia but indicated in its response to the Peer Review questionnaire that bilateral negotiations would be pursued in respect of its agreement with Germany. These agreements will therefore not, at this stage, be modified by the MLI. North Macedonia have listed their agreements with Latvia under the MLI.

Latvia is generally implementing the minimum standard through the inclusion of the preamble statement and the PPT.[82]

The agreements that will be modified by the MLI will come into compliance with the minimum standard once the provisions of the MLI take effect.

B. Implementation issues

As mentioned above, Latvia has not listed its agreement with North Macedonia under the MLI. Listing the agreement under the MLI or entering into bilateral renegotiations to implement the minimum standard would ensure that the minimum standard could be implemented in that non-covered agreement.

Summary of the jurisdiction response - Latvia

	Treaty partners	Compliance with the standard	If compliant, the alternative implemented	Signature of a complying instrument	The alternative implemented through the complying instrument (if not the MLI)	Comments
1	Albania	No	N/A	Yes	N/A	
2	Armenia	No	N/A	Yes	N/A	
3	Austria	No	N/A	Yes	N/A	
4	Azerbaijan*	No	N/A	Yes	N/A	
5	Belarus*	No	N/A	Yes	N/A	
6	Belgium	No	N/A	Yes	N/A	
7	Bulgaria	No	N/A	Yes	N/A	
8	Canada	No	N/A	Yes	N/A	
9	China (People's Republic of)	No	N/A	Yes	N/A	
10	Croatia	No	N/A	Yes	N/A	
11	Cyprus*	No	N/A	Yes	N/A	
12	Czech Republic	No	N/A	Yes	N/A	
13	Denmark	No	N/A	Yes	N/A	
14	Estonia	No	N/A	Yes	N/A	

82 For its agreements listed under the MLI, Latvia is implementing the preamble statement (Article 6 of the MLI) and the PPT (Article 7 of the MLI).

15	Finland	No	N/A	Yes	N/A	
16	France	No	N/A	Yes	N/A	
17	Georgia	No	N/A	Yes	N/A	
18	Germany	No	N/A	No	N/A	
19	Greece	No	N/A	Yes	N/A	
20	Hong Kong (China)	No	N/A	Yes	N/A	
21	Hungary	No	N/A	Yes	N/A	
22	Iceland	No	N/A	Yes	N/A	
23	India	No	N/A	Yes	N/A	
24	Ireland	No	N/A	Yes	N/A	
25	Israel	No	N/A	Yes	N/A	
26	Italy	No	N/A	Yes	N/A	
27	Japan	Yes	PPT and LOB	N/A	N/A	
28	Kazakhstan	No	N/A	Yes	N/A	
29	Korea	No	N/A	Yes	N/A	
30	Kuwait*	No	N/A	Yes	N/A	
31	Kyrgyzstan*	No	N/A	Yes	N/A	
32	Lithuania	No	N/A	Yes	N/A	
33	Luxembourg	No	N/A	Yes	N/A	
34	Malta	No	N/A	Yes	N/A	
35	Mexico	No	N/A	Yes	N/A	
36	Moldova*	No	N/A	Yes	N/A	
37	Montenegro	No	N/A	Yes	N/A	
38	Morocco	No	N/A	Yes	N/A	
39	Netherlands	No	N/A	Yes	N/A	
40	North Macedonia	No	N/A	No	N/A	
41	Norway	No	N/A	Yes	N/A	
42	Poland	No	N/A	Yes	N/A	
43	Portugal	No	N/A	Yes	N/A	
44	Qatar	No	N/A	Yes	N/A	
45	Romania	No	N/A	Yes	N/A	
46	Russia	No	N/A	Yes	N/A	
47	Serbia	No	N/A	Yes	N/A	
48	Singapore	No	N/A	Yes	N/A	
49	Slovak Republic	No	N/A	Yes	N/A	
50	Slovenia	No	N/A	Yes	N/A	
51	Spain	No	N/A	Yes	N/A	
52	Sweden	No	N/A	Yes	N/A	
53	Switzerland	Yes	PPT alone	N/A	N/A	
54	Tajikistan*	No	N/A	Yes	N/A	
55	Turkey	No	N/A	Yes	N/A	
56	Turkmenistan*	No	N/A	Yes	N/A	
57	Ukraine	No	N/A	Yes	N/A	
58	United Arab Emirates	No	N/A	Yes	N/A	
59	United Kingdom	No	N/A	Yes	N/A	
60	United States	No	N/A	Yes	N/A	
61	Uzbekistan*	No	N/A	Yes	N/A	
62	Viet Nam	No	N/A	Yes	N/A	

Liberia

A. Progress in the implementation of the minimum standard

Liberia has one tax agreement in force with Germany, as reported in its response to the Peer Review questionnaire.

Liberia's agreement does not comply with the minimum standard and is not subject to any complying instrument.

Liberia has not signed the MLI.

Liberia indicated in its response to the Peer Review questionnaire that bilateral negotiations would be pursued to bring its agreement with German into compliance with the minimum standard.

B. Implementation issues

As Liberia has not signed the MLI or implemented anti-treaty-shopping measures in its agreement, the Secretariat will offer its support to design a plan for the implementation of the minimum standard to strengthen its treaty network.

Summary of the jurisdiction response - Liberia

	Treaty partners	Compliance with the standard	If compliant, the alternative implemented	Signature of a complying instrument	The alternative implemented through the complying instrument (if not the MLI)	Comments
1	Germany	No	N/A	No	N/A	

Liechtenstein

A. Progress in the implementation of the minimum standard

Liechtenstein has 20 tax agreements in force, as reported in its response to the Peer Review questionnaire. Five of those agreements, the agreements with Austria, Iceland, Jersey, Lithuania and Monaco, comply with the minimum standard.

Liechtenstein signed the MLI in 2017 and deposited its instrument of ratification on 19 December 2019. The MLI entered into force for Liechtenstein on 1 April 2020. Liechtenstein's agreements with Germany and Switzerland are subject to a complying instrument.

Liechtenstein is implementing the minimum standard through the inclusion of the preamble statement and the PPT.[83]

The agreements that will be modified by the MLI will come into compliance with the minimum standard once the provisions of the MLI take effect.

B. Implementation issues

No jurisdiction has raised any concerns about their agreements with Liechtenstein.

Summary of the jurisdiction response - Liechtenstein

	Treaty partners	Compliance with the standard	If compliant, the alternative implemented	Signature of a complying instrument	The alternative implemented through the complying instrument (if not the MLI)	Comments
1	Andorra	No	N/A	Yes	N/A	
2	Austria	Yes	PPT alone	N/A	N/A	
3	Czech Republic	No	N/A	Yes	N/A	
4	Georgia	No	N/A	Yes	N/A	
5	Germany	No	N/A	Yes	N/A	Listed under MLI, however, Protocol signed in October 2020
6	Guernsey	No	N/A	Yes	N/A	
7	Hong Kong (China)	No	N/A	Yes	N/A	
8	Hungary	No	N/A	Yes	N/A	
9	Iceland	Yes	PPT alone	N/A	N/A	
10	Jersey	Yes	PPT alone	N/A	N/A	
11	Lithuania	Yes	PPT alone	N/A	N/A	
12	Luxembourg	No	N/A	Yes	N/A	
13	Malta	No	N/A	Yes	N/A	
14	Monaco	Yes	PPT alone	N/A	N/A	
15	San Marino	No	N/A	Yes	N/A	
16	Singapore	No	N/A	Yes	N/A	
17	Switzerland	No	N/A	Yes	PPT alone	
18	United Arab Emirates	No	N/A	Yes	N/A	
19	United Kingdom	No	N/A	Yes	N/A	
20	Uruguay	No	N/A	Yes	N/A	

[83] For its agreements listed under the MLI, Liechtenstein is implementing the preamble statement (Article 6 of the MLI) and the PPT (Article 7 of the MLI).

Lithuania

A. Progress in the implementation of the minimum standard

Lithuania has 57 tax agreements in force, as reported in its response to the Peer Review questionnaire. Twenty-five of those agreements, the agreements with Austria, Belgium, Canada, Denmark, Finland, France, Georgia, Israel, Iceland, India, Ireland, Japan, Liechtenstein, Luxembourg, Malta, the Netherlands, Norway, Poland, Serbia, Singapore, the Slovak Republic, Slovenia, Ukraine, the United Arab Emirates and the United Kingdom, comply with the minimum standard.

Lithuania signed the MLI in 2017 and deposited its instrument of ratification on 11 September 2018. The MLI entered into force for the Lithuania on 1 January 2019.

Lithuania is generally implementing the minimum standard through the inclusion of the preamble statement and the PPT.[84]

The agreements modified by the MLI come into compliance with the minimum standard once the provisions of the MLI take effect.

B. Implementation issues

No jurisdiction has raised any concerns about their agreements with Lithuania.

Summary of the jurisdiction response - Lithuania

	Treaty partners	Compliance with the standard	If compliant, the alternative implemented	Signature of a complying instrument	The alternative implemented through the complying instrument (if not the MLI)	Comments
1	Armenia	No	N/A	Yes	N/A	
2	Austria	Yes	PPT alone	N/A	N/A	
3	Azerbaijan*	No	N/A	Yes	N/A	
4	Belarus*	No	N/A	Yes	N/A	
5	Belgium	Yes	PPT alone	N/A	N/A	
6	Bulgaria	No	N/A	Yes	N/A	
7	Canada	Yes	PPT alone	N/A	N/A	
8	China (People's Republic of)	No	N/A	Yes	N/A	
9	Croatia	No	N/A	Yes	N/A	
10	Cyprus*	No	N/A	Yes	N/A	
11	Czech Republic	No	N/A	Yes	N/A	
12	Denmark	Yes	PPT alone	N/A	N/A	
13	Estonia	No	N/A	Yes	N/A	Preamble missing, partial compliance in respect of PPT.
14	Finland	Yes	PPT alone	N/A	N/A	
15	France	Yes	PPT alone	N/A	N/A	

[84] For its agreements listed under the MLI, Lithuania is implementing the preamble statement (Article 6 of the MLI) and the PPT (Article 7 of the MLI).

16	Georgia	Yes	PPT alone	N/A	N/A	
17	Germany	No	N/A	Yes	N/A	
18	Greece	No	N/A	Yes	N/A	
19	Hungary	No	N/A	Yes	N/A	
20	Iceland	Yes	PPT alone	N/A	N/A	
21	India	Yes	PPT alone	N/A	N/A	
22	Ireland	Yes	PPT alone	N/A	N/A	
23	Israel	Yes	PPT alone	N/A	N/A	
24	Italy	No	N/A	Yes	N/A	Preamble missing, partial compliance in respect of PPT.
25	Japan	Yes	PPT and LOB	N/A	N/A	The agreement was signed on 13 July 2017 and entered into effect on 1 January 2019.
26	Kazakhstan	No	N/A	Yes	N/A	Preamble missing, partial compliance in respect of PPT.
27	Korea	No	N/A	Yes	N/A	
28	Kuwait*	No	N/A	Yes	N/A	
29	Kyrgyzstan*	No	N/A	Yes	N/A	
30	Latvia	No	N/A	Yes	N/A	Preamble missing, partial compliance in respect of PPT.
31.	Liechtenstein	Yes	PPT alone	N/A	N/A	The agreement was signed on 15 February 2019 and entered into force on 19 February 2020. It will enter into effect on 1 January 2021.
32	Luxembourg	Yes	PPT alone	N/A	N/A	
33	Malta	Yes	PPT alone	N/A	N/A	
34	Mexico	No	N/A	Yes	N/A	Preamble missing, partial compliance in respect of PPT.
35	Moldova*	No	N/A	Yes	N/A	
36	Morocco	No	N/A	Yes	N/A	
37	Netherlands	Yes	PPT alone	N/A	N/A	
38	North Macedonia	No	N/A	Yes	N/A	Preamble missing, partial compliance in respect of PPT.
39	Norway	Yes	PPT alone	N/A	N/A	
40	Poland	Yes	PPT alone	N/A	N/A	
41	Portugal	No	N/A	Yes	N/A	
42	Romania	No	N/A	Yes	N/A	
43	Russia	No	N/A	Yes	N/A	Preamble missing, partial compliance in respect of PPT.
44	Serbia	Yes	PPT alone	N/A	N/A	
45	Singapore	Yes	PPT alone	N/A	N/A	
46	Slovak Republic	Yes	PPT alone	N/A	N/A	
47	Slovenia	Yes	PPT alone	N/A	N/A	
48	Spain	No	N/A	Yes	N/A	
49	Sweden	No	N/A	Yes	N/A	
50	Switzerland	No	N/A	Yes	N/A	
51	Turkey	No	N/A	Yes	N/A	
52	Turkmenistan*	No	N/A	Yes	N/A	

53	Ukraine	Yes	PPT alone	N/A	N/A	
54	United Arab Emirates	Yes	PPT alone	N/A	N/A	
55	United Kingdom	Yes	PPT alone	N/A	N/A	
56	United States	No	N/A	Yes	N/A	Preamble missing, partial compliance in respect of LOB.
57	Uzbekistan*	No	N/A	Yes	N/A	Preamble missing, partial compliance in respect of PPT.

Luxembourg

A. Progress in the implementation of the minimum standard

Luxembourg has 83 tax agreements in force, as reported in its response to the Peer Review questionnaire. 32 of those agreements, the agreements with Austria, Belgium, Canada, Cyprus*, Denmark, Finland, France, Georgia, Guernsey, Iceland, India, Ireland, the Isle of Man, Israel, Japan, Jersey, Kosovo*, Lithuania, Malta, Monaco, the Netherlands, Norway, Poland, Senegal, Serbia, Singapore, the Slovak Republic, Slovenia, Ukraine, the United Arab Emirates, the United Kingdom and Uzbekistan*, comply with the minimum standard.

Luxembourg signed the MLI in 2017 and deposited its instrument of ratification on 9 April 2019. The MLI entered into force for Luxembourg on 1 August 2019.

Luxembourg is implementing the minimum standard through the inclusion of the preamble statement and the PPT.[85]

The agreements modified by the MLI come into compliance with the minimum standard once the provisions of the MLI take effect.

B. Implementation issues

No jurisdiction has raised any concerns about their agreements with Luxembourg.

Summary of the jurisdiction response - Luxembourg

	Treaty partners	Compliance with the standard	If compliant, the alternative implemented	Signature of a complying instrument	The alternative implemented through the complying instrument (if not the MLI)	Comments
1	Andorra	No	N/A	Yes	N/A	
2	Armenia	No	N/A	Yes	N/A	
3	Austria	Yes	PPT alone	N/A	N/A	
4	Azerbaijan*	No	N/A	Yes	N/A	
5	Bahrain	No	N/A	Yes	N/A	
6	Barbados	No	N/A	Yes	N/A	
7	Belgium	Yes	PPT alone	N/A	N/A	
8	Brazil	No	N/A	Yes	N/A	
9	Brunei Darussalam	No	N/A	Yes	N/A	
10	Bulgaria	No	N/A	Yes	N/A	
11	Canada	Yes	PPT alone	N/A	N/A	
12	China (People's Republic of)	No	N/A	Yes	N/A	
13	Chinese Taipei*	No	N/A	Yes	N/A	
14	Croatia	No	N/A	Yes	N/A	
15	Cyprus*	Yes	PPT alone	N/A	N/A	

[85] For its agreements listed under the MLI, Luxembourg is implementing the preamble statement (Article 6 of the MLI) and the PPT (Article 7 of the MLI).

16	Czech Republic	No	N/A	Yes	N/A	
17	Denmark	Yes	PPT alone	N/A	N/A	
18	Estonia	No	N/A	Yes	N/A	
19	Finland	Yes	PPT alone	N/A	N/A	
20	France	Yes	PPT alone	N/A	N/A	
21	Georgia	Yes	PPT alone	N/A	N/A	
22	Germany	No	N/A	Yes	N/A	
23	Greece	No	N/A	Yes	N/A	
24	Guernsey	Yes	PPT alone	N/A	N/A	
25	Hong Kong (China)	No	N/A	Yes	N/A	
26	Hungary	No	N/A	Yes	N/A	
27	Iceland	Yes	PPT alone	N/A	N/A	
28	India	Yes	PPT alone	N/A	N/A	
29	Indonesia	No	N/A	Yes	N/A	
30	Ireland	Yes	PPT alone	N/A	N/A	
31	Isle of Man	Yes	PPT alone	N/A	N/A	
32	Israel	Yes	PPT alone	N/A	N/A	
33	Italy	No	N/A	Yes	N/A	
34	Japan	Yes	PPT alone	N/A	N/A	
35	Jersey	Yes	PPT alone	N/A	N/A	
36	Kazakhstan	No	N/A	Yes	N/A	
37	Korea	No	N/A	Yes	N/A	
38	Kosovo*	Yes	PPT alone	N/A	N/A	
39	Lao People's Democratic Republic*	No	N/A	Yes	N/A	
40	Latvia	No	N/A	Yes	N/A	
41	Liechtenstein	No	N/A	Yes	N/A	
42	Lithuania	Yes	PPT alone	N/A	N/A	
43	Malaysia	No	N/A	Yes	N/A	
44	Malta	Yes	PPT alone	N/A	N/A	
45	Mauritius	No	N/A	Yes	N/A	
46	Mexico	No	N/A	Yes	N/A	
47	Moldova*	No	N/A	Yes	N/A	
48	Monaco	Yes	PPT alone	N/A	N/A	
49	Morocco	No	N/A	Yes	N/A	
50	Netherlands	Yes	PPT alone	N/A	N/A	
51	North Macedonia	No	N/A	Yes	N/A	
52	Norway	Yes	PPT alone	N/A	N/A	
53	Panama	No	N/A	Yes	N/A	
54	Poland	Yes	PPT alone	N/A	N/A	
55	Portugal	No	N/A	Yes	N/A	
56	Qatar	No	N/A	Yes	N/A	
57	Romania	No	N/A	Yes	N/A	
58	Russia	No	N/A	Yes	N/A	
59	San Marino	No	N/A	Yes	N/A	
60	Saudi Arabia	No	N/A	Yes	N/A	
61	Senegal	Yes	PPT alone	N/A	N/A	
62	Serbia	Yes	PPT alone	N/A	N/A	
63	Seychelles	No	N/A	Yes	N/A	
64	Singapore	Yes	PPT alone	N/A	N/A	
65	Slovak Republic	Yes	PPT alone	N/A	N/A	
66	Slovenia	Yes	PPT alone	N/A	N/A	

67	South Africa	No	N/A	Yes	N/A	
68	Spain	No	N/A	Yes	N/A	
69	Sri Lanka	No	N/A	Yes	N/A	
70	Sweden	No	N/A	Yes	N/A	
71	Switzerland	No	N/A	Yes	N/A	
72	Tajikistan*	No	N/A	Yes	N/A	
73	Thailand	No	N/A	Yes	N/A	
74	Trinidad and Tobago	No	N/A	Yes	N/A	
75	Tunisia	No	N/A	Yes	N/A	
76	Turkey	No	N/A	Yes	N/A	
77	Ukraine	Yes	PPT alone	N/A	N/A	
78	United Arab Emirates	Yes	PPT alone	N/A	N/A	
79	United Kingdom	Yes	PPT alone	N/A	N/A	
80	United States	No	N/A	Yes	N/A	
81	Uruguay	No	N/A	Yes	N/A	
82	Uzbekistan*	Yes	PPT alone	N/A	N/A	
83	Viet Nam	No	N/A	Yes	N/A	

Macau (China)

A. Progress in the implementation of the minimum standard

Macau (China) has four tax agreements in force, as reported in its response to the Peer Review questionnaire.

None of Macau (China)'s agreements comply with the minimum standard or are subject to a complying instrument.

Macau (China) has not joined the MLI.

B. Implementation issues

As Macau (China) has not joined the MLI or implemented anti-treaty-shopping measures in its agreements, the Secretariat will offer its support to design a plan for the implementation of the minimum standard to strengthen its network of agreements.

Summary of the jurisdiction response – Macau (China)

	Treaty partners	Compliance with the standard	If compliant, the alternative implemented	Signature of a complying instrument	The alternative implemented through the complying instrument (if not the MLI)	Comments
1	Cabo Verde	No	N/A	No	N/A	
2	Mozambique*	No	N/A	No	N/A	
3	Portugal	No	N/A	No	N/A	
4	Viet Nam	No	N/A	No	N/A	

Malaysia

A. Progress in the implementation of the minimum standard

Malaysia has 72 tax agreements in force, as reported in its response to the Peer Review questionnaire.

Malaysia signed the MLI in 2018, listing its non-compliant bilateral agreements.

Malaysia indicated in its response to the Peer Review questionnaire that bilateral negotiations would be used with respect to its agreement with Austria, Germany, Norway and Switzerland.

Malaysia is implementing the minimum standard through the inclusion of the preamble statement and the PPT.[86]

The agreements that will be modified by the MLI will come into compliance with the minimum standard once the provisions of the MLI take effect.

B. Implementation issues

Malaysia's listed agreements under the MLI will start to be compliant after Malaysia's ratification of the MLI. Malaysia indicated that it expected to deposit its instrument of ratification of the MLI early in 2021.

Summary of the jurisdiction response - Malaysia

	Treaty partners	Compliance with the standard	If compliant, the alternative implemented	Signature of a complying instrument	The alternative implemented through the complying instrument (if not the MLI)	Comments
1	Albania	No	N/A	Yes	N/A	
2	Australia	No	N/A	Yes	N/A	
3	Austria	No	N/A	Yes	N/A	
4	Bahrain	No	N/A	Yes	N/A	
5	Bangladesh*	No	N/A	Yes	N/A	
6	Belgium	No	N/A	Yes	N/A	
7	Bosnia-Herzegovina	No	N/A	Yes	N/A	
8	Brunei Darussalam	No	N/A	Yes	N/A	
9	Canada	No	N/A	Yes	N/A	
10	Chile	No	N/A	Yes	N/A	
11	China (People's Republic of)	No	N/A	Yes	N/A	
12	Croatia	No	N/A	Yes	N/A	
13	Czech Republic	No	N/A	Yes	N/A	
14	Denmark	No	N/A	Yes	N/A	
15	Egypt	No	N/A	Yes	N/A	
16	Fiji*	No	N/A	Yes	N/A	

[86] For its agreements listed under the MLI, Malaysia is implementing the preamble statement (Article 6 of the MLI) and the PPT (Article 7 of the MLI).

17	Finland	No	N/A	Yes	N/A	
18	France	No	N/A	Yes	N/A	
19	Germany	No	N/A	Yes	N/A	
20	Hong Kong (China)	No	N/A	Yes	N/A	
21	Hungary	No	N/A	Yes	N/A	
22	India	No	N/A	Yes	N/A	
23	Indonesia	No	N/A	Yes	N/A	
24	Iran*	No	N/A	Yes	N/A	
25	Ireland	No	N/A	Yes	N/A	
26	Italy	No	N/A	Yes	N/A	
27	Japan	No	N/A	Yes	N/A	
28	Jordan	No	N/A	Yes	N/A	
29	Kazakhstan	No	N/A	Yes	N/A	
30	Korea	No	N/A	Yes	N/A	
31	Kuwait*	No	N/A	Yes	N/A	
32	Kyrgyzstan*	No	N/A	Yes	N/A	
33	Lao People's Democratic Republic*	No	N/A	Yes	N/A	
34	Lebanon*	No	N/A	Yes	N/A	
35	Luxembourg	No	N/A	Yes	N/A	
36	Malta	No	N/A	Yes	N/A	
37	Mauritius	No	N/A	Yes	N/A	
38	Mongolia	No	N/A	Yes	N/A	
39	Morocco	No	N/A	Yes	N/A	
40	Myanmar*	No	N/A	Yes	N/A	
41	Namibia	No	N/A	Yes	N/A	
42	Netherlands	No	N/A	Yes	N/A	
43	New Zealand	No	N/A	Yes	N/A	
44	Norway	No	N/A	Yes	N/A	
45	Pakistan	No	N/A	Yes	N/A	
46	Papua New Guinea	No	N/A	Yes	N/A	
47	Philippines*	No	N/A	Yes	N/A	
48	Poland	No	N/A	Yes	N/A	Malaysia and Poland signed a new tax agreement which has not yet entered into force. The new agreement is listed in Malaysia's MLI position.
49	Qatar	No	N/A	Yes	N/A	
50	Romania	No	N/A	Yes	N/A	
51	Russia	No	N/A	Yes	N/A	
52	San Marino	No	N/A	Yes	N/A	
53	Saudi Arabia	No	N/A	Yes	N/A	
54	Seychelles	No	N/A	Yes	N/A	
55	Singapore	No	N/A	Yes	N/A	
56	Slovak Republic	No	N/A	Yes	N/A	
57	South Africa	No	N/A	Yes	N/A	
58	Spain	No	N/A	Yes	N/A	
59	Sri Lanka	No	N/A	Yes	N/A	
60	Sudan*	No	N/A	Yes	N/A	
61	Sweden	No	N/A	Yes	N/A	
62	Switzerland	No	N/A	Yes	N/A	

63	Syrian Arab Republic*	No	N/A	Yes	N/A	
64	Thailand	No	N/A	Yes	N/A	
65	Turkey	No	N/A	Yes	N/A	
66	Turkmenistan*	No	N/A	Yes	N/A	
67	United Arab Emirates	No	N/A	Yes	N/A	
68	United Kingdom	No	N/A	Yes	N/A	
69	Uzbekistan*	No	N/A	Yes	N/A	
70	Venezuela*	No	N/A	Yes	N/A	
71	Viet Nam	No	N/A	Yes	N/A	
72	Zimbabwe*	No	N/A	Yes	N/A	

Maldives

A. Progress in the implementation of the minimum standard

The Maldives has one agreement in force, as reported in its response to the Peer Review questionnaire.

The Maldives' agreement does not comply with the minimum standard and is not subject to a complying instrument.

The Maldives has not signed the MLI.

B. Implementation issues

As the Maldives has not signed the MLI or implemented anti-treaty-shopping measures in its agreements, the Secretariat will offer its support to design a plan for the implementation of the minimum standard to strengthen its network of agreements.

Summary of the jurisdiction response - Maldives

	Treaty partners	Compliance with the standard	If compliant, the alternative implemented	Signature of a complying instrument	The alternative implemented through the complying instrument (if not the MLI)	Comments
1	United Arab Emirates	No	N/A	No	N/A	

Malta

A. Progress in the implementation of the minimum standard

Malta has 77 tax agreements in force, as reported in its response to the Peer Review questionnaire. Twenty-seven of those agreements, the agreements with Australia, Austria, Belgium, Canada, Denmark, Finland, France, Guernsey, Iceland, India, Ireland, the Isle of Man, Israel, Jersey, Kosovo*, Lithuania, Luxembourg, the Netherlands, Norway, Poland, Serbia, Singapore, the Slovak Republic, Slovenia, Ukraine, the United Arab Emirates and the United Kingdom comply with the minimum standard.

Malta signed the MLI in 2017 and deposited its instrument of ratification on 18 December 2018. The MLI entered into force for Malta on 1 April 2019. Malta has not listed its agreements with Botswana, Bulgaria and Monaco. These agreements will therefore not, at this stage, be modified by the MLI.

Malta is implementing the minimum standard through the inclusion of the preamble statement and the PPT.[87]

The agreements modified by the MLI come into compliance with the minimum standard once the provisions of the MLI take effect.[88]

B. Implementation issues

As mentioned above, Malta has not listed its agreements with Botswana, Bulgaria, and Monaco under the MLI. Listing the agreements under the MLI or entering into bilateral renegotiations to implement the minimum standard would ensure that the minimum standard could be implemented in those non-covered agreements.

Summary of the jurisdiction response - Malta

	Treaty partners	Compliance with the standard	If compliant, the alternative implemented	Signature of a complying instrument	The alternative implemented through the complying instrument (if not the MLI)	Comments
1	Albania	No	N/A	Yes	N/A	
2	Andorra	No	N/A	Yes	N/A	
3	Australia	Yes	PPT alone	N/A	N/A	
4	Austria	Yes	PPT alone	N/A	N/A	
5	Azerbaijan*	No	N/A	Yes	N/A	
6	Bahrain	No	N/A	Yes	N/A	
7	Barbados	No	N/A	Yes	N/A	
8	Belgium	Yes	PPT alone	N/A	N/A	
9	Botswana	No	N/A	No	N/A	

[87] For its agreements listed under the MLI, Malta is implementing the preamble statement (Article 6 of the MLI) and the PPT (Article 7 of the MLI).

[88] Malta chose to replace, under Article 35(3) of the MLI, the reference to "taxable periods beginning on or after the expiration of a period" with a reference to "taxable periods beginning on or after 1 January of the next calendar year beginning on or after the expiration of a period" for the purposes of its own application of Article 35(1)(b) and (5)(b) of the MLI.

10	Bulgaria	No	N/A	No	N/A	
11	Canada	Yes	PPT alone	N/A	N/A	
12	China (People's Republic of)	No	N/A	Yes	N/A	
13	Croatia	No	N/A	Yes	N/A	
14	Cyprus*	No	N/A	Yes	N/A	
15	Czech Republic	No	N/A	Yes	N/A	
16	Denmark	Yes	PPT alone	N/A	N/A	
17	Egypt	No	N/A	Yes	N/A	
18	Estonia	No	N/A	Yes	N/A	
19	Finland	Yes	PPT alone	N/A	N/A	
20	France	Yes	PPT alone	N/A	N/A	
21	Georgia	No	N/A	Yes	N/A	
22	Germany	No	N/A	Yes	N/A	
23	Greece	No	N/A	Yes	N/A	
24	Guernsey	Yes	PPT alone	N/A	N/A	
25	Hong Kong (China)	No	N/A	Yes	N/A	
26	Hungary	No	N/A	Yes	N/A	
27	Iceland	Yes	PPT alone	N/A	N/A	
28	India	Yes	PPT alone	N/A	N/A	
29	Ireland	Yes	PPT alone	N/A	N/A	
30	Isle of Man	Yes	PPT alone	N/A	N/A	
31	Israel	Yes	PPT alone	N/A	N/A	
32	Italy	No	N/A	Yes	N/A	
33	Jersey	Yes	PPT alone	N/A	N/A	
34	Jordan	No	N/A	Yes	N/A	
35	Korea	No	N/A	Yes	N/A	
36	Kosovo*	Yes	PPT alone	N/A	N/A	
37	Kuwait*	No	N/A	Yes	N/A	
38	Latvia	No	N/A	Yes	N/A	
39	Lebanon*	No	N/A	Yes	N/A	
40	Libya*	No	N/A	Yes	N/A	
41	Liechtenstein	No	N/A	Yes	N/A	
42	Lithuania	Yes	PPT alone	N/A	N/A	
43	Luxembourg	Yes	PPT alone	N/A	N/A	
44	Malaysia	No	N/A	Yes	N/A	
45	Mauritius	No	N/A	Yes	N/A	
46	Mexico	No	N/A	Yes	N/A	
47	Moldova*	No	N/A	Yes	N/A	
48	Monaco	No	N/A	No	N/A	
49	Montenegro	No	N/A	Yes	N/A	
50	Morocco	No	N/A	Yes	N/A	
51	Netherlands	Yes	PPT alone	N/A	N/A	
52	Norway	Yes	PPT alone	N/A	N/A	
53	Pakistan	No	N/A	Yes	N/A	
54	Poland	Yes	PPT alone	N/A	N/A	
55	Portugal	No	N/A	Yes	N/A	
56	Qatar	No	N/A	Yes	N/A	
57	Romania	No	N/A	Yes	N/A	
58	Russia	No	N/A	Yes	N/A	
59	San Marino	No	N/A	Yes	N/A	
60	Saudi Arabia	No	N/A	Yes	N/A	
61	Serbia	Yes	PPT alone	N/A	N/A	
62	Singapore	Yes	PPT alone	N/A	N/A	

63	Slovak Republic	Yes	PPT alone	N/A	N/A	
64	Slovenia	Yes	PPT alone	N/A	N/A	
65	South Africa	No	N/A	Yes	N/A	
66	Spain	No	N/A	Yes	N/A	
67	Sweden	No	N/A	Yes	N/A	
68	Switzerland	No	N/A	Yes	N/A	
69	Syrian Arab Republic*	No	N/A	Yes	N/A	
70	Tunisia	No	N/A	Yes	N/A	
71	Turkey	No	N/A	Yes	N/A	
72	Ukraine	Yes	PPT alone	N/A	N/A	
73	United Arab Emirates	Yes	PPT alone	N/A	N/A	
74	United Kingdom	Yes	PPT alone	N/A	N/A	
75	United States	No	N/A	No	N/A	
76	Uruguay	No	N/A	Yes	N/A	
77	Viet Nam	No	N/A	Yes	N/A	

Mauritius

A. Progress in the implementation of the minimum standard

Mauritius has 44 tax agreements in force, as reported in its response to the Peer Review questionnaire.

Mauritius signed the MLI in 2017 and deposited its instrument of ratification on 18 October 2019. The MLI entered into force for Mauritius on 1 February 2020. Mauritius has not listed its agreement with India but indicated in its response to the Peer Review questionnaire that bilateral negotiations would be used with respect to its agreement with India. This agreement will therefore not, at this stage, be modified by the MLI. India has listed its agreement with Mauritius under the MLI.

Mauritius is implementing the minimum standard in its tax agreements through the inclusion of the preamble statement and the PPT.[89]

The agreements that will be modified by the MLI will come into compliance with the minimum standard once the provisions of the MLI take effect.

B. Implementation issues

No jurisdiction has raised any concerns about their agreements with Mauritius.

Summary of the jurisdiction response - Mauritius

	Treaty partners	Compliance with the standard	If compliant, the alternative implemented	Signature of a complying instrument	The alternative implemented through the complying instrument (if not the MLI)	Comments
1	Bangladesh*	No	N/A	Yes	N/A	
2	Barbados	No	N/A	Yes	N/A	
3	Belgium	No	N/A	Yes	N/A	
4	Botswana	No	N/A	Yes	N/A	
5	Cabo Verde	No	N/A	Yes	N/A	
6	China (People's Republic of)	No	N/A	Yes	N/A	
7	Congo	No	N/A	Yes	N/A	
8	Croatia	No	N/A	Yes	N/A	
9	Cyprus*	No	N/A	Yes	N/A	
10	Egypt	No	N/A	Yes	N/A	
11	Eswatini	No	N/A	Yes	N/A	
12	France	No	N/A	Yes	N/A	
13	Germany	No	N/A	Yes	N/A	
14	Ghana*	No	N/A	Yes	N/A	
15	Guernsey	No	N/A	Yes	N/A	
16	India	No	N/A	No	N/A	
17	Italy	No	N/A	Yes	N/A	

[89] For its agreements listed under the MLI, Mauritius is implementing the preamble statement (Article 6 of the MLI) and the PPT (Article 7 of the MLI). Mauritius stated that while it accepts the application of the PPT under the MLI, it intends where possible to adopt an LOB provision through bilateral negotiation.

18	Jersey	No	N/A	Yes	N/A	
19	Kuwait*	No	N/A	Yes	N/A	
20	Lesotho*	No	N/A	Yes	N/A	
21	Luxembourg	No	N/A	Yes	N/A	
22	Madagascar*	No	N/A	Yes	N/A	
23	Malaysia	No	N/A	Yes	N/A	
24	Malta	No	N/A	Yes	N/A	
25	Monaco	No	N/A	Yes	N/A	
26	Mozambique*	No	N/A	Yes	N/A	
27	Namibia	No	N/A	Yes	N/A	
28	Nepal*	No	N/A	Yes	N/A	
29	Oman	No	N/A	Yes	N/A	
30	Pakistan	No	N/A	Yes	N/A	
31	Qatar	No	N/A	Yes	N/A	
32	Rwanda*	No	N/A	Yes	N/A	
33	Seychelles	No	N/A	Yes	N/A	
34	Singapore	No	N/A	Yes	N/A	
35	South Africa	No	N/A	Yes	N/A	
36	Sri Lanka	No	N/A	Yes	N/A	
37	Sweden	No	N/A	Yes	N/A	
38	Thailand	No	N/A	Yes	N/A	
39	Tunisia	No	N/A	Yes	N/A	
40	Uganda*	No	N/A	Yes	N/A	
41	United Arab Emirates	No	N/A	Yes	N/A	
42	United Kingdom	No	N/A	Yes	N/A	
43	Zambia	No	N/A	Yes	N/A	
44	Zimbabwe*	No	N/A	Yes	N/A	

Mexico

A. Progress in the implementation of the minimum standard

Mexico has 60 tax agreements in force, as reported in its response to the Peer Review questionnaire. Three of those agreements, the agreements with Argentina, the Philippines* and Spain, comply with the minimum standard.

Mexico signed the MLI in 2017, listing its non-compliant agreements.

Mexico is implementing the minimum standard through the inclusion of the preamble statement and the PPT combined with the LOB.[90]

The agreements that will be modified by the MLI will come into compliance with the minimum standard once the provisions of the MLI take effect.

B. Implementation issues

Mexico's listed agreements under the MLI will start to be compliant after Mexico's ratification of the MLI. Mexico is encouraged to ratify the MLI as soon as possible. Mexico indicated that the MLI had been presented to its Parliament in November 2018.

Summary of the jurisdiction response - Mexico

	Treaty partners	Compliance with the standard	If compliant, the alternative implemented	Signature of a complying instrument	The alternative implemented through the complying instrument (if not the MLI)	Comments
1	Argentina	Yes	PPT and LOB	N/A	N/A	
2	Australia	No	N/A	Yes	N/A	
3	Austria	No	N/A	Yes	N/A	
4	Bahrain	No	N/A	Yes	N/A	
5	Barbados	No	N/A	Yes	N/A	
6	Belgium	No	N/A	Yes	N/A	
7	Brazil	No	N/A	Yes	N/A	
8	Canada	No	N/A	Yes	N/A	
9	Chile	No	N/A	Yes	N/A	
10	China (People's Republic of)	No	N/A	Yes	N/A	
11	Colombia	No	N/A	Yes	N/A	
12	Costa Rica	No	N/A	Yes	N/A	
13	Czech Republic	No	N/A	Yes	N/A	
14	Denmark	No	N/A	Yes	N/A	

90 For 57 of its agreements listed under the MLI, Mexico is implementing the preamble statement (Article 6 of the MLI) and the PPT (Article 7 of the MLI). Mexico also opted for the simplified LOB under Article 7(6) of the MLI. Mexico made a reservation pursuant to Article 6(4) of the MLI not to apply Article 6(1) of the MLI with respect to agreements which already contain the relevant preamble language and a reservation pursuant to Article 7(15)(b) of the MLI not to apply Article 7(1) of the MLI with respect to agreements which already contain a PPT Three of Mexico's agreements are within the scope of the reservations.

15	Ecuador*	No	N/A	Yes	N/A
16	Estonia	No	N/A	Yes	N/A
17	Finland	No	N/A	Yes	N/A
18	France	No	N/A	Yes	N/A
19	Germany	No	N/A	Yes	N/A
20	Greece	No	N/A	Yes	N/A
21	Hong Kong (China)	No	N/A	Yes	N/A
22	Hungary	No	N/A	Yes	N/A
23	Iceland	No	N/A	Yes	N/A
24	India	No	N/A	Yes	N/A
25	Indonesia	No	N/A	Yes	N/A
26	Ireland	No	N/A	Yes	N/A
27	Israel	No	N/A	Yes	N/A
28	Italy	No	N/A	Yes	N/A
29	Jamaica	No	N/A	Yes	N/A
30	Japan	No	N/A	Yes	N/A
31	Korea	No	N/A	Yes	N/A
32	Kuwait*	No	N/A	Yes	N/A
33	Latvia	No	N/A	Yes	N/A
34	Lithuania	No	N/A	Yes	N/A
35	Luxembourg	No	N/A	Yes	N/A
36	Malta	No	N/A	Yes	N/A
37	Netherlands	No	N/A	Yes	N/A
38	New Zealand	No	N/A	Yes	N/A
39	Norway	No	N/A	Yes	N/A
40	Panama	No	N/A	Yes	N/A
41	Peru	No	N/A	Yes	N/A
42	Philippines*	Yes	PPT alone	N/A	N/A
43	Poland	No	N/A	Yes	N/A
44	Portugal	No	N/A	Yes	N/A
45	Qatar	No	N/A	Yes	N/A
46	Romania	No	N/A	Yes	N/A
47	Russia	No	N/A	Yes	N/A
48	Saudi Arabia	No	N/A	Yes	N/A
49	Singapore	No	N/A	Yes	N/A
50	Slovak Republic	No	N/A	Yes	N/A
51	South Africa	No	N/A	Yes	N/A
52	Spain	Yes	PPT alone	N/A	N/A
53	Sweden	No	N/A	Yes	N/A
54	Switzerland	No	N/A	Yes	N/A
55	Turkey	No	N/A	Yes	N/A
56	Ukraine	No	N/A	Yes	N/A
57	United Arab Emirates	No	N/A	Yes	N/A
58	United Kingdom	No	N/A	Yes	N/A
59	United States	No	N/A	Yes	N/A
60	Uruguay	No	N/A	Yes	N/A

Monaco

A. Progress in the implementation of the minimum standard

Monaco has ten tax agreements in force, as reported in its response to the Peer Review questionnaire. Four of those agreements, the agreements with France, Guernsey, Liechtenstein and Luxembourg, comply with the minimum standard.

Monaco signed the MLI in 2017 and deposited its instrument of ratification on 10 January 2019. The MLI entered into force for Monaco on 1 May 2019. Monaco has not listed its agreement with Malta. This agreement will therefore not, at this stage, be modified by the MLI.

Monaco is implementing the minimum standard through the inclusion of the preamble statement and the PPT.[91]

The agreements modified by the MLI come into compliance with the minimum standard once the provisions of the MLI take effect.

B. Implementation issues

As mentioned above, Monaco has not listed its agreement with Malta under the MLI. Listing the agreement under the MLI or entering into bilateral renegotiations to implement the minimum standard would ensure that the minimum standard could be implemented in that non-covered agreement.

Summary of the jurisdiction response - Monaco

	Treaty partners	Compliance with the standard	If compliant, the alternative implemented	Signature of a complying instrument	The alternative implemented through the complying instrument (if not the MLI)	Comments
1	France	Yes	PPT alone	N/A	N/A	
2	Guernsey	Yes	PPT alone	N/A	N/A	
3	Liechtenstein	Yes	PPT alone	N/A	N/A	
4	Luxembourg	Yes	PPT alone	N/A	N/A	
5	Mali*	No	N/A	Yes	N/A	
6	Malta	No	N/A	No	N/A	
7	Mauritius	No	N/A	Yes	N/A	
8	Qatar	No	N/A	Yes	N/A	
9	Saint Kitts and Nevis	No	N/A	Yes	N/A	
10	Seychelles	No	N/A	Yes	N/A	

[91] For its agreements listed under the MLI, Monaco is implementing the preamble statement (Article 6 of the MLI) and the PPT (Article 7 of the MLI).

Mongolia

A. Progress in the implementation of the minimum standard

Mongolia has 25 tax agreements in force as reported in its response to the Peer Review questionnaire.

None of Mongolia's agreements comply with the minimum standard or are subject to a complying instrument.

Mongolia has not signed the MLI.

Mongolia indicated in its response to the Peer Review questionnaire that it is currently working towards signing the MLI.

B. Implementation issues

As Mongolia has not signed the MLI or implemented anti-treaty-shopping measures in its agreements, the Secretariat will offer its support to design a plan for the implementation of the minimum standard to strengthen its network of agreements.

Summary of the jurisdiction response - Mongolia

	Treaty partners	Compliance with the standard	If compliant, the alternative implemented	Signature of a complying instrument	The alternative implemented through the complying instrument (if not the MLI)	Comments
1	Austria	No	N/A	No	N/A	
2	Belarus*	No	N/A	No	N/A	
3	Belgium	No	N/A	No	N/A	
4	Bulgaria	No	N/A	No	N/A	
5	Canada	No	N/A	No	N/A	
6	China (People's Republic of)	No	N/A	No	N/A	
7	Czech Republic	No	N/A	No	N/A	
8	Democratic People's Republic of Korea*	No	N/A	No	N/A	
9	France	No	N/A	No	N/A	
10	Germany	No	N/A	No	N/A	
11	Hungary	No	N/A	No	N/A	
12	India	No	N/A	No	N/A	
13	Indonesia	No	N/A	No	N/A	
14	Kazakhstan	No	N/A	No	N/A	
15	Korea	No	N/A	No	N/A	
16	Kyrgyzstan*	No	N/A	No	N/A	
17	Malaysia	No	N/A	No	N/A	
18	Poland	No	N/A	No	N/A	
19	Russia	No	N/A	No	N/A	
20	Singapore	No	N/A	No	N/A	
21	Switzerland	No	N/A	No	N/A	

22	Turkey	No	N/A	No	N/A	
23	Ukraine	No	N/A	No	N/A	
24	United Kingdom	No	N/A	No	N/A	
25	Viet Nam	No	N/A	No	N/A	

Montenegro

A. Progress in the implementation of the minimum standard

Montenegro has 43 tax agreements in force, as reported in its response to the Peer Review questionnaire.

None of Montenegro's agreements comply with the minimum standard or are subject to a complying instrument.

Montenegro has not signed the MLI.

B. Implementation issues

As Montenegro has not signed the MLI or implemented anti-treaty-shopping measures in its agreements, the Secretariat will offer its support to design a plan for the implementation of the minimum standard to strengthen its network of agreements.

Summary of the jurisdiction response - Montenegro

	Treaty partners	Compliance with the standard	If compliant, the alternative implemented	Signature of a complying instrument	The alternative implemented through the complying instrument (if not the MLI)	Comments
1	Albania	No	N/A	No	N/A	
2	Austria	No	N/A	No	N/A	
3	Azerbaijan*	No	N/A	No	N/A	
4	Belarus*	No	N/A	No	N/A	
5	Belgium	No	N/A	No	N/A	
6	Bosnia-Herzegovina	No	N/A	No	N/A	
7	Bulgaria	No	N/A	No	N/A	
8	China (People's Rep.)	No	N/A	No	N/A	
9	Croatia	No	N/A	No	N/A	
10	Cyprus*	No	N/A	No	N/A	
11	Czech Republic	No	N/A	No	N/A	
12	Denmark	No	N/A	No	N/A	
13	Egypt	No	N/A	No	N/A	
14	Finland	No	N/A	No	N/A	
15	France	No	N/A	No	N/A	
16	Germany	No	N/A	No	N/A	
17	Greece	No	N/A	No	N/A	
18	Hungary	No	N/A	No	N/A	
19	India	No	N/A	No	N/A	
20	Iran*	No	N/A	No	N/A	
21	Ireland	No	N/A	No	N/A	
22	Italy	No	N/A	No	N/A	
23	Korea (Dem. People's Rep.)*	No	N/A	No	N/A	
24	Kuwait*	No	N/A	No	N/A	

25	Latvia	No	N/A	No	N/A	
26	Malaysia	No	N/A	No	N/A	
27	Moldova*	No	N/A	No	N/A	
28	Netherlands	No	N/A	No	N/A	
29	North Macedonia	No	N/A	No	N/A	
30	Norway	No	N/A	No	N/A	
31	Poland	No	N/A	No	N/A	
32	Portugal	No	N/A	No	N/A	
33	Romania	No	N/A	No	N/A	
34	Russia	No	N/A	No	N/A	
35	Slovak Republic	No	N/A	No	N/A	
36	Slovenia	No	N/A	No	N/A	
37	Sri Lanka	No	N/A	No	N/A	
38	Sweden	No	N/A	No	N/A	
39	Switzerland	No	N/A	No	N/A	
40	Turkey	No	N/A	No	N/A	
41	Ukraine	No	N/A	No	N/A	
42	United Arab Emirates	No	N/A	No	N/A	
43	United Kingdom	No	N/A	No	N/A	

Montserrat

A. Progress in the implementation of the minimum standard

Montserrat has two tax agreements in force, as reported in its response to the Peer Review questionnaire.

Neither of Montserrat's agreements comply with the minimum standard or are subject to a complying instrument.

Montserrat has not joined the MLI.

Montserrat indicated in its response to the Peer Review questionnaire that its agreement with the United Kingdom is an arrangement that cannot be modified with the MLI.

B. Implementation issues

As Montserrat has not joined the MLI or implemented anti-treaty-shopping measures in its agreements, the Secretariat will offer its support to design a plan for the implementation of the minimum standard to strengthen its network of agreements.

Summary of the jurisdiction response - Montserrat

	Treaty partners	Compliance with the standard	If compliant, the alternative implemented	Signature of a complying instrument	The alternative implemented through the complying instrument (if not the MLI)	Comments
1	Switzerland	No	N/A	No	N/A	
2	United Kingdom	No	N/A	No	N/A	

Morocco

A. Progress in the implementation of the minimum standard

Morocco has 53 tax agreements in force, as reported in its response to the Peer Review questionnaire, including the Arab Maghreb Union Income Agreement concluded with four treaty partners (the UMA Agreement).[92]

Morocco signed the MLI in 2019, listing its non-compliant tax agreements.

Morocco is implementing the minimum standard through the inclusion of the preamble statement and the PPT.[93]

The agreements that will be modified by the MLI will come into compliance with the minimum standard once the provisions of the MLI take effect.

B. Implementation issues

Morocco's listed agreements under the MLI will start to be compliant after Morocco's ratification of the MLI. Morocco is encouraged to ratify the MLI as soon as possible. Morocco indicated that the approval of the MLI by the Moroccan Chamber of Representatives (first chamber of the parliament) was in progress. Morocco also reiterated its engagement to deposit the instrument of ratification of the MLI as soon as possible.

Summary of the jurisdiction response - Morocco

	Treaty partners	Compliance with the standard	If compliant, the alternative implemented	Signature of a complying instrument	The alternative implemented through the complying instrument (if not the MLI)	Comments
1	Algeria*	No	N/A	Yes	N/A	UMA Agreement
2	Austria	No	N/A	Yes	N/A	
3	Bahrain	No	N/A	Yes	N/A	
4	Belgium	No	N/A	Yes	N/A	
5	Bulgaria	No	N/A	Yes	N/A	
6	Canada	No	N/A	Yes	N/A	
7	China (People's Republic of)	No	N/A	Yes	N/A	
8	Côte d'Ivoire	No	N/A	Yes	N/A	
9	Croatia	No	N/A	Yes	N/A	
10	Czech Republic	No	N/A	Yes	N/A	
11	Denmark	No	N/A	Yes	N/A	
12	Egypt	No	N/A	Yes	N/A	
13	Finland	No	N/A	Yes	N/A	

[92] In total, Morocco identified 56 "agreements" in its List of Tax agreements: 52 bilateral agreements and the UMA Agreement concluded with four of its treaty partners.

[93] For its agreements listed under the MLI, Morocco is implementing the preamble statement (Article 6 of the MLI) and the PPT (Article 7 of the MLI).

14	France	No	N/A	Yes	N/A	
15	Gabon	No	N/A	Yes	N/A	
16	Germany	No	N/A	Yes	N/A	
17	Greece	No	N/A	Yes	N/A	
18	Guinea*	No	N/A	Yes	N/A	
19	Hungary	No	N/A	Yes	N/A	
20	India	No	N/A	Yes	N/A	
21	Indonesia	No	N/A	Yes	N/A	
22	Ireland	No	N/A	Yes	N/A	
23	Italy	No	N/A	Yes	N/A	
24	Jordan	No	N/A	Yes	N/A	
25	Korea	No	N/A	Yes	N/A	
26	Kuwait*	No	N/A	Yes	N/A	
27	Latvia	No	N/A	Yes	N/A	
28	Lebanon*	No	N/A	Yes	N/A	
29	Libya*	No	N/A	Yes	N/A	UMA Agreement
30	Luxembourg	No	N/A	Yes	N/A	
31	Malaysia	No	N/A	Yes	N/A	
32	Mali*	No	N/A	Yes	N/A	
33	Malta	No	N/A	Yes	N/A	
34	Mauritania*	No	N/A	Yes	N/A	UMA Agreement
35	Netherlands	No	N/A	Yes	N/A	
36	North Macedonia	No	N/A	Yes	N/A	
37	Norway	No	N/A	Yes	N/A	
38	Oman	No	N/A	Yes	N/A	
39	Pakistan	No	N/A	Yes	N/A	
40	Poland	No	N/A	Yes	N/A	
41	Portugal	No	N/A	Yes	N/A	
42	Qatar (new)	No	N/A	Yes	N/A	
43	Romania	No	N/A	Yes	N/A	
44	Russia	No	N/A	Yes	N/A	
45	Senegal	No	N/A	Yes	N/A	
46	Singapore	No	N/A	Yes	N/A	
47	Spain	No	N/A	Yes	N/A	
48	Switzerland	No	N/A	Yes	N/A	
49	Syrian Arab Republic*	No	N/A	Yes	N/A	
50	Tunisia	No	N/A	Yes	N/A	UMA Agreement
51	Turkey	No	N/A	Yes	N/A	
52	United Arab Emirates	No	N/A	Yes	N/A	
53	United Kingdom	No	N/A	Yes	N/A	
54	Ukraine	No	N/A	Yes	N/A	
55	United States	No	N/A	Yes	N/A	
56	Viet Nam	No	N/A	Yes	N/A	

Namibia

A. Progress in the implementation of the minimum standard

Namibia has eleven tax agreements in force, as reported in its response to the Peer Review questionnaire.

None of Namibia's agreements comply with the minimum standard or are subject to a complying instrument.

Namibia has not signed the MLI.

B. Implementation issues

As Namibia has not signed the MLI or implemented anti-treaty-shopping measures in its agreements, the Secretariat will offer its support to design a plan for the implementation of the minimum standard to strengthen its network of agreements.

Summary of the jurisdiction response - Namibia

	Treaty partners	Compliance with the standard	If compliant, the alternative implemented	Signature of a complying instrument	The alternative implemented through the complying instrument (if not the MLI)	Comments
1	Botswana	No	N/A	No	N/A	
2	France	No	N/A	No	N/A	
3	Germany	No	N/A	No	N/A	
4	India	No	N/A	No	N/A	
5	Malaysia	No	N/A	No	N/A	
6	Mauritius	No	N/A	No	N/A	
7	Romania	No	N/A	No	N/A	
8	Russia	No	N/A	No	N/A	
9	South Africa	No	N/A	No	N/A	
10	Sweden	No	N/A	No	N/A	
11	United Kingdom	No	N/A	No	N/A	

Netherlands

A. Progress in the implementation of the minimum standard

The Netherlands has 92 tax agreements in force, as reported in its response to the Peer Review questionnaire. Twenty-five of those agreements, the agreements with Australia, Austria, Canada, Denmark, Finland, France, Georgia, Ghana*, Iceland, India, Ireland, Israel, Japan, Lithuania, Luxembourg, Malta, New Zealand, Norway, Serbia, Singapore, the Slovak Republic, Slovenia, the United Arab Emirates, the United Kingdom and Uzbekistan*, comply with the minimum standard.

The Netherlands signed the MLI in 2017 and deposited its instrument of acceptance in 2019. The MLI entered into force for the Netherlands on 1 July 2019. The Netherlands has not listed its agreements with Belgium, Brazil, Bulgaria, Poland, Spain, Switzerland and Ukraine. These agreements will therefore not, at this stage, be modified by the MLI. Belgium, Poland and Ukraine have listed their agreements with the Netherlands under the MLI.

The Netherlands' arrangements with Aruba, Curaçao and Sint Maarten* are arrangements governed by the domestic law of the Kingdom of the Netherlands.

The Netherlands signed a bilateral complying instrument with respect to its agreements, the agreements with Algeria*, Iraq*[94], Ghana*, Switzerland, Ukraine and Uzbekistan*.[95]

The Netherlands indicated in its response to the Peer Review questionnaire that bilateral negotiations would be pursued with respect to its agreements with Belgium, Brazil, Bulgaria, Poland and Spain.

The Netherlands is implementing the minimum standard through the inclusion of the preamble statement and the PPT.[96]

The agreements modified by the MLI come into compliance with the minimum standard once the provisions of the MLI take effect.

B. Implementation issues

No jurisdiction has raised any concerns about their agreements with the Netherlands.

Summary of the jurisdiction response - Netherlands

	Treaty partners	Compliance with the standard	If compliant, the alternative implemented	Signature of a complying instrument	The alternative implemented through the complying instrument (if not the MLI)	Comments
1	Albania	No	N/A	Yes	N/A	
2	Argentina	No	N/A	Yes	N/A	

[94] The agreement with Iraq* is not yet in force.

[95] The agreements with Ghana* and Uzbekistan* are subject to a bilateral complying instrument and listed under the MLI.

[96] For its agreements listed under the MLI, the Netherlands is implementing the preamble statement (Article 6 of the MLI) and the PPT (Article 7 of the MLI). The Netherlands' agreements with Aruba, Curaçao and Sint Maarten* are not listed under the MLI as they are arrangements governed by the domestic law of the Kingdom of the Netherlands.

3	Armenia	No	N/A	Yes	N/A	
4	Aruba	No	N/A	No	N/A	
5	Australia	Yes	PPT alone	N/A	N/A	
6	Austria	Yes	PPT alone	N/A	N/A	
7	Azerbaijan*	No	N/A	Yes	N/A	
8	Bahrain	No	N/A	Yes	N/A	
9	Bangladesh*	No	N/A	Yes	N/A	
10	Barbados	No	N/A	Yes	N/A	
11	Belarus*	No	N/A	Yes	N/A	
12	Belgium	No	N/A	No	N/A	
13	Bosnia-Herzegovina	No	N/A	Yes	N/A	
14	Brazil	No	N/A	No	N/A	
15	Bulgaria	No	N/A	No	N/A	
16	Canada	Yes	PPT alone	N/A	N/A	
17	China (People's Republic of)	No	N/A	Yes	N/A	
18	Chinese Taipei*	No	N/A	No	N/A	
19	Croatia	No	N/A	Yes	N/A	
20	Curaçao	No	N/A	No	N/A	
21	Czech Republic	No	N/A	Yes	N/A	
22	Denmark	Yes	PPT alone	N/A	N/A	
23	Egypt	No	N/A	Yes	N/A	
24	Estonia	No	N/A	Yes	N/A	
25	Ethiopia*	No	N/A	Yes	N/A	
26	Finland	Yes	PPT alone	N/A	N/A	
27	France	Yes	PPT alone	N/A	N/A	
28	Georgia	Yes	PPT alone	N/A	N/A	
29	Germany	No	N/A	Yes	N/A	
30	Ghana*	Yes	PPT alone	N/A	N/A	
31	Greece	No	N/A	Yes	N/A	
32	Hong Kong (China)	No	N/A	Yes	N/A	
33	Hungary	No	N/A	Yes	N/A	
34	Iceland	Yes	PPT alone	N/A	N/A	
35	India	Yes	PPT alone	N/A	N/A	
36	Indonesia	No	N/A	Yes	N/A	
37	Ireland	Yes	PPT alone	N/A	N/A	
38	Israel	Yes	PPT alone	N/A	N/A	
39	Italy	No	N/A	Yes	N/A	
40	Japan	Yes	PPT and LOB	N/A	N/A	
41	Jordan	No	N/A	Yes	N/A	
42	Kazakhstan	No	N/A	Yes	N/A	
43	Korea	No	N/A	Yes	N/A	
44	Kuwait*	No	N/A	Yes	N/A	
45	Latvia	No	N/A	Yes	N/A	
46	Lithuania	Yes	PPT alone	N/A	N/A	
47	Luxembourg	Yes	PPT alone	N/A	N/A	
48	Malaysia	No	N/A	Yes	N/A	
49	Malta	Yes	PPT alone	N/A	N/A	
50	Mexico	No	N/A	Yes	N/A	
51	Moldova*	No	N/A	Yes	N/A	
52	Montenegro	No	N/A	Yes	N/A	
53	Morocco	No	N/A	Yes	N/A	
54	New Zealand	Yes	PPT alone	N/A	N/A	

55	Nigeria	No	N/A	Yes	N/A	
56	North Macedonia	No	N/A	Yes	N/A	
57	Norway	Yes	PPT alone	N/A	N/A	
58	Oman	No	N/A	Yes	N/A	
59	Pakistan	No	N/A	Yes	N/A	
60	Panama	No	N/A	Yes	N/A	
61	Philippines*	No	N/A	Yes	N/A	
62	Poland	No	N/A	No	N/A	
63	Portugal	No	N/A	Yes	N/A	
64	Qatar	No	N/A	Yes	N/A	
65	Romania	No	N/A	Yes	N/A	
66	Russia	No	N/A	Yes	N/A	
67	Saudi Arabia	No	N/A	Yes	N/A	
68	Serbia	Yes	PPT alone	N/A	N/A	
69	Singapore	Yes	PPT alone	N/A	N/A	
70	Sint Maarten*	No	N/A	No	N/A	
71	Slovak Republic	Yes	PPT alone	N/A	N/A	
72	Slovenia	Yes	PPT alone	N/A	N/A	
73	South Africa	No	N/A	Yes	N/A	
74	Spain	No	N/A	No	N/A	
75	Sri Lanka	No	N/A	Yes	N/A	
76	Suriname*	No	N/A	Yes	N/A	
77	Sweden	No	N/A	Yes	N/A	
78	Switzerland	No	N/A	Yes	PPT alone	
79	Tajikistan*	No	N/A	Yes	N/A	
80	Thailand	No	N/A	Yes	N/A	
81	Tunisia	No	N/A	Yes	N/A	
82	Turkey	No	N/A	Yes	N/A	
83	Uganda*	No	N/A	Yes	N/A	
84	Ukraine	No	N/A	Yes	PPT alone	
85	United Arab Emirates	Yes	PPT alone	N/A	N/A	
86	United Kingdom	Yes	PPT alone	N/A	N/A	
87	United States	No	N/A	Yes	N/A	
88	Uzbekistan*	Yes	PPT alone	N/A	N/A	
89	Venezuela*	No	N/A	Yes	N/A	
90	Viet Nam	No	N/A	Yes	N/A	
91	Zambia	No	N/A	Yes	N/A	
92	Zimbabwe*	No	N/A	Yes	N/A	

New Zealand

A. Progress in the implementation of the minimum standard

New Zealand has 40 tax agreements in force, as reported in its response to the Peer Review questionnaire. Sixteen of those agreements, the agreements with Australia, Belgium, Canada, China, Denmark, Finland, France, India, Ireland, Japan, the Netherlands, Poland, Samoa*, Singapore, the United Arab Emirates and the United Kingdom, comply with the minimum standard.

New Zealand signed the MLI in 2017 and deposited its instrument of ratification on the 27 June 2018. The MLI entered into force for New Zealand on 1 October 2018.

New Zealand indicated in its response to the Peer Review questionnaire that bilateral negotiations would be used for its agreements with Austria, the Slovak Republic and Switzerland.

New Zealand is implementing the minimum standard through the inclusion of the preamble statement and the PPT.[97]

The agreements modified by the MLI come into compliance with the minimum standard once the provisions of the MLI take effect.

B. Implementation issues

No jurisdiction has raised any concerns about their agreements with New Zealand.

Summary of the jurisdiction response – New Zealand

	Treaty partners	Compliance with the standard	If compliant, the alternative implemented	Signature of a complying instrument	The alternative implemented through the complying instrument (if not the MLI)	Comments
1	Australia	Yes	PPT alone	N/A	N/A	
2	Austria	No	N/A	Yes	N/A	
3	Belgium	Yes	PPT alone	N/A	N/A	
4	Canada	Yes	PPT alone	N/A	N/A	
5	Chile	No	N/A	Yes	N/A	
6	China (People's Republic of)	Yes	PPT alone	N/A	N/A	2019 China-NZ treaty contains preamble and PPT article.
7	Chinese Taipei*	No	N/A	No	N/A	
8	Czech Republic	No	N/A	Yes	N/A	
9	Denmark	Yes	PPT alone	N/A	N/A	
10	Fiji*	No	N/A	Yes	N/A	
11	Finland	Yes	PPT alone	N/A	N/A	
12	France	Yes	PPT alone	N/A	N/A	
13	Germany	No	N/A	Yes	N/A	
14	Hong Kong (China)	No	N/A	Yes	N/A	

[97] For its agreements listed under the MLI, New Zealand is implementing the preamble statement (Article 6 of the MLI) and the PPT (Article 7 of the MLI).

15	India	Yes	PPT alone	N/A	N/A	
16	Indonesia	No	N/A	Yes	N/A	
17	Ireland	Yes	PPT alone	N/A	N/A	
18	Italy	No	N/A	Yes	N/A	
19	Japan	Yes	PPT and LOB	N/A	N/A	The treaty already contained an LOB and this is unaffected by the MLI
20	Korea	No	N/A	Yes	N/A	
21	Malaysia	No	N/A	Yes	N/A	
22	Mexico	No	N/A	Yes	N/A	
23	Netherlands	Yes	PPT alone	N/A	N/A	
24	Norway	No	N/A	Yes	N/A	
25	Papua New Guinea	No	N/A	Yes	N/A	
26	Philippines*	No	N/A	Yes	N/A	
27	Poland	Yes	PPT alone	N/A	N/A	
28	Russia	No	N/A	Yes	N/A	
29	Samoa*	Yes	PPT alone	N/A	N/A	
30	Singapore	Yes	PPT alone	N/A	N/A	
31	South Africa	No	N/A	Yes	N/A	
32	Spain	No	N/A	Yes	N/A	
33	Sweden	No	N/A	Yes	N/A	
34	Switzerland	No	N/A	Yes	N/A	
35	Thailand	No	N/A	Yes	N/A	
36	Turkey	No	N/A	Yes	N/A	
37	United Arab Emirates	Yes	PPT alone	N/A	N/A	
38	United Kingdom	Yes	PPT alone	N/A	N/A	
39	United States	No	N/A	No	N/A	Contains an LOB as per US treaty policy
40	Viet Nam	No	N/A	Yes	N/A	

Nigeria

A. Progress in the implementation of the minimum standard

Nigeria has 15 tax agreements in force, as reported in its response to the Peer Review questionnaire.

Nigeria signed the MLI in 2017, listing its non-compliant agreements.

Nigeria is implementing the minimum standard through the inclusion of the preamble statement and the PPT.

The agreements that will be modified by the MLI will come into compliance with the minimum standard once the provisions of the MLI take effect.[98]

B. Implementation issues

Nigeria's listed agreements under the MLI will start to be compliant after Nigeria's ratification of the MLI. Nigeria is encouraged to ratify the MLI as soon as possible.

Summary of the jurisdiction response - Nigeria

	Treaty partners	Compliance with the standard	If compliant, the alternative implemented	Signature of a complying instrument	The alternative implemented through the complying instrument (if not the MLI)	Comments
1	Belgium	No	N/A	Yes	N/A	
2	Canada	No	N/A	Yes	N/A	
3	China (People's Republic of)	No	N/A	Yes	N/A	
4	Czech Republic	No	N/A	Yes	N/A	
5	France	No	N/A	Yes	N/A	
6	Netherlands	No	N/A	Yes	N/A	
7	Pakistan	No	N/A	Yes	N/A	
8	Philippines*	No	N/A	Yes	N/A	
9	Romania	No	N/A	Yes	N/A	
10	Slovak Republic	No	N/A	Yes	N/A	
11	South Africa	No	N/A	Yes	N/A	
12	Spain	No	N/A	Yes	N/A	
13	Singapore	No	N/A	Yes	N/A	
14	Sweden	No	N/A	Yes	N/A	
15	United Kingdom	No	N/A	Yes	N/A	

[98] For its agreements listed under the MLI, Nigeria is implementing the preamble statement (Article 6 of the MLI) and the PPT (Article 7 of the MLI).

North Macedonia

A. Progress in the implementation of the minimum standard

The Republic of North Macedonia has 48 tax agreements in force, as reported in its response to the Peer Review questionnaire.

The Republic of North Macedonia signed the MLI in 2020, listing its non-compliant agreements.

The Republic of North Macedonia is implementing the minimum standard through the inclusion of the preamble statement and the PPT.[99]

The agreements that will be modified by the MLI will come into compliance with the minimum standard once the provisions of the MLI take effect.

B. Implementation issues

The Republic of North Macedonia's listed agreements under the MLI will start to be compliant after the Republic of North Macedonia's ratification of the MLI. The Republic of North Macedonia indicated that it expected to deposit its instrument of ratification of the MLI early in 2021.

Summary of the jurisdiction response – North Macedonia

	Treaty partners	Compliance with the standard	If compliant, the alternative implemented	Signature of a complying instrument	The alternative implemented through the complying instrument (if not the MLI)	Comments
1	Albania	No	N/A	Yes	N/A	
2	Austria	No	N/A	Yes	N/A	
3	Azerbaijan*	No	N/A	Yes	N/A	
4	Belarus*	No	N/A	Yes	N/A	
5	Belgium	No	N/A	Yes	N/A	Partial compliance with respect to PPT
6	Bosnia-Herzegovina	No	N/A	Yes	N/A	
7	Bulgaria	No	N/A	Yes	N/A	
8	China (People's Republic of)	No	N/A	Yes	N/A	
9	Chinese Taipei*	No	N/A	Yes	N/A	
10	Croatia	No	N/A	Yes	N/A	
11	Czech Republic	No	N/A	Yes	N/A	
12	Denmark	No	N/A	Yes	N/A	
13	Estonia	No	N/A	Yes	N/A	
14	Finland	No	N/A	Yes	N/A	
15	France	No	N/A	Yes	N/A	
16	Germany	No	N/A	Yes	N/A	
17	Hungary	No	N/A	Yes	N/A	

[99] For its agreements listed under the MLI, the Republic of North Macedonia is implementing the preamble statement (Article 6 of the MLI) and the PPT (Article 7 of the MLI).

18	India	No	N/A	Yes	N/A	Partial compliance with respect to PPT
19	Iran*	No	N/A	Yes	N/A	
20	Ireland	No	N/A	Yes	N/A	
21	Israel	No	N/A	Yes	N/A	
22	Italy	No	N/A	Yes	N/A	
23	Kazakhstan	No	N/A	Yes	N/A	
24	Kosovo*	No	N/A	Yes	N/A	
25	Kuwait*	No	N/A	Yes	N/A	
26	Latvia	No	N/A	Yes	N/A	
27	Lithuania	No	N/A	Yes	N/A	Partial compliance with respect to PPT
28	Luxembourg	No	N/A	Yes	N/A	
29	Moldova*	No	N/A	Yes	N/A	
30	Montenegro[100]	No	N/A	Yes	N/A	
31	Morocco	No	N/A	Yes	N/A	
32	Netherlands	No	N/A	Yes	N/A	
33	Norway	No	N/A	Yes	N/A	
34	Poland	No	N/A	Yes	N/A	
35	Qatar	No	N/A	Yes	N/A	
36	Romania	No	N/A	Yes	N/A	
37	Russia	No	N/A	Yes	N/A	
38	Saudi Arabia	No	N/A	Yes	N/A	
39	Serbia[101]	No	N/A	Yes	N/A	
40	Slovak Republic	No	N/A	Yes	N/A	
41	Slovenia	No	N/A	Yes	N/A	
42	Spain	No	N/A	Yes	N/A	
43	Sweden	No	N/A	Yes	N/A	
44	Switzerland	No	N/A	No	N/A	Protocol concluded to meet minimum standard (preamble and PPT) and is awaiting signature
45	Turkey	No	N/A	Yes	N/A	
46	Ukraine	No	N/A	Yes	N/A	PPT with respect to interest and royalty articles
47	United Arab Emirates	No	N/A	Yes	N/A	
48	United Kingdom	No	N/A	Yes	N/A	PPT with respect to dividend, interest, royalty and other income articles

[100] North Macedonia signed the agreement with the former Federal Republic of Yugoslavia.

[101] North Macedonia signed the agreement with the former Federal Republic of Yugoslavia.

Norway

A. Progress in the implementation of the minimum standard

Norway has 84 tax agreements in force, as reported in its response to the Peer Review questionnaire, including the multilateral Nordic Convention concluded with Denmark, the Faroe Islands, Finland, Iceland and Sweden (the "Nordic Convention").[102] Fifteen of those agreements, the agreements with Australia, Estonia, Georgia, India, Ireland, Japan, Lithuania, Luxembourg, Malta, the Netherlands, Poland, Serbia, Slovenia and the United Kingdom as well as the Nordic Convention, comply with the minimum standard.

Norway signed the MLI in 2017 and deposited its instrument of ratification on the 17 July 2019. The MLI entered into force for Norway on 1 November 2019. Norway has not listed its agreements with Albania, Austria, Barbados, Belgium, Benin, Bosnia-Herzegovina, Brazil, Canada, Côte d'Ivoire, Croatia, Curaçao, Egypt, France, Germany, Greenland, Hungary, Indonesia, Israel, Italy, Jamaica, Kazakhstan, Kenya, Korea, Malaysia, Montenegro, Morocco, New Zealand, North Macedonia, Pakistan, Qatar, Senegal, Sierra Leone, Singapore, the Slovak Republic, Spain, Sri Lanka, Switzerland, Thailand, Trinidad and Tobago, Tunisia, Ukraine, Viet Nam and Zambia. These agreements will therefore not, at this stage, be modified by the MLI. Albania, Barbados, Bosnia-Herzegovina, Canada, Côte d'Ivoire, Croatia, Curaçao, Egypt, France, Hungary, Indonesia, Israel, Italy, Jamaica, Kazakhstan, Kenya, Korea, Malaysia, Morocco, New Zealand, North Macedonia, Pakistan, Senegal, Singapore, the Slovak Republic, Tunisia and Ukraine have listed their agreements with Norway under the MLI.

Norway indicated in its response to the Peer Review questionnaire that bilateral negotiations would be used with respect to its agreements with Austria, Belgium, Brazil, Canada, France, Germany, Israel, Italy, Kazakhstan, Korea, Malaysia, New Zealand, Pakistan, Singapore, the Slovak Republic, Spain, Thailand, and Tunisia.

The Parties to the Nordic Convention signed a complying instrument in 2018. The protocol entered into force on 28 November 2019 and its provisions took effect which became effective as of 1 January 2020.

Norway is implementing the minimum standard through the inclusion of the preamble statement and the PPT.[103]

The agreements modified by the MLI come into compliance with the minimum standard once the provisions of the MLI take effect.

B. Implementation issues

As mentioned above, Norway has not listed its agreements with Albania, Barbados, Benin, Bosnia-Herzegovina, Côte d'Ivoire, Croatia, Curaçao, Egypt, Greenland, Hungary, Indonesia, Jamaica, Kenya, Montenegro, Morocco, North Macedonia, Qatar, Senegal, Sierra Leone, Sri Lanka, Trinidad and Tobago,

[102] See the Multilateral convention concluded by Denmark, Finland, the Faroe Islands, Iceland, Norway and Sweden: for the avoidance of double taxation with respect to taxes on income and on capital (1996, 1997, 2008 and 2018). In total, Norway identified 88 "agreements" in its List of Tax agreements: 83 bilateral agreements and the Nordic Convention concluded with five of its treaty partners.

[103] For its agreements listed under the MLI, Norway is implementing the preamble statement (Article 6 of the MLI) and the PPT (Article 7 of the MLI). Norway stated that while it accepts the application of the PPT under the MLI, it intends where possible to adopt an LOB provision through bilateral negotiation. Norway has also accepted to implement a simplified LOB in agreements concluded with partners that opted in for the simplified LOB under Article 7(7)(a) of the MLI.

Ukraine, Viet Nam and Zambia under the MLI. Listing the agreements under the MLI or entering into bilateral renegotiations to implement the minimum standard would ensure that the minimum standard could be implemented in those non-covered agreements.

Summary of the jurisdiction response - Norway

	Treaty partners	Compliance with the standard	If compliant, the alternative implemented	Signature of a complying instrument	The alternative implemented through the complying instrument (if not the MLI)	Comments
1	Albania	No	N/A	No	N/A	
2	Argentina	No	N/A	Yes	N/A	
3	Australia	Yes	PPT alone	N/A	N/A	
4	Austria	No	N/A	No	N/A	Bilateral negotiations
5	Azerbaijan*	No	N/A	No	N/A	
6	Bangladesh*	No	N/A	No	N/A	
7	Barbados	No	N/A	No	N/A	
8	Belgium	No	N/A	No	N/A	Bilateral negotiations
9	Benin	No	N/A	No	N/A	
10	Bosnia-Herzegovina	No	N/A	No	N/A	
11	Brazil	No	N/A	No	N/A	Bilateral negotiations
12	Bulgaria	No	N/A	Yes	N/A	
13	Canada	No	N/A	No	N/A	Bilateral negotiations
14	Chile	No	N/A	Yes	N/A	
15	China (People's Republic of)	No	N/A	Yes	N/A	
16	Côte d'Ivoire	No	N/A	No	N/A	
17	Croatia	No	N/A	No	N/A	
18	Curaçao	No	N/A	No	N/A	
19	Cyprus*	No	N/A	Yes	N/A	
20	Czech Republic	No	N/A	Yes	N/A	
21	Denmark	Yes	PPT alone	N/A	N/A	Nordic Convention
22	Egypt	No	N/A	No	N/A	
23	Estonia	Yes	PPT alone	N/A	N/A	
24	Faroe Islands	Yes	PPT alone	N/A	N/A	Nordic Convention
25	Finland	Yes	PPT alone	N/A	N/A	Nordic Convention
26	France	No	N/A	No	N/A	Bilateral negotiations
27	Gambia*	No	N/A	No	N/A	
28	Georgia	Yes	PPT alone	N/A	N/A	
29	Germany	No	N/A	No	N/A	Bilateral negotiations
30	Greece	No	N/A	Yes	N/A	
31	Greenland	No	N/A	No	N/A	
32	Hungary	No	N/A	No	N/A	
33	Iceland	Yes	PPT alone	N/A	N/A	Nordic Convention
34	India	Yes	PPT and LOB	N/A	N/A	
35	Indonesia	No	N/A	No	N/A	
36	Ireland	Yes	PPT alone	N/A	N/A	
37	Israel	No	N/A	No	N/A	Bilateral negotiations
38	Italy	No	N/A	No	N/A	Bilateral negotiations
39	Jamaica	No	N/A	No	N/A	
40	Japan	Yes	PPT alone	N/A	N/A	
41	Kazakhstan	No	N/A	No	N/A	Bilateral negotiations

42	Kenya	No	N/A	No	N/A	
43	Korea	No	N/A	No	N/A	Bilateral negotiations
44	Latvia	No	N/A	Yes	N/A	
45	Lithuania	Yes	PPT alone	N/A	N/A	
46	Luxembourg	Yes	PPT alone	N/A	N/A	
47	Malawi*	No	N/A	No	N/A	
48	Malaysia	No	N/A	No	N/A	Bilateral negotiations
49	Malta	Yes	PPT alone	N/A	N/A	
50	Mexico	No	N/A	Yes	N/A	
51	Montenegro	No	N/A	No	N/A	
52	Morocco	No	N/A	No	N/A	
53	Nepal*	No	N/A	No	N/A	
54	Netherlands	Yes	PPT alone	N/A	N/A	
55	New Zealand	No	N/A	No	N/A	Bilateral negotiations
56	North Macedonia	No	N/A	No	N/A	
57	Pakistan	No	N/A	No	N/A	Bilateral negotiations
58	Philippines*	No	N/A	No	N/A	
59	Poland	Yes	PPT alone	N/A	N/A	
60	Portugal	No	N/A	Yes	N/A	
61	Qatar	No	N/A	No	N/A	
62	Romania	No	N/A	Yes	N/A	
63	Russia	No	N/A	Yes	N/A	
64	Senegal	No	N/A	No	N/A	
65	Serbia	Yes	PPT alone	N/A	N/A	
66	Sierra Leone	No	N/A	No	N/A	
67	Singapore	No	N/A	No	N/A	Bilateral negotiations
68	Sint Maarten*	No	N/A	No	N/A	
69	Slovak Republic	No	N/A	No	N/A	Bilateral negotiations
70	Slovenia	Yes	PPT alone	N/A	N/A	
71	South Africa	No	N/A	Yes	N/A	
72	Spain	No	N/A	No	N/A	Bilateral negotiations
73	Sri Lanka	No	N/A	No	N/A	
74	Sweden	Yes	PPT alone	N/A	N/A	Nordic Convention
75	Switzerland	No	N/A	Yes	PPT alone	
76	Tanzania*	No	N/A	No	N/A	
77	Thailand	No	N/A	No	N/A	Bilateral negotiations
78	Trinidad and Tobago	No	N/A	No	N/A	
79	Tunisia	No	N/A	No	N/A	Bilateral negotiations
80	Turkey	No	N/A	Yes	N/A	
81	Uganda*	No	N/A	No	N/A	
82	Ukraine	No	N/A	No	N/A	
83	United Kingdom	Yes	PPT alone	N/A	N/A	
84	United States	No	N/A	No	N/A	Bilateral negotiations
85	Venezuela*	No	N/A	No	N/A	
86	Viet Nam	No	N/A	No	N/A	
87	Zambia	No	N/A	No	N/A	
88	Zimbabwe*	No	N/A	No	N/A	

Oman

A. Progress in the implementation of the minimum standard

Oman has 34 tax agreements in force, as reported in its response to the Peer Review questionnaire.

Oman signed the MLI in 2019 and deposited its instrument of ratification on the 7 July 2020. The MLI will enter into force for Oman on 1 November 2020. Oman has not listed its agreement with India but indicated in its response to the Peer Review questionnaire that bilateral negotiations would be used with respect to the agreement.

Oman is implementing the minimum standard through the inclusion of the preamble statement and the PPT.[104]

The agreements that will be modified by the MLI will come into compliance with the minimum standard once the provisions of the MLI take effect.

B. Implementation issues

No jurisdiction has raised any concerns about their agreements with Oman.

Summary of the jurisdiction response - Oman

	Treaty partners	Compliance with the standard	If compliant, the alternative implemented	Signature of a complying instrument	The alternative implemented through the complying instrument (if not the MLI)	Comments
1	Algeria*	No	N/A	Yes	N/A	
2	Belarus*	No	N/A	Yes	N/A	
3	Brunei Darussalam	No	N/A	Yes	N/A	
4	Canada	No	N/A	Yes	N/A	
5	China (People's Republic of)	No	N/A	Yes	N/A	
6	Croatia	No	N/A	Yes	N/A	
7	France	No	N/A	Yes	N/A	
8	Hungary	No	N/A	Yes	N/A	
9	India	No	N/A	No	N/A	
10	Iran*	No	N/A	Yes	N/A	
11	Italy	No	N/A	Yes	N/A	
12	Japan	No	N/A	Yes	N/A	
13	Korea	No	N/A	Yes	N/A	
14	Lebanon*	No	N/A	Yes	N/A	
15	Mauritius	No	N/A	Yes	N/A	
16	Moldova*	No	N/A	Yes	N/A	
17	Morocco	No	N/A	Yes	N/A	
18	Netherlands	No	N/A	Yes	N/A	
19	Pakistan	No	N/A	Yes	N/A	

[104] For its agreements listed under the MLI, Oman is implementing the preamble statement (Article 6 of the MLI) and the PPT (Article 7 of the MLI).

20	Portugal	No	N/A	Yes	N/A	
21	Seychelles	No	N/A	Yes	N/A	
22	Singapore	No	N/A	Yes	N/A	
23	South Africa	No	N/A	Yes	N/A	
24	Spain	No	N/A	Yes	N/A	
25	Sudan*	No	N/A	Yes	N/A	
26	Switzerland	No	N/A	Yes	N/A	
27	Syrian Arab Republic*	No	N/A	Yes	N/A	
28	Thailand	No	N/A	Yes	N/A	
29	Tunisia	No	N/A	Yes	N/A	
30	Turkey	No	N/A	Yes	N/A	
31	United Kingdom	No	N/A	Yes	N/A	
32	Uzbekistan*	No	N/A	Yes	N/A	
33	Viet Nam	No	N/A	Yes	N/A	
34	Yemen*	No	N/A	Yes	N/A	

Pakistan

A. Progress in the implementation of the minimum standard

Pakistan has 66 tax agreements in force, as reported in its response to the Peer Review questionnaire. One of those agreements, the agreement with Bulgaria, complies with the minimum standard.

Pakistan signed the MLI in 2017 and deposited its instrument of ratification on 18 December 2020. The MLI will enter into force for Pakistan on 1 April 2021.

Pakistan is implementing the minimum standard through the inclusion of the preamble statement and the PPT.[105]

The agreements that will be modified by the MLI will come into compliance with the minimum standard once the provisions of the MLI take effect.

B. Implementation issues

No jurisdiction has raised any concerns about their agreements with Pakistan.

Summary of the jurisdiction response - Pakistan

	Treaty partners	Compliance with the standard	If compliant, the alternative implemented	Signature of a complying instrument	The alternative implemented through the complying instrument (if not the MLI)	Comments
1	Austria	No	N/A	Yes	N/A	
2	Azerbaijan*	No	N/A	Yes	N/A	
3	Bahrain	No	N/A	Yes	N/A	
4	Bangladesh*	No	N/A	Yes	N/A	
5	Belarus*	No	N/A	Yes	N/A	
6	Belgium	No	N/A	Yes	N/A	
7	Bosnia-Herzegovina	No	N/A	Yes	N/A	
8	Brunei Darussalam	No	N/A	No	N/A	Pakistan will include this agreement in the CTA list on depositing the Instrument of Ratification of MLI.
9	Bulgaria	Yes	PPT alone	N/A	N/A	The agreement includes the new Preamble as well as the PPT
10	Canada	No	N/A	Yes	N/A	
11	China (People's Republic of)	No	N/A	Yes	N/A	
12	Czech Republic	No	N/A	Yes	N/A	
13	Denmark	No	N/A	Yes	N/A	
14	Egypt	No	N/A	Yes	N/A	
15	Finland	No	N/A	Yes	N/A	
16	France	No	N/A	Yes	N/A	

105 For its agreements listed under the MLI, Pakistan is implementing the preamble statement (Article 6 of the MLI) and the PPT (Article 7 of the MLI).

17	Germany	No	N/A	Yes	N/A	
18	Hong Kong (China)	No	N/A	Yes	N/A	
19	Hungary	No	N/A	Yes	N/A	
20	Indonesia	No	N/A	Yes	N/A	
21	Iran*	No	N/A	Yes	N/A	
22	Ireland	No	N/A	Yes	N/A	
23	Italy	No	N/A	Yes	N/A	
24	Japan	No	N/A	Yes	N/A	
25	Jordan	No	N/A	Yes	N/A	
26	Kazakhstan	No	N/A	Yes	N/A	
27	Korea	No	N/A	Yes	N/A	
28	Kuwait*	No	N/A	Yes	N/A	
29	Kyrgyzstan*	No	N/A	Yes	N/A	
30	Lebanon*	No	N/A	Yes	N/A	
31	Libya*	No	N/A	Yes	N/A	
32	Malaysia	No	N/A	Yes	N/A	
33	Malta	No	N/A	Yes	N/A	
34	Mauritius	No	N/A	Yes	N/A	
35	Morocco	No	N/A	Yes	N/A	
36	Nepal*	No	N/A	Yes	N/A	
37	Netherlands	No	N/A	Yes	N/A	
38	Nigeria	No	N/A	Yes	N/A	
39	Norway	No	N/A	Yes	N/A	
40	Oman	No	N/A	Yes	N/A	
41	Philippines*	No	N/A	Yes	N/A	
42	Poland	No	N/A	Yes	N/A	
43	Portugal	No	N/A	Yes	N/A	
44	Qatar	No	N/A	Yes	N/A	
45	Romania	No	N/A	Yes	N/A	
46	Saudi Arabia	No	N/A	Yes	N/A	
47	Serbia	No	N/A	Yes	N/A	
48	Singapore	No	N/A	Yes	N/A	
49	South Africa	No	N/A	Yes	N/A	
50	Spain	No	N/A	Yes	N/A	
51	Sri Lanka	No	N/A	Yes	N/A	
52	Sweden	No	N/A	Yes	N/A	
53	Switzerland	No	N/A	Yes	N/A	
54	Syrian Arab Republic*	No	N/A	Yes	N/A	
55	Tajikistan*	No	N/A	Yes	N/A	
56	Thailand	No	N/A	Yes	N/A	
57	Tunisia	No	N/A	Yes	N/A	
58	Turkey	No	N/A	Yes	N/A	
59	Turkmenistan*	No	N/A	Yes	N/A	
60	Ukraine	No	N/A	Yes	N/A	
61	United Arab Emirates	No	N/A	Yes	N/A	
62	United Kingdom	No	N/A	Yes	N/A	
63	United States	No	N/A	Yes	N/A	
64	Uzbekistan*	No	N/A	Yes	N/A	
65	Viet Nam	No	N/A	Yes	N/A	
66	Yemen*	No	N/A	Yes	N/A	

Panama

A. Progress in the implementation of the minimum standard

Panama has 17 tax agreements in force, as reported in its response to the Peer Review questionnaire.

Panama signed the MLI in 2018 and deposited its instrument of ratification on 5 November 2020. The MLI will enter into force for Panama on 1 March 2021.

Panama is implementing the minimum standard through the inclusion of the preamble statement and the PPT.[106]

The agreements that will be modified by the MLI will come into compliance with the minimum standard once the provisions of the MLI take effect.

B. Implementation issues

No jurisdiction has raised any concerns about their agreements with Panama.

Summary of the jurisdiction response - Panama

	Treaty partners	Compliance with the standard	If compliant, the alternative implemented	Signature of a complying instrument	The alternative implemented through the complying instrument (if not the MLI)	Comments
1	Barbados	No	N/A	Yes	N/A	
2	Czech Republic	No	N/A	Yes	N/A	
3	France	No	N/A	Yes	N/A	
4	Ireland	No	N/A	Yes	N/A	
5	Israel	No	N/A	Yes	N/A	
6	Italy	No	N/A	Yes	N/A	
7	Korea	No	N/A	Yes	N/A	
8	Luxembourg	No	N/A	Yes	N/A	
9	Mexico	No	N/A	Yes	N/A	
10	Netherlands	No	N/A	Yes	N/A	
11	Portugal	No	N/A	Yes	N/A	
12	Qatar	No	N/A	Yes	N/A	
13	Singapore	No	N/A	Yes	N/A	
14	Spain	No	N/A	Yes	N/A	
15	United Arab Emirates	No	N/A	Yes	N/A	
16	United Kingdom	No	N/A	Yes	N/A	
17	Viet Nam	No	N/A	Yes	N/A	

[106] For its agreements listed under the MLI, Panama is implementing the preamble statement (Article 6 of the MLI) and the PPT (Article 7 of the MLI).

Papua New Guinea

A. Progress in the implementation of the minimum standard

Papua New Guinea has ten tax agreements in force, as reported in its response to the Peer Review questionnaire.

Papua New Guinea signed the MLI in 2019, listing its non-compliant agreements.

Papua New Guinea is implementing the minimum standard through the inclusion of the preamble statement and the PPT.[107]

The agreements that will be modified by the MLI will come into compliance with the minimum standard once the provisions of the MLI take effect.

B. Implementation issues

Papua New Guinea's listed agreements under the MLI will start to be compliant after Papua New Guinea's ratification of the MLI. Papua New Guinea is encouraged to ratify the MLI as soon as possible. Papua New Guinea indicated that it expected to commence its ratification process of the MLI in 2021.

Summary of the jurisdiction response - Papua New Guinea

	Treaty partners	Compliance with the standard	If compliant, the alternative implemented	Signature of a complying instrument	The alternative implemented through the complying instrument (if not the MLI)	Comments
1	Australia	No	N/A	Yes	N/A	
2	Canada	No	N/A	Yes	N/A	
3	China (People's Republic of)	No	N/A	Yes	N/A	
4	Fiji*	No	N/A	Yes	N/A	
5	Indonesia	No	N/A	Yes	N/A	Indonesia has not listed our agreement in their MLI Position to be a CTA.
6	Korea	No	N/A	Yes	N/A	
7	Malaysia	No	N/A	Yes	N/A	
8	New Zealand	No	N/A	Yes	N/A	
9	Singapore	No	N/A	Yes	N/A	
10	United Kingdom	No	N/A	Yes	N/A	

107 For its agreements listed under the MLI, Papua New Guinea is implementing the preamble statement (Article 6 of the MLI) and the PPT (Article 7 of the MLI).

Paraguay

A. Progress in the implementation of the minimum standard

Paraguay has three tax agreements in force, as reported in its response to the Peer Review questionnaire. One of those agreements, the agreement with Uruguay, complies with the minimum standard.

Paraguay has not signed the MLI.

Paraguay is implementing the minimum standard through the inclusion of the preamble statement and the PPT combined with the LOB.

B. Implementation issues

As Paraguay has not signed the MLI or implemented anti-treaty-shopping measures in its agreements, the Secretariat will offer its support to design a plan for the implementation of the minimum standard to strengthen its network of agreements.

Summary of the jurisdiction response - Paraguay

	Treaty partners	Compliance with the standard	If compliant, the alternative implemented	Signature of a complying instrument	The alternative implemented through the complying instrument (if not the MLI)	Comments
1	Chile	No	N/A	No	N/A	
2	Chinese Taipei*	No	N/A	No	N/A	
3	Uruguay	Yes	PPT and LOB	N/A	N/A	

Peru

A. Progress in the implementation of the minimum standard

Peru has eight tax agreements in force, as reported in its response to the Peer Review questionnaire, including the Decision 578 of the Andean Community Commission (Decision 578) for the members of the Andean Community (the Andean Community Agreement).[108]

Peru signed the MLI in 2018, listing its non-compliant bilateral agreements.

Peru is implementing the minimum standard through the inclusion of the preamble statement and the PPT.[109]

The agreements that will be modified by the MLI will come into compliance with the minimum standard once the provisions of the MLI take effect.

Peru indicated in its response to the Peer Review questionnaire that the Andean Community Agreement has not been listed under the MLI as it is a decision of the Andean Community Commission and that it will renegotiate the agreement with its treaty partners.[110]

B. Implementation issues

Peru's listed agreements under the MLI will start to be compliant after Peru's ratification of the MLI. Peru is encouraged to ratify the MLI as soon as possible.

Summary of the jurisdiction response – Peru

	Treaty partners	Compliance with the standard	If compliant, the alternative implemented	Signature of a complying instrument	The alternative implemented through the complying instrument (if not the MLI)	Comments
1	Bolivia*	No	N/A	No	N/A	Currently renegotiating Decision 578
2	Brazil	No	N/A	Yes	N/A	
3	Canada	No	N/A	Yes	N/A	
4	Chile	No	N/A	Yes	N/A	
5	Colombia	No	N/A	No	N/A	Currently renegotiating Decision 578
6	Ecuador*	No	N/A	No	N/A	Currently renegotiating Decision 578
7	Korea	No	N/A	Yes	N/A	
8	Mexico	No	N/A	Yes	N/A	
9	Portugal	No	N/A	Yes	N/A	
10	Switzerland	No	N/A	Yes	N/A	

108 The Decision of the Commission of the Andean Community 578 on the regime for the avoidance of double taxation and the prevention of fiscal evasion, adopted on 4 May 2004. The current members of the Andean Community are Bolivia*, Colombia, Ecuador* and Peru. In total, Peru identified ten "agreements" in its List of Tax agreements: seven bilateral agreements and the Andean Community.

109 For its agreements listed under the MLI, Peru is implementing the preamble statement (Article 6 of the MLI) and the PPT (Article 7 of the MLI). Peru expressed a statement that while it accepts the application of the PPT under the MLI, it intends where possible to adopt an LOB provision through bilateral negotiation.

110 Bolivia* and Ecuador* are not members of the BEPS Inclusive Framework.

Poland

A. Progress in the implementation of the minimum standard

Poland has 82 tax agreements in force, as reported in its response to the Peer Review questionnaire. Twenty-four of those agreements, the agreements with Australia, Austria, Belgium, Canada, Denmark, Finland, France, Iceland, India, Ireland, Israel, Japan, Lithuania, Luxembourg, Malta, New Zealand, Norway, Serbia, Singapore, the Slovak Republic, Slovenia, Ukraine, the United Arab Emirates, and the United Kingdom, comply with the minimum standard.

Poland signed the MLI in 2017 and deposited its instrument of ratification of the MLI on 23 January 2018. The MLI entered into force for Poland on 1 July 2018. Poland has not listed its agreements with Georgia, Germany and Montenegro but indicated in its response to the Peer Review questionnaire that bilateral negotiations would be pursued with respect to those agreement.

Poland is implementing the minimum standard through the inclusion of the preamble statement and the PPT.[111]

The agreements modified by the MLI come into compliance with the minimum standard once the provisions of the MLI take effect.

B. Implementation issues

No jurisdiction has raised any concerns about their agreements with Poland.

Summary of the jurisdiction response - Poland

	Treaty partners	Compliance with the standard	If compliant, the alternative implemented	Signature of a complying instrument	The alternative implemented through the complying instrument (if not the MLI)	Comments
1	Albania	No	N/A	Yes	N/A	
2	Armenia	No	N/A	Yes	N/A	
3	Australia	Yes	PPT alone	N/A	N/A	The express statement in the preamble and the PPT (equivalent to paragraph 9 of Article 29 of the 2017 OECD MTC)
4	Austria	Yes	PPT alone	N/A	N/A	The express statement in the preamble and the PPT (equivalent to paragraph 9 of Article 29 of the 2017 OECD MTC)
5	Azerbaijan*	No	N/A	Yes	N/A	
6	Bangladesh*	No	N/A	Yes	N/A	
7	Belarus*	No	N/A	Yes	N/A	
8	Belgium	Yes	PPT alone	N/A	N/A	The express statement in the preamble and the PPT (equivalent to paragraph 9 of Article 29 of the 2017 OECD MTC)

[111] For its agreements listed under the MLI, Poland is implementing the preamble statement (Article 6 of the MLI) and the PPT (Article 7 of the MLI). Poland expressed a statement that while it accepts the application of the PPT under the MLI, it intends where possible to adopt an LOB provision through bilateral negotiation.

9	Bosnia-Herzegovina	No	N/A	Yes	N/A	
10	Bulgaria	No	N/A	Yes	N/A	
11	Canada	Yes	PPT alone	N/A	N/A	The express statement in the preamble and the PPT (equivalent to paragraph 9 of Article 29 of the 2017 OECD MTC)
12	Chile	No	N/A	Yes	N/A	
13	China (People's Republic of)	No	N/A	Yes	N/A	
14	Croatia	No	N/A	Yes	N/A	
15	Cyprus*	No	N/A	Yes	N/A	
16	Czech Republic	No	N/A	Yes	N/A	
17	Denmark	Yes	PPT alone	N/A	N/A	The express statement in the preamble and the PPT (equivalent to paragraph 9 of Article 29 of the 2017 OECD MTC)
18	Egypt	No	N/A	Yes	N/A	
19	Estonia	No	N/A	Yes	N/A	
20	Ethiopia*	No	N/A	Yes	N/A	
21	Finland	Yes	PPT alone	N/A	N/A	The express statement in the preamble and the PPT (equivalent to paragraph 9 of Article 29 of the 2017 OECD MTC)
22	France	Yes	PPT alone	N/A	N/A	The express statement in the preamble and the PPT (equivalent to paragraph 9 of Article 29 of the 2017 OECD MTC)
23	Georgia	No	N/A	No	N/A	
24	Germany	No	N/A	No	N/A	The Protocol will amend the text of the title of the DTA as well as the preamble. It will introduce also the PPT provision.
25	Greece	No	N/A	Yes	N/A	
26	Hungary	No	N/A	Yes	N/A	
27	Iceland	Yes	PPT alone	N/A	N/A	The express statement in the preamble and the PPT (equivalent to paragraph 9 of Article 29 of the 2017 OECD MTC)
28	India	Yes	PPT alone	N/A	N/A	The express statement in the preamble and the PPT (equivalent to paragraph 9 of Article 29 of the 2017 OECD MTC)
29	Indonesia	No	N/A	Yes	N/A	
30	Iran*	No	N/A	Yes	N/A	
31	Ireland	Yes	PPT alone	N/A	N/A	The express statement in the preamble and the PPT (equivalent to paragraph 9 of Article 29 of the 2017 OECD MTC)
32	Israel	Yes	PPT alone	N/A	N/A	The express statement in the preamble and the PPT (equivalent to paragraph 9

						of Article 29 of the 2017 OECD MTC)
33	Italy	No	N/A	Yes	N/A	
34	Japan	Yes	PPT alone	N/A	N/A	The express statement in the preamble and the PPT (equivalent to paragraph 9 of Article 29 of the 2017 OECD MTC)
35	Jordan	No	N/A	Yes	N/A	
36	Kazakhstan	No	N/A	Yes	N/A	
37	Korea	No	N/A	Yes	N/A	
38	Kuwait*	No	N/A	Yes	N/A	
39	Kyrgyzstan*	No	N/A	Yes	N/A	
40	Latvia	No	N/A	Yes	N/A	
41	Lebanon*	No	N/A	Yes	N/A	
42	Lithuania	Yes	PPT alone	N/A	N/A	The express statement in the preamble and the PPT (equivalent to paragraph 9 of Article 29 of the 2017 OECD MTC)
43	Luxembourg	Yes	PPT alone	N/A	N/A	The express statement in the preamble and the PPT (equivalent to paragraph 9 of Article 29 of the 2017 OECD MTC)
44	Malaysia (old)	No	N/A	No	N/A	
45	Malta	Yes	PPT alone	N/A	N/A	The express statement in the preamble and the PPT (equivalent to paragraph 9 of Article 29 of the 2017 OECD MTC)
46	Mexico	No	N/A	Yes	N/A	
47	Moldova*	No	N/A	Yes	N/A	
48	Mongolia	No	N/A	Yes	N/A	
49	Montenegro	No	N/A	No	N/A	Invitation letter sent for bilateral negotiation
50	Morocco	No	N/A	Yes	N/A	
51	Netherlands	No	N/A	Yes[112]	N/A	
52	New Zealand	Yes	PPT alone	N/A	N/A	The express statement in the preamble and the PPT (equivalent to paragraph 9 of Article 29 of the 2017 OECD MTC)
53	North Macedonia	No	N/A	Yes	N/A	
54	Norway	Yes	PPT alone	N/A	N/A	The express statement in the preamble and the PPT (equivalent to paragraph 9 of Article 29 of the 2017 OECD MTC)
55	Pakistan	No	N/A	Yes	N/A	
56	Philippines*	No	N/A	Yes	N/A	
57	Portugal	No	N/A	Yes	N/A	

[112] The tax agreement concluded between Poland and the Netherlands in 2002 has been notified by Poland as "covered" under the MLI. The Netherlands didn't notify the tax treaty with Poland as "covered". In order to introduce to the above DTA the minimum standard provided for in the BEPS Action 6, bilateral negotiations were held. On 29 October 2020, the Protocol amending this tax agreement was signed. The Protocol provides for, amongst others, the inclusion of the preamble statement and the PPT clause in the DTA. As soon as the Protocol comes into force and is effective, this DTA will include the minimum standard resulting from the BEPS Action 6.

58	Qatar	No	N/A	Yes	N/A	
59	Romania	No	N/A	Yes	N/A	
60	Russia	No	N/A	Yes	N/A	
61	Saudi Arabia	No	N/A	Yes	N/A	
62	Serbia	Yes	PPT alone	N/A	N/A	The express statement in the preamble and the PPT (equivalent to paragraph 9 of Article 29 of the 2017 OECD MTC)
63	Singapore	Yes	PPT alone	N/A	N/A	The express statement in the preamble and the PPT (equivalent to paragraph 9 of Article 29 of the 2017 OECD MTC)
64	Slovak Republic	Yes	PPT alone	N/A	N/A	The express statement in the preamble and the PPT (equivalent to paragraph 9 of Article 29 of the 2017 OECD MTC)
65	Slovenia	Yes	PPT alone	N/A	N/A	The express statement in the preamble and the PPT (equivalent to paragraph 9 of Article 29 of the 2017 OECD MTC)
66	South Africa	No	N/A	Yes	N/A	
67	Spain	No	N/A	Yes	N/A	
68	Sri Lanka	No	N/A	Yes	N/A	
69	Sweden	No	N/A	Yes	N/A	
70	Switzerland	No	N/A	Yes	N/A	
71	Syrian Arab Republic*	No	N/A	Yes	N/A	
72	Tajikistan*	No	N/A	Yes	N/A	
73	Thailand	No	N/A	Yes	N/A	
74	Tunisia	No	N/A	Yes	N/A	
75	Turkey	No	N/A	Yes	N/A	
76	Ukraine	Yes	PPT alone	N/A	N/A	The express statement in the preamble and the PPT (equivalent to paragraph 9 of Article 29 of the 2017 OECD MTC)
77	United Arab Emirates	Yes	PPT alone	N/A	N/A	The express statement in the preamble and the PPT (equivalent to paragraph 9 of Article 29 of the 2017 OECD MTC)
78	United Kingdom	Yes	PPT alone	N/A	N/A	The express statement in the preamble and the PPT (equivalent to paragraph 9 of Article 29 of the 2017 OECD MTC)
79	United States	No	N/A	No	N/A	Invitation letter sent for bilateral negotiation
80	Uzbekistan*	No	N/A	Yes	N/A	
81	Viet Nam	No	N/A	Yes	N/A	
82	Zimbabwe*	No	N/A	Yes	N/A	

Portugal

A. Progress in the implementation of the minimum standard

Portugal has 78 tax agreements in force, as reported in its response to the Peer Review questionnaire. One of those agreements, the agreement with Angola, complies with the minimum standard.

Portugal signed the MLI in 2017 and deposited its instrument of ratification on 28 February 2020. The MLI entered into force for Portugal on 1 June 2020.

Portugal is implementing the minimum standard through the inclusion of the preamble statement and the PPT.[113]

The agreements that will be modified by the MLI will come into compliance with the minimum standard once the provisions of the MLI take effect.

B. Implementation issues

No jurisdiction has raised any concerns about their agreements with Portugal.

Summary of the jurisdiction response - Portugal

	Treaty partners	Compliance with the standard	If compliant, the alternative implemented	Signature of a complying instrument	The alternative implemented through the complying instrument (if not the MLI)	Comments
1	Algeria*	No	N/A	Yes	N/A	
2	Andorra	No	N/A	Yes	N/A	
3	Angola	Yes	PPT alone	N/A	N/A	
4	Austria	No	N/A	Yes	N/A	
5	Bahrain	No	N/A	Yes	N/A	
6	Barbados	No	N/A	Yes	N/A	
7	Belgium	No	N/A	Yes	N/A	
8	Brazil	No	N/A	Yes	N/A	
9	Bulgaria	No	N/A	Yes	N/A	
10	Cabo Verde	No	N/A	Yes	N/A	
11	Canada	No	N/A	Yes	N/A	
12	Chile	No	N/A	Yes	N/A	
13	China (People's Republic of)	No	N/A	Yes	N/A	
14	Colombia	No	N/A	Yes	N/A	
15	Côte d'Ivoire	No	N/A	Yes	N/A	
16	Croatia	No	N/A	Yes	N/A	
17	Cuba*	No	N/A	Yes	N/A	
18	Cyprus*	No	N/A	Yes	N/A	
19	Czech Republic	No	N/A	Yes	N/A	
20	Denmark	No	N/A	Yes	N/A	

[113] For its agreements listed under the MLI, Portugal is implementing the preamble statement (Article 6 of the MLI) and the PPT (Article 7 of the MLI).

21	Estonia	No	N/A	Yes	N/A	
22	Ethiopia*	No	N/A	Yes	N/A	
23	France	No	N/A	Yes	N/A	
24	Georgia	No	N/A	Yes	N/A	
25	Germany	No	N/A	Yes	N/A	
26	Greece	No	N/A	Yes	N/A	
27	Guinea-Bissau*	No	N/A	Yes	N/A	
28	Hong Kong (China)	No	N/A	Yes	N/A	
29	Hungary	No	N/A	Yes	N/A	
30	Iceland	No	N/A	Yes	N/A	
31	India	No	N/A	Yes	N/A	
32	Indonesia	No	N/A	Yes	N/A	
33	Ireland	No	N/A	Yes	N/A	
34	Israel	No	N/A	Yes	N/A	
35	Italy	No	N/A	Yes	N/A	
36	Japan	No	N/A	Yes	N/A	
37	Korea	No	N/A	Yes	N/A	
38	Kuwait*	No	N/A	Yes	N/A	
39	Latvia	No	N/A	Yes	N/A	
40	Lithuania	No	N/A	Yes	N/A	
41	Luxembourg	No	N/A	Yes	N/A	
42	Macau (China)	No	N/A	Yes	N/A	
43	Malta	No	N/A	Yes	N/A	
44	Mexico	No	N/A	Yes	N/A	
45	Moldova*	No	N/A	Yes	N/A	
46	Montenegro	No	N/A	Yes	N/A	
47	Morocco	No	N/A	Yes	N/A	
48	Mozambique*	No	N/A	Yes	N/A	
49	Netherlands	No	N/A	Yes	N/A	
50	Norway	No	N/A	Yes	N/A	
51	Oman	No	N/A	Yes	N/A	
52	Pakistan	No	N/A	Yes	N/A	
53	Panama	No	N/A	Yes	N/A	
54	Peru	No	N/A	Yes	N/A	
55	Poland	No	N/A	Yes	N/A	
56	Qatar	No	N/A	Yes	N/A	
57	Romania	No	N/A	Yes	N/A	
58	Russia	No	N/A	Yes	N/A	
59	San Marino	No	N/A	Yes	N/A	
60	Sao Tome and Principe*	No	N/A	Yes	N/A	
61	Saudi Arabia	No	N/A	Yes	N/A	
62	Senegal	No	N/A	Yes	N/A	
63	Singapore	No	N/A	Yes	N/A	
64	Slovak Republic	No	N/A	Yes	N/A	
65	Slovenia	No	N/A	Yes	N/A	
66	South Africa	No	N/A	Yes	N/A	
67	Spain	No	N/A	Yes	N/A	
68	Sweden	No	N/A	Yes	PPT alone	
69	Switzerland	No	N/A	Yes	N/A	
70	Tunisia	No	N/A	Yes	N/A	
71	Turkey	No	N/A	Yes	N/A	
72	Ukraine	No	N/A	Yes	N/A	
73	United Arab	No	N/A	Yes	N/A	

	Emirates					
74	United Kingdom	No	N/A	Yes	N/A	
75	United States	No	N/A	Yes	N/A	
76	Uruguay	No	N/A	Yes	N/A	
77	Venezuela*	No	N/A	Yes	N/A	
78	Viet Nam	No	N/A	Yes	N/A	

Qatar

A. Progress in the implementation of the minimum standard

Qatar has 77 tax agreements in force, as reported in its response to the Peer Review questionnaire.

Qatar signed the MLI in 2018 and deposited its instrument of ratification on 23 December 2019. The MLI entered into force for Qatar on April 1 2020. Qatar has not listed its agreements with Austria, Georgia, Guernsey, Kazakhstan, Norway, Switzerland, Tunisia and Ukraine. These agreements will therefore not, at this stage, be modified by the MLI. Kazakhstan and Tunisia have listed their agreements with Qatar under the MLI.

Qatar indicated in its response to the Peer Review questionnaire that bilateral negotiations would be pursued with respect to its agreement with Austria and Guernsey.

Qatar is implementing the minimum standard through the inclusion of the preamble statement and the PPT.[114]

The agreements that will be modified by the MLI will come into compliance with the minimum standard once the provisions of the MLI take effect.

B. Implementation issues

As mentioned above, Qatar has not listed its agreements with Georgia, Kazakhstan Norway, Switzerland, Tunisia and Ukraine under the MLI. Listing the agreements under the MLI or entering into bilateral renegotiations to implement the minimum standard would ensure that the minimum standard could be implemented in those non-covered agreements.

Summary of the jurisdiction response - Qatar

	Treaty partners	Compliance with the standard	If compliant, the alternative implemented	Signature of a complying instrument	The alternative implemented through the complying instrument (if not the MLI)	Comments
1	Albania	No	N/A	Yes	N/A	
2	Algeria*	No	N/A	Yes	N/A	
3	Armenia	No	N/A	Yes	N/A	
4	Austria	No	N/A	Yes	N/A	Amending instrument ensuring compliance with standards under negotiation
5	Azerbaijan*	No	N/A	Yes	N/A	
6	Barbados	No	N/A	Yes	N/A	
7	Belarus*	No	N/A	Yes	N/A	
8	Bermuda	No	N/A	Yes	N/A	
9	Bosnia-Herzegovina	No	N/A	Yes	N/A	

114 For its agreements listed under the MLI, Qatar is implementing the preamble statement (Article 6 of the MLI) and the PPT (Article 7 of the MLI).

10	Brunei Darussalam	No	N/A	Yes	N/A	
11	Bulgaria	No	N/A	Yes	N/A	
12	Chad*	No	N/A	Yes	N/A	
13	China (People's Republic of)	No	N/A	Yes	N/A	
14	Croatia	No	N/A	Yes	N/A	
15	Cuba*	No	N/A	Yes	N/A	
16	Cyprus*	No	N/A	Yes	N/A	
17	Ecuador*	No	N/A	Yes	N/A	
18	Fiji*	No	N/A	Yes	N/A	
19	France	No	N/A	Yes	N/A	
20	Georgia	No	N/A	No	N/A	
21	Greece	No	N/A	Yes	N/A	
22	Guernsey	No	N/A	Yes	PPT alone	Amending instrument ensuring compliance with standards initialled
23	Hong Kong (China)	No	N/A	Yes	N/A	
24	Hungary	No	N/A	Yes	N/A	
25	India	No	N/A	Yes	N/A	A new tax treaty compliant with the Standards initialled
26	Indonesia	No	N/A	Yes	N/A	
27	Iran*	No	N/A	Yes	N/A	
28	Ireland	No	N/A	Yes	N/A	
29	Isle of Man	No	N/A	Yes	N/A	
30	Italy	No	N/A	Yes	N/A	
31	Japan	No	N/A	Yes	N/A	
32	Jersey	No	N/A	Yes	N/A	
33	Jordan	No	N/A	Yes	N/A	
34	Kazakhstan	No	N/A	No	N/A	
35	Kenya	No	N/A	Yes	N/A	
36	Korea	No	N/A	Yes	N/A	
37	Kyrgyzstan*	No	N/A	Yes	N/A	
38	Latvia	No	N/A	Yes	N/A	
39	Lebanon*	No	N/A	Yes	N/A	
40	Luxembourg	No	N/A	Yes	N/A	
41	Malaysia	No	N/A	Yes	N/A	
42	Malta	No	N/A	Yes	N/A	
43	Mauritius	No	N/A	Yes	N/A	
44	Mexico	No	N/A	Yes	N/A	
45	Monaco	No	N/A	Yes	N/A	
46	Morocco	No	N/A	Yes	N/A	The new agreement expected to be in force on 30 June 2019
47	Nepal*	No	N/A	Yes	N/A	
48	Netherlands	No	N/A	Yes	N/A	
49	Nigeria	No	N/A	Yes	N/A	
50	North Macedonia	No	N/A	Yes	N/A	
51	Norway	No	N/A	No	N/A	
52	Pakistan	No	N/A	Yes	N/A	
53	Panama	No	N/A	Yes	N/A	
54	Philippines*	No	N/A	Yes	N/A	
55	Poland	No	N/A	Yes	N/A	
56	Portugal	No	N/A	Yes	N/A	
57	Romania	No	N/A	Yes	N/A	

58	Russia	No	N/A	Yes	N/A	
59	San Marino	No	N/A	Yes	N/A	
60	Senegal	No	N/A	Yes	N/A	
61	Serbia	No	N/A	Yes	N/A	
62	Seychelles	No	N/A	Yes	N/A	
63	Singapore	No	N/A	Yes	N/A	
64	Slovenia	No	N/A	Yes	N/A	
65	South Africa	No	N/A	Yes	N/A	
66	Spain	No	N/A	Yes	N/A	
67	Sri Lanka	No	N/A	Yes	N/A	
68	Sudan*	No	N/A	Yes	N/A	
69	Switzerland	No	N/A	No	N/A	
70	Syrian Arab Republic*	No	N/A	Yes	N/A	
71	Tunisia	No	N/A	No	N/A	
72	Turkey	No	N/A	Yes	N/A	
73	Ukraine	No	N/A	No	N/A	
74	United Kingdom	No	N/A	Yes	N/A	
75	Venezuela*	No	N/A	Yes	N/A	
76	Viet Nam	No	N/A	Yes	N/A	
77	Yemen*	No	N/A	Yes	N/A	

Romania

A. Progress in the implementation of the minimum standard

Romania has 88 tax agreements in force, as reported in its response to the Peer Review questionnaire.

Romania signed the MLI in 2017, listing its non-compliant agreements.[115]

Romania signed a bilateral complying instrument with respect to its agreement with Spain.

Romania is implementing the minimum standard through the inclusion of the preamble statement and the PPT.[116]

The agreements that will be modified by the MLI will come into compliance with the minimum standard once the provisions of the MLI take effect.

B. Implementation issues

Romania's listed agreements under the MLI will start to be compliant after Romania's ratification of the MLI. Romania is encouraged to ratify the MLI as soon as possible. Romania indicated that it was working towards the ratification of the MLI and that it expected to deposit its instrument of ratification of the MLI by mid-2021.

Summary of the jurisdiction response - Romania

	Treaty partners	Compliance with the standard	If compliant, the alternative implemented	Signature of a complying instrument	The alternative implemented through the complying instrument (if not the MLI)	Comments
1	Albania	No	N/A	Yes	N/A	
2	Algeria*	No	N/A	Yes	N/A	
3	Armenia	No	N/A	Yes	N/A	
4	Australia	No	N/A	Yes	N/A	
5	Austria	No	N/A	Yes	N/A	
6	Azerbaijan*	No	N/A	Yes	N/A	
7	Bangladesh*	No	N/A	Yes	N/A	
8	Belarus*	No	N/A	Yes	N/A	
9	Belgium	No	N/A	Yes	N/A	
10	Bosnia-Herzegovina	No	N/A	Yes	N/A	
11	Bulgaria	No	N/A	Yes	N/A	
12	Canada	No	N/A	Yes	N/A	
13	China (People's Republic of)	No	N/A	Yes	N/A	

115 Romania's new agreements with China and Italy entered into force in 2018 and the agreement with Bosnia and Herzegovina entered into force in 2019. The old agreements with those jurisdictions will be removed from the list of notified agreements to be covered by the MLI.

116 For its agreements listed under the MLI, Romania is implementing the preamble statement (Article 6 of the MLI) and the PPT (Article 7 of the MLI).

14	Croatia	No	N/A	Yes	N/A	
15	Cyprus*	No	N/A	Yes	N/A	
16	Czech Republic	No	N/A	Yes	N/A	
17	Democratic People's Republic of Korea*	No	N/A	Yes	N/A	
18	Denmark	No	N/A	Yes	N/A	
19	Ecuador*	No	N/A	Yes	N/A	
20	Egypt	No	N/A	Yes	N/A	
21	Estonia	No	N/A	Yes	N/A	
22	Ethiopia*	No	N/A	Yes	N/A	
23	Finland	No	N/A	Yes	N/A	
24	France	No	N/A	Yes	N/A	
25	Georgia	No	N/A	Yes	N/A	
26	Germany	No	N/A	Yes	N/A	
27	Greece	No	N/A	Yes	N/A	
28	Hong Kong (China)	No	N/A	Yes	N/A	
29	Hungary	No	N/A	Yes	N/A	
30	Iceland	No	N/A	Yes	N/A	
31	India	No	N/A	Yes	N/A	
32	Indonesia	No	N/A	Yes	N/A	
33	Iran*	No	N/A	Yes	N/A	
34	Ireland	No	N/A	Yes	N/A	
35	Israel	No	N/A	Yes	N/A	
36	Italy	No	N/A	Yes	N/A	
37	Japan	No	N/A	Yes	N/A	
38	Jordan	No	N/A	Yes	N/A	
39	Kazakhstan	No	N/A	Yes	N/A	
40	Korea	No	N/A	Yes	N/A	
41	Kuwait*	No	N/A	Yes	N/A	
42	Latvia	No	N/A	Yes	N/A	
43	Lebanon*	No	N/A	Yes	N/A	
44	Lithuania	No	N/A	Yes	N/A	
45	Luxembourg	No	N/A	Yes	N/A	
46	Malaysia	No	N/A	Yes	N/A	
47	Malta	No	N/A	Yes	N/A	
48	Mexico	No	N/A	Yes	N/A	
49	Moldova*	No	N/A	Yes	N/A	
50	Montenegro	No	N/A	Yes	N/A	
51	Morocco	No	N/A	Yes	N/A	
52	Namibia	No	N/A	Yes	N/A	
53	Netherlands	No	N/A	Yes	N/A	
54	Nigeria	No	N/A	Yes	N/A	
55	North Macedonia	No	N/A	Yes	N/A	
56	Norway	No	N/A	Yes	N/A	
57	Pakistan	No	N/A	Yes	N/A	
58	Philippines*	No	N/A	Yes	N/A	
59	Poland	No	N/A	Yes	N/A	
60	Portugal	No	N/A	Yes	N/A	
61	Qatar	No	N/A	Yes	N/A	
62	Russia	No	N/A	Yes	N/A	
63	San Marino	No	N/A	Yes	N/A	
64	Saudi Arabia	No	N/A	Yes	N/A	
65	Serbia	No	N/A	Yes	N/A	

66	Singapore	No	N/A	Yes	N/A	
67	Slovak Republic	No	N/A	Yes	N/A	
68	Slovenia	No	N/A	Yes	N/A	
69	South Africa	No	N/A	Yes	N/A	
70	Spain	No	N/A	Yes	PPT alone	
71	Sri Lanka	No	N/A	Yes	N/A	
72	Sudan*	No	N/A	Yes	N/A	
73	Sweden	No	N/A	Yes	N/A	
74	Switzerland	No	N/A	Yes	N/A	
75	Syrian Arab Republic*	No	N/A	Yes	N/A	
76	Tajikistan*	No	N/A	Yes	N/A	
77	Thailand	No	N/A	Yes	N/A	
78	Tunisia	No	N/A	Yes	N/A	
79	Turkey	No	N/A	Yes	N/A	
80	Turkmenistan*	No	N/A	Yes	N/A	
81	Ukraine	No	N/A	Yes	N/A	
82	United Arab Emirates	No	N/A	Yes	N/A	
83	United Kingdom	No	N/A	Yes	N/A	
84	United States	No	N/A	Yes	N/A	
85	Uruguay	No	N/A	Yes	N/A	
86	Uzbekistan*	No	N/A	Yes	N/A	
87	Viet Nam	No	N/A	Yes	N/A	
88	Zambia	No	N/A	Yes	N/A	

Russian Federation

A. Progress in the implementation of the minimum standard

The Russian Federation has 85 tax agreements in force, as reported in its response to the Peer Review questionnaire. Two of those agreements, the agreements with Japan and Sweden, comply with the minimum standard.

The Russian Federation signed the MLI in 2017 and deposited its instrument of ratification on 18 June 2019. The MLI entered into force for Russia on 1 October 2019. The Russian Federation has not listed its agreements with Brazil, Germany, Namibia, North Macedonia and Switzerland but indicated in its response to the Peer Review questionnaire that bilateral negotiations would be used with respect to its agreements with Brazil, Germany and Switzerland. These agreements will therefore not, at this stage, be modified by the MLI. North Macedonia has listed its agreement with the Russian Federation under the MLI.

The Russian Federation has made a reservation under the MLI that delays its entry into effect after completing its internal procedures for this purpose for each of its listed agreements.[117] The Russian Federation notified that it completed its internal procedures for the entry into effect of the MLI with respect to its agreements with Australia, Austria, Belgium (old), Canada, Denmark, Finland, France, Iceland, India, Ireland, Israel, Latvia, Lithuania, Luxembourg, Malta, the Netherlands, New Zealand, Norway, Poland, Qatar, Serbia, Singapore, the Slovak Republic, Slovenia, Ukraine, the United Arab Emirates and the United Kingdom on 30 April 2020, and with respect to its agreements with Cyprus*, the Czech Republic, Indonesia, Kazakhstan, Korea, Portugal and Saudi Arabia on 26 November 2020.

The Russian Federation is implementing the minimum standard through the inclusion of the preamble statement and the PPT combined with the LOB.[118]

The agreements that will be modified by the MLI will come into compliance with the minimum standard once the provisions of the MLI take effect.

B. Implementation issues

As mentioned above, the Russian Federation has not listed its agreements with Namibia and North Macedonia under the MLI. Listing the agreements under the MLI or entering into bilateral renegotiations to implement the minimum standard would ensure that the minimum standard could be implemented in those non-covered agreements.

Summary of the jurisdiction response – Russian Federation

	Treaty partners	Compliance with the standard	If compliant, the alternative implemented	Signature of a complying instrument	The alternative implemented through the complying instrument (if not the MLI)	Comments
1	Albania	No	N/A	Yes	N/A	

[117] The reservation was made under Article 35(7)(a) of the MLI.

[118] For its agreements listed under the MLI, the Russian Federation is implementing the preamble statement (Article 6 of the MLI) and the PPT (Article 7 of the MLI). The Russian Federation also opted for the simplified LOB under Article 7(6) of the MLI.

2	Algeria*	No	N/A	Yes	N/A	
3	Argentina	No	N/A	Yes	N/A	
4	Armenia	No	N/A	Yes	N/A	
5	Australia	No	N/A	Yes	N/A	
6	Austria	No	N/A	Yes	N/A	
7	Azerbaijan*	No	N/A	Yes	N/A	
8	Belarus*	No	N/A	Yes	N/A	
9	Belgium (old)	No	N/A	Yes	N/A	
10	Botswana	No	N/A	Yes	N/A	
11	Brazil	No	N/A	No	N/A	
12	Bulgaria	No	N/A	Yes	N/A	
13	Canada	No	N/A	Yes	N/A	
14	Chile	No	N/A	Yes	N/A	
15	China (People's Republic of)	No	N/A	Yes	N/A	
16	Croatia	No	N/A	Yes	N/A	
17	Cuba*	No	N/A	Yes	N/A	
18	Cyprus*	No	N/A	Yes	N/A	
19	Czech Republic	No	N/A	Yes	N/A	
20	Democratic People's Republic of Korea*	No	N/A	No	N/A	
21	Denmark	No	N/A	Yes	N/A	
22	Ecuador*	No	N/A	Yes	N/A	
23	Egypt	No	N/A	Yes	N/A	
24	Finland	No	N/A	Yes	N/A	
25	France	No	N/A	Yes	N/A	
26	Germany	No	N/A	No	N/A	
27	Greece	No	N/A	Yes	N/A	
28	Hong Kong (China)	No	N/A	Yes	N/A	
29	Hungary	No	N/A	Yes	N/A	
30	Iceland	No	N/A	Yes	N/A	
31	India	No	N/A	Yes	N/A	
32	Indonesia	No	N/A	Yes	N/A	
33	Iran*	No	N/A	No	N/A	
34	Ireland	No	N/A	Yes	N/A	
35	Israel	No	N/A	Yes	N/A	
36	Italy	No	N/A	Yes	N/A	
37	Japan	Yes	PPT and LOB	N/A	N/A	
38	Kazakhstan	No	N/A	Yes	N/A	
39	Korea	No	N/A	Yes	N/A	
40	Kuwait*	No	N/A	Yes	N/A	
41	Kyrgyzstan*	No	N/A	No	N/A	
42	Latvia	No	N/A	Yes	N/A	
43	Lebanon*	No	N/A	Yes	N/A	
44	Lithuania	No	N/A	Yes	N/A	
45	Luxembourg	No	N/A	Yes	N/A	
46	Malaysia	No	N/A	Yes	N/A	
47	Mali*	No	N/A	No	N/A	
48	Malta	No	N/A	Yes	N/A	
49	Mexico	No	N/A	Yes	N/A	
50	Moldova*	No	N/A	Yes	N/A	
51	Mongolia	No	N/A	Yes	N/A	
52	Montenegro	No	N/A	Yes	N/A	

53	Morocco	No	N/A	Yes	N/A	
54	Namibia	No	N/A	No	N/A	
55	Netherlands	No	N/A	Yes	N/A	
56	New Zealand	No	N/A	Yes	N/A	
57	North Macedonia	No	N/A	No	N/A	
58	Norway	No	N/A	Yes	N/A	
59	Philippines*	No	N/A	Yes	N/A	
60	Poland	No	N/A	Yes	N/A	
61	Portugal	No	N/A	Yes	N/A	
62	Qatar	No	N/A	Yes	N/A	
63	Romania	No	N/A	Yes	N/A	
64	Saudi Arabia	No	N/A	Yes	N/A	
65	Serbia	No	N/A	Yes	N/A	
66	Singapore	No	N/A	Yes	N/A	
67	Slovak Republic	No	N/A	Yes	N/A	
68	Slovenia	No	N/A	Yes	N/A	
69	South Africa	No	N/A	Yes	N/A	
70	Spain	No	N/A	Yes	N/A	
71	Sri Lanka	No	N/A	Yes	N/A	
72	Sweden	Yes	PPT alone	N/A	N/A	
73	Switzerland	No	N/A	No	N/A	
74	Syrian Arab Republic*	No	N/A	No	N/A	
75	Tajikistan*	No	N/A	No	N/A	
76	Thailand	No	N/A	Yes	N/A	
77	Turkey	No	N/A	Yes	N/A	
78	Turkmenistan*	No	N/A	No	N/A	
79	Ukraine	No	N/A	Yes	N/A	
80	United Arab Emirates	No	N/A	Yes	N/A	
81	United Kingdom	No	N/A	Yes	N/A	
82	United States	No	N/A	Yes	N/A	
83	Uzbekistan*	No	N/A	No	N/A	
84	Venezuela*	No	N/A	Yes	N/A	
85	Viet Nam	No	N/A	Yes	N/A	

Saint Kitts and Nevis

A. Progress in the implementation of the minimum standard

Saint Kitts and Nevis has five tax agreements in force, as reported in its response to the Peer Review questionnaire, including the multilateral agreement among the members of the CARICOM concluded with ten treaty partners (the CARICOM Agreement).[119]

None of Saint Kitts and Nevis' agreements comply with the minimum standard or are subject to a complying instrument.

Saint Kitts and Nevis has not signed the MLI.

B. Implementation issues

As Saint Kitts and Nevis has not signed the MLI or implemented anti-treaty-shopping measures in its agreements, the Secretariat will offer its support to design a plan for the implementation of the minimum standard to strengthen its network of agreements.

Saint Kitts and Nevis is encouraged to bring the CARICOM Agreement up to date by commencing talks among all the treaty partners.[120]

Summary of the jurisdiction response – Saint Kitts and Nevis

	Treaty partners	Compliance with the standard	If compliant, the alternative implemented	Signature of a complying instrument	The alternative implemented through the complying instrument (if not the MLI)	Comments
1	Antigua and Barbuda	No	N/A	No	N/A	CARICOM
2	Barbados	No	N/A	No	N/A	CARICOM
3	Belize	No	N/A	No	N/A	CARICOM
4	Dominica	No	N/A	No	N/A	CARICOM
5	Grenada	No	N/A	No	N/A	CARICOM
6	Guyana*	No	N/A	No	N/A	CARICOM
7	Jamaica	No	N/A	No	N/A	CARICOM
8	Monaco	No	N/A	No	N/A	
9	Saint Lucia	No	N/A	No	N/A	CARICOM
10	Saint Vincent and the Grenadines	No	N/A	No	N/A	CARICOM
11	San Marino	No	N/A	No	N/A	
12	Switzerland	No	N/A	No	N/A	
13	Trinidad and Tobago	No	N/A	No	N/A	CARICOM
14	United Kingdom	No	N/A	No	N/A	

119 In total, Saint Kitts and Nevis identified 14 "agreements" in its List of Tax agreements: four bilateral agreements and the CARICOM Agreement concluded with ten of its treaty partners.

120 Revisions to the CARICOM Agreement require an agreement from its eleven treaty partners.

Saint Lucia

A. Progress in the implementation of the minimum standard

Saint Lucia has two tax agreements, including the multilateral agreement among the members of the CARICOM concluded with ten treaty partners (the CARICOM Agreement).[121]

Neither of Saint Lucia's agreements comply with the minimum standard or are subject to a complying instrument.

Saint Lucia has not signed the MLI.

Saint Lucia indicated in its response to the Peer Review questionnaire that it contacted Switzerland in late 2019 to discuss revising their agreement.

B. Implementation issues

As Saint Lucia has not signed the MLI or implemented anti-treaty-shopping measures in its agreements, the Secretariat will offer its support to design a plan for the implementation of the minimum standard to strengthen its network of agreements.

Saint Lucia is encouraged to bring the CARICOM Agreement up to date by commencing talks among all the treaty partners.[122]

Summary of the jurisdiction response – Saint Lucia

	Treaty partners	Compliance with the standard	If compliant, the alternative implemented	Signature of a complying instrument	The alternative implemented through the complying instrument (if not the MLI)	Comments
1	Antigua and Barbuda	No	N/A	No	N/A	CARICOM
2	Barbados	No	N/A	No	N/A	CARICOM
3	Belize	No	N/A	No	N/A	CARICOM
4	Dominica	No	N/A	No	N/A	CARICOM
5	Grenada	No	N/A	No	N/A	CARICOM
6	Guyana*	No	N/A	No	N/A	CARICOM
7	Jamaica	No	N/A	No	N/A	CARICOM
8	Saint Kitts and Nevis	No	N/A	No	N/A	CARICOM
9	Saint Vincent and the Grenadines	No	N/A	No	N/A	CARICOM
10	Switzerland	No	N/A	No	N/A	
11	Trinidad and Tobago	No	N/A	No	N/A	CARICOM

[121] In total, Saint Lucia identified 11 "agreements" in its List of Tax agreements: one bilateral agreement and the CARICOM Agreement concluded with ten of its treaty partners.

[122] Revisions to the CARICOM Agreement require an agreement from its eleven treaty partners.

Saint Vincent and the Grenadines

A. Progress in the implementation of the minimum standard

Saint Vincent and the Grenadines has two tax agreements, as reported in its response to the Peer Review questionnaire, including the multilateral agreement among the members of the CARICOM concluded with ten treaty partners (the CARICOM Agreement).[123]

Neither of Saint Vincent and the Grenadines' agreements comply with the minimum standard or are subject to a complying instrument.

Saint Vincent and the Grenadines has not signed the MLI.

B. Implementation issues

As Saint Vincent and the Grenadines has not signed the MLI or implemented anti-treaty-shopping measures in its agreements, the Secretariat will offer its support to design a plan for the implementation of the minimum standard to strengthen its network of agreements.

Saint Vincent and the Grenadines is encouraged to bring the CARICOM Agreement up to date by commencing talks among all the treaty partners.[124]

Summary of the jurisdiction response – Saint Vincent and the Grenadines

	Treaty partners	Compliance with the standard	If compliant, the alternative implemented	Signature of a complying instrument	The alternative implemented through the complying instrument (if not the MLI)	Comments
1	Antigua and Barbuda	No	N/A	No	N/A	CARICOM
2	Barbados	No	N/A	No	N/A	CARICOM
3	Belize	No	N/A	No	N/A	CARICOM
4	Dominica	No	N/A	No	N/A	CARICOM
5	Grenada	No	N/A	No	N/A	CARICOM
6	Guyana*	No	N/A	No	N/A	CARICOM
7	Jamaica	No	N/A	No	N/A	CARICOM
8	Saint Kitts and Nevis	No	N/A	No	N/A	CARICOM
9	Saint Lucia	No	N/A	No	N/A	CARICOM
10	Switzerland	No	N/A	No	N/A	
11	Trinidad and Tobago	No	N/A	No	N/A	CARICOM

[123] In total, Saint Vincent and the Grenadines identified eleven "agreements" in its List of Tax agreements: one bilateral agreement and the CARICOM Agreement concluded with ten of its treaty partners.

[124] Revisions to the CARICOM Agreement require an agreement from its eleven treaty partners.

San Marino

A. Progress in the implementation of the minimum standard

San Marino has 23 tax agreements in force, as reported in its response to the Peer Review questionnaire. One of those agreements, the agreement with Serbia, complies with the minimum standard.

San Marino signed the MLI in 2017 and deposited its instrument of ratification on 11 March 2020, listing its non-compliant agreements. The MLI will enter into force for San Marino on 1 July 2020.

San Marino is implementing the minimum standard through the inclusion of the preamble statement and the PPT.[125]

The agreements that will be modified by the MLI will come into compliance with the minimum standard once the provisions of the MLI take effect.

B. Implementation issues

No jurisdiction has raised any concerns about their agreements with San Marino.

Summary of the jurisdiction response – San Marino

	Treaty partners	Compliance with the standard	If compliant, the alternative implemented	Signature of a complying instrument	The alternative implemented through the complying instrument (if not the MLI)	Comments
1	Austria	No	N/A	Yes	N/A	The treaty partner has not listed this agreement in its MLI position.
2	Azerbaijan*	No	N/A	Yes	N/A	Partial compliance (the treaty just lacks the new preamble).
3	Barbados	No	N/A	Yes	N/A	Partial compliance (the treaty just lacks the new preamble).
4	Belgium	No	N/A	Yes	N/A	
5	Croatia	No	N/A	Yes	N/A	
6	Cyprus*	No	N/A	Yes	N/A	
7	Georgia	No	N/A	Yes	N/A	
8	Greece	No	N/A	Yes	N/A	
9	Hungary	No	N/A	Yes	N/A	
10	Italy	No	N/A	Yes	N/A	Partial compliance (the treaty just lacks the new preamble)
11	Liechtenstein	No	N/A	Yes	N/A	
12	Luxembourg	No	N/A	Yes	N/A	

[125] For its agreements listed under the MLI, San Marino is implementing the preamble statement (Article 6 of the MLI). For 19 of its agreements listed under the MLI, San Marino is implementing the PPT (Article 7 of the MLI). San Marino made a reservation pursuant to Article 7(15)(b) of the MLI not to apply Article 7(1) of the MLI with respect to agreements which already contain a PPT. Three of San Marino's agreements are within the scope of this reservation.

13	Malaysia	No	N/A	Yes	N/A	
14	Malta	No	N/A	Yes	N/A	
15	Portugal	No	N/A	Yes	N/A	
16	Qatar	No	N/A	Yes	N/A	
17	Romania	No	N/A	Yes	N/A	
18	Saint Kitts and Nevis	No	N/A	Yes	N/A	
19	Serbia	Yes	PPT alone	N/A	N/A	
20	Seychelles	No	N/A	Yes	N/A	
21	Singapore	No	N/A	Yes	N/A	
22	United Arab Emirates	No	N/A	Yes	N/A	The treaty partner has not listed this agreement in its MLI position.
23	Viet Nam	No	N/A	Yes	N/A	

Saudi Arabia

A. Progress in the implementation of the minimum standard

Saudi Arabia has 51 tax agreements in force, as reported in its response to the Peer Review questionnaire. Two of those agreements, the agreements with Bulgaria and the United Arab Emirates, comply with the minimum standard.

Saudi Arabia signed the MLI in 2018 and deposited its instrument of ratification on 23 January 2020, listing its non-compliant agreements. The MLI entered into force for Saudi Arabia on 1 May 2020.

Saudi Arabia is implementing the minimum standard through the inclusion of the preamble statement and the PPT.[126]

The agreements that will be modified by the MLI will come into compliance with the minimum standard once the provisions of the MLI take effect.

B. Implementation issues

No jurisdiction has raised any concerns about their agreements with Saudi Arabia.

Summary of the jurisdiction response – Saudi Arabia

	Treaty partners	Compliance with the standard	If compliant, the alternative implemented	Signature of a complying instrument	The alternative implemented through the complying instrument (if not the MLI)	Comments
1	Albania	No	N/A	Yes	N/A	
2	Algeria*	No	N/A	Yes	N/A	
3	Austria	No	N/A	Yes	N/A	
4	Azerbaijan*	No	N/A	Yes	N/A	
5	Bangladesh*	No	N/A	Yes	N/A	
6	Belarus*	No	N/A	Yes	N/A	
7	Bulgaria	Yes	PPT alone	N/A	N/A	
8	China (People's Republic of)	No	N/A	Yes	N/A	
9	Cyprus*	No	N/A	Yes	N/A	
10	Czech Republic	No	N/A	Yes	N/A	
11	Egypt	No	N/A	Yes	N/A	
12	Ethiopia*	No	N/A	Yes	N/A	
13	France	No	N/A	Yes	N/A	
14	Georgia	No	N/A	Yes	N/A	
15	Greece	No	N/A	Yes	N/A	
16	Hong Kong (China)	No	N/A	Yes	N/A	
17	Hungary	No	N/A	Yes	N/A	
18	India	No	N/A	Yes	N/A	
19	Ireland	No	N/A	Yes	N/A	

[126] For its agreements listed under the MLI, Saudi Arabia is implementing the preamble statement (Article 6 of the MLI) and the PPT (Article 7 of the MLI).

20	Italy	No	N/A	Yes	N/A	
21	Japan	No	N/A	Yes	N/A	
22	Jordan	No	N/A	Yes	N/A	
23	Kazakhstan	No	N/A	Yes	N/A	
24	Korea	No	N/A	Yes	N/A	
25	Kyrgyzstan*	No	N/A	Yes	N/A	
26	Luxembourg	No	N/A	Yes	N/A	
27	Malaysia	No	N/A	Yes	N/A	
28	Malta	No	N/A	Yes	N/A	
29	Mexico	No	N/A	Yes	N/A	
30	Netherlands	No	N/A	Yes	N/A	
31	North Macedonia	No	N/A	Yes	N/A	
32	Pakistan	No	N/A	Yes	N/A	
33	Poland	No	N/A	Yes	N/A	
34	Portugal	No	N/A	Yes	N/A	
35	Romania	No	N/A	Yes	N/A	
36	Russia	No	N/A	Yes	N/A	
37	Singapore	No	N/A	Yes	N/A	
38	South Africa	No	N/A	Yes	N/A	
39	Spain	No	N/A	Yes	N/A	
40	Sweden	No	N/A	Yes	N/A	
41	Syrian Arab Republic*	No	N/A	Yes	N/A	
42	Tajikistan*	No	N/A	Yes	N/A	
43	Tunisia	No	N/A	Yes	N/A	
44	Turkey	No	N/A	Yes	N/A	
45	Turkmenistan*	No	N/A	Yes	N/A	
46	Ukraine	No	N/A	Yes	N/A	
47	United Arab Emirates	Yes	PPT alone	N/A	N/A	
48	United Kingdom	No	N/A	Yes	N/A	
49	Uzbekistan*	No	N/A	Yes	N/A	
50	Venezuela*	No	N/A	Yes	N/A	
51	Viet Nam	No	N/A	Yes	N/A	

Senegal

A. Progress in the implementation of the minimum standard

Senegal has 18 tax agreements in force, as reported in its response to the Peer Review questionnaire, including the multilateral Regulation 08/2008/COM adopting the rules for the avoidance of double taxation within the West African Economic and Monetary Union and the rule for assistance in tax matters (the UEMOA) concluded with seven partners. [127] One of those agreements, the agreement with Luxembourg, complies with the minimum standard.

Senegal signed the MLI in 2017, listing its non-compliant bilateral agreements.

Senegal indicated in its response to the Peer Review questionnaire that the UEMOA has not been listed under the MLI as it is a regulation of the West African Economic and Monetary Union.

Senegal is implementing the minimum standard through the inclusion of the preamble statement and the PPT combined with the LOB.[128]

The agreements that will be modified by the MLI will come into compliance with the minimum standard once the provisions of the MLI take effect.

B. Implementation issues

Senegal's listed agreements under the MLI will start to be compliant after Senegal's ratification of the MLI. Senegal is encouraged to ratify the MLI as soon as possible. Senegal indicated that a bill for the ratification of the MLI that had been approved by its Council of Ministers on 14 October 2020 would be submitted to its Parliament in 2020. Senegal further indicated that it expected to deposit its instrument of ratification of the MLI in 2021.

Senegal is encouraged to consider entering into bilateral renegotiations with respect to the UEMOA to implement the minimum standard.

Summary of the jurisdiction response – Senegal

	Treaty partners	Compliance with the standard	If compliant, the alternative implemented	Signature of a complying instrument	The alternative implemented through the complying instrument (if not the MLI)	Comments
1	Belgium	No	N/A	Yes	N/A	
2	Benin	No	N/A	No	N/A	UEMOA
3	Burkina Faso	No	N/A	No	N/A	UEMOA
4	Canada	No	N/A	Yes	N/A	
5	Chinese Taipei*	No	N/A	No	N/A	
6	Côte d'Ivoire	No	N/A	No	N/A	UEMOA

[127] Règlement n°08/2008/CM des pays de l'Union économique et monétaire Ouest Africaine (UEMOA) du 26 septembre 2008 portant adoption des règles visant à éviter la double imposition au sein de l'UEMOA et des règles d'assistance en matière fiscale. In total, Senegal identified 24 "agreements" in its List of Tax agreements: 17 bilateral agreements and the UEMOA with seven partners

[128] For its agreements listed under the MLI, Senegal is implementing the preamble statement (Article 6 of the MLI) and the PPT (Article 7 of the MLI). Senegal also opted for the simplified LOB under Article 7(6) of the MLI and stated that, while it accepts the application of the PPT under the MLI, it intends where possible to adopt an LOB provision through bilateral negotiation.

7	France	No	N/A	Yes	N/A	
8	Guinea-Bissau*	No	N/A	No	N/A	UEMOA
9	Italy	No	N/A	Yes	N/A	
10	Lebanon*	No	N/A	Yes	N/A	
11	Luxembourg	Yes	PPT alone	N/A	N/A	
12	Malaysia	No	N/A	Yes	N/A	
13	Mali*	No	N/A	No	N/A	UEMOA
14	Mauritania*	No	N/A	Yes	N/A	
15	Morocco	No	N/A	Yes	N/A	
16	Niger*	No	N/A	No	N/A	UEMOA
17	Norway	No	N/A	Yes	N/A	
18	Portugal	No	N/A	Yes	N/A	
19	Qatar	No	N/A	Yes	N/A	
20	Spain	No	N/A	Yes	N/A	
21	Togo*	No	N/A	No	N/A	UEMOA
22	Tunisia	No	N/A	Yes	N/A	
23	United Arab Emirates	No	N/A	Yes	N/A	
24	United Kingdom	No	N/A	Yes	N/A	

Serbia

A. Progress in the implementation of the minimum standard

Serbia has 60 tax agreements in force, as reported in its response to the Peer Review questionnaire. 22 of those agreements, the agreements with Austria, Belgium, Canada, Denmark, Finland, France, Georgia, India, Ireland, Israel, Lithuania, Luxembourg, Malta, the Netherlands, Norway, Poland, San Marino, the Slovak Republic, Slovenia, Ukraine, the United Arab Emirates and the United Kingdom, comply with the minimum standard.

Serbia signed the MLI in 2017 and deposited its instrument of ratification on 5 June 2018, listing its non-compliant agreements. The MLI has entered into force for Serbia on 1 October 2018.

Serbia is implementing the minimum standard through the inclusion of the preamble statement and the PPT.[129]

The agreements modified by the MLI come into compliance with the minimum standard once the provisions of the MLI take effect.

B. Implementation issues

No jurisdiction has raised any concerns about their agreements with Serbia.

Summary of the jurisdiction response - Serbia

	Treaty partners	Compliance with the standard	If compliant, the alternative implemented	Signature of a complying instrument	The alternative implemented through the complying instrument (if not the MLI)	Comments
1	Albania	No	N/A	Yes	N/A	
2	Armenia	No	N/A	Yes	N/A	
3	Austria	Yes	PPT alone	N/A	N/A	
4	Azerbaijan*	No	N/A	Yes	N/A	
5	Belarus*	No	N/A	Yes	N/A	
6	Belgium	Yes	PPT alone	N/A	N/A	
7	Bosnia-Herzegovina	No	N/A	Yes	N/A	
8	Bulgaria	No	N/A	Yes	N/A	
9	Canada	Yes	PPT alone	N/A	N/A	
10	China (People's Republic of)	No	N/A	Yes	N/A	
11	Croatia	No	N/A	Yes	N/A	
12	Cyprus*	No	N/A	Yes	N/A	
13	Czech Republic	No	N/A	Yes	N/A	
14	Democratic	No	N/A	Yes	N/A	

[129] For its agreements listed under the MLI, Serbia is implementing the preamble statement (Article 6 of the MLI) and the PPT (Article 7 of the MLI).

	People's Republic of Korea*					
15	Denmark	Yes	PPT alone	N/A	N/A	
16	Egypt	No	N/A	Yes	N/A	
17	Estonia	No	N/A	Yes	N/A	
18	Finland	Yes	PPT alone	N/A	N/A	
19	France	Yes	PPT alone	N/A	N/A	
20	Georgia	Yes	PPT alone	N/A	N/A	
21	Germany	No	N/A	Yes	N/A	
22	Greece	No	N/A	Yes	N/A	
23	Hungary	No	N/A	Yes	N/A	
24	India	Yes	PPT alone	N/A	N/A	
25	Indonesia	No	N/A	Yes	N/A	
26	Iran*	No	N/A	Yes	N/A	
27	Ireland	Yes	PPT alone	N/A	N/A	
28	Israel	Yes	PPT alone	N/A	N/A	
29	Italy	No	N/A	Yes	N/A	
30	Kazakhstan	No	N/A	Yes	N/A	
31	Korea	No	N/A	Yes	N/A	
32	Kuwait*	No	N/A	Yes	N/A	
33	Latvia	No	N/A	Yes	N/A	
34	Libya*	No	N/A	Yes	N/A	
35	Lithuania	Yes	PPT alone	N/A	N/A	
36	Luxembourg	Yes	PPT alone	N/A	N/A	
37	Malta	Yes	PPT alone	N/A	N/A	
38	Moldova*	No	N/A	Yes	N/A	
39	Montenegro	No	N/A	Yes	N/A	
40	Netherlands	Yes	PPT alone	N/A	N/A	
41	North Macedonia	No	N/A	Yes	N/A	
42	Norway	Yes	PPT alone	N/A	N/A	
43	Pakistan	No	N/A	Yes	N/A	
44	Poland	Yes	PPT alone	N/A	N/A	
45	Qatar	No	N/A	Yes	N/A	
46	Romania	No	N/A	Yes	N/A	
47	Russia	No	N/A	Yes	N/A	
48	San Marino	Yes	PPT alone	N/A	N/A	
49	Slovak Republic	Yes	PPT alone	N/A	N/A	
50	Slovenia	Yes	PPT alone	N/A	N/A	
51	Spain	No	N/A	Yes	N/A	
52	Sri Lanka	No	N/A	Yes	N/A	
53	Sweden	No	N/A	Yes	N/A	
54	Switzerland	No	N/A	Yes	N/A	
55	Tunisia	No	N/A	Yes	N/A	
56	Turkey	No	N/A	Yes	N/A	
57	Ukraine	Yes	PPT alone	N/A	N/A	
58	United Arab Emirates	Yes	PPT alone	N/A	N/A	
59	United Kingdom	Yes	PPT alone	N/A	N/A	
60	Viet Nam	No	N/A	Yes	N/A	

Seychelles

A. Progress in the implementation of the minimum standard

The Seychelles has 28 tax agreements in force, as reported in its response to the Peer Review questionnaire.

The Seychelles signed the MLI in 2017, listing its non-compliant agreements.

The Seychelles is implementing the minimum standard through the inclusion of the preamble statement and the PPT.[130]

The agreements that will be modified by the MLI will come into compliance with the minimum standard once the provisions of the MLI take effect.

B. Implementation issues

The Seychelles' listed agreements under the MLI will start to be compliant after the Seychelles' ratification of the MLI. The Seychelles is encouraged to ratify the MLI as soon as possible.

Summary of the jurisdiction response - Seychelles

	Treaty partners	Compliance with the standard	If compliant, the alternative implemented	Signature of a complying instrument	The alternative implemented through the complying instrument (if not the MLI)	Comments
1	Bahrain	No	N/A	Yes	N/A	
2	Barbados	No	N/A	Yes	N/A	
3	Belgium	No	N/A	Yes	N/A	
4	Bermuda	No	N/A	Yes	N/A	
5	Botswana	No	N/A	Yes	N/A	
6	China (People's Republic of)	No	N/A	Yes	N/A	
7	Cyprus*	No	N/A	Yes	N/A	
8	Eswatini	No	N/A	Yes	N/A	
9	Ethiopia*	No	N/A	Yes	N/A	
10	Guernsey	No	N/A	Yes	N/A	
11	Indonesia	No	N/A	Yes	N/A	
12	Isle of Man	No	N/A	Yes	N/A	
13	Jersey	No	N/A	Yes	N/A	
14	Kenya	No	N/A	Yes	N/A	
15	Luxembourg	No	N/A	Yes	N/A	
16	Malaysia	No	N/A	Yes	N/A	
17	Mauritius	No	N/A	Yes	N/A	
18	Monaco	No	N/A	Yes	N/A	
19	Oman	No	N/A	Yes	N/A	

130 For its agreements listed under the MLI, the Seychelles is implementing the preamble statement (Article 6 of the MLI) and the PPT (Article 7 of the MLI). The Seychelles expressed a statement that while it accepts the application of the PPT under the MLI, it intends where possible to adopt an LOB provision through bilateral negotiation.

20	Qatar	No	N/A	Yes	N/A	
21	San Marino	No	N/A	Yes	N/A	
22	Singapore	No	N/A	Yes	N/A	
23	South Africa	No	N/A	Yes	N/A	
24	Sri Lanka	No	N/A	Yes	N/A	
25	Thailand	No	N/A	Yes	N/A	
26	United Arab Emirates	No	N/A	Yes	N/A	
27	Viet Nam	No	N/A	Yes	N/A	
28	Zambia	No	N/A	Yes	N/A	

Sierra Leone

A. Progress in the implementation of the minimum standard

Sierra Leone has three tax agreements in force, as reported in its response to the Peer Review questionnaire.

None of Sierra Leone's agreements comply with the minimum standard or are subject to a complying instrument.

Sierra Leone has not signed the MLI.

B. Implementation issues

As Sierra Leone has not signed the MLI or implemented anti-treaty-shopping measures in its agreements, the Secretariat will offer its support to design a plan for the implementation of the minimum standard to strengthen its network of agreements.

Summary of the jurisdiction response – Sierra Leone

	Treaty partners	Compliance with the standard	If compliant, the alternative implemented	Signature of a complying instrument	The alternative implemented through the complying instrument (if not the MLI)	Comments
1	Norway	No	N/A	No	N/A	
2	South Africa	No	N/A	No	N/A	
3	United Kingdom	No	N/A	No	N/A	

Singapore

A. Progress in the implementation of the minimum standard

Singapore has 88 tax agreements in force, as reported in its response to the Peer Review questionnaire. 28 of those agreements, the agreement with Australia, Austria, Belgium, Canada, Denmark, Finland, France, Georgia, Guernsey, India, Ireland, the Isle of Man, Israel, Japan, Jersey, Korea, Lithuania, Luxembourg, Malta, the Netherlands, New Zealand, Poland, the Slovak Republic, Slovenia, Turkmenistan*, Ukraine, the United Arab Emirates, and the United Kingdom, comply with the minimum standard[131].

Singapore signed the MLI in 2017 and deposited its instrument of ratification on 21 December 2018. The MLI entered into force for Singapore on 1 April 2019.

Singapore is implementing the minimum standard in its tax agreements through the inclusion of the preamble statement and the PPT.[132]

The agreements modified by the MLI come into compliance with the minimum standard once the provisions of the MLI take effect.

B. Implementation issues

No jurisdiction has raised any concerns about their agreements with Singapore.

Summary of the jurisdiction response - Singapore

	Treaty partners	Compliance with the standard	If compliant, the alternative implemented	Signature of a complying instrument	The alternative implemented through the complying instrument (if not the MLI)	Comments
1	Albania	No	N/A	Yes	N/A	Singapore has included this treaty to be covered by MLI. However, treaty partner has not ratified MLI.
2	Australia	Yes	PPT alone	N/A	N/A	
3	Austria	Yes	PPT alone	N/A	N/A	
4	Bahrain	No	N/A	Yes	N/A	Singapore has included this treaty to be covered by MLI. However, treaty partner has not signed MLI.
5	Bangladesh*	No	N/A	Yes	N/A	Singapore has included this treaty to be covered by MLI. Treaty partner is not an IF member and has not

[131] Out of the 28 tax agreements, 26 are amended via the MLI, one is a new agreement signed with a new partner (Turkmenistan*), and one is a revised agreement signed with an existing partner (Korea).

[132] For its agreements listed under the MLI, Singapore is implementing the preamble statement (Article 6 of the MLI) and the PPT (Article 7 of the MLI).

						signed MLI. (See Note 1)
6	Barbados	No	N/A	Yes	N/A	Singapore has included this treaty to be covered by MLI. However, treaty partner has not ratified MLI.
7	Belarus*	No	N/A	Yes	N/A	Singapore has included this treaty to be covered by MLI. Treaty partner is not an IF member and has not signed MLI. (See Note 1)
8	Belgium	Yes	PPT alone	N/A	N/A	
9	Brunei Darussalam	No	N/A	Yes	N/A	Singapore has included this treaty to be covered by MLI. However, treaty partner has not signed MLI.
10	Bulgaria	No	N/A	Yes	N/A	Singapore has included this treaty to be covered by MLI. However, treaty partner has not ratified MLI.
11	Cambodia*	No	N/A	Yes	N/A	Singapore has included this treaty to be covered by MLI. Treaty partner is not an IF member and has not signed MLI. (See Note 1)
12	Canada	Yes	PPT alone	N/A	N/A	
13	China (People's Republic of)	No	N/A	Yes	N/A	Singapore has included this treaty to be covered by MLI. However, treaty partner has not ratified MLI.
14	Chinese Taipei*	No	N/A	No	N/A	Treaty partner is not an IF member and has not signed MLI. (See Note 1)
15	Cyprus*	No	N/A	Yes	N/A	MLI will enter into effect after 30 June 2020.
16	Czech Republic	No	N/A	Yes	N/A	MLI will enter into force after 30 June 2020.
17	Denmark	Yes	PPT alone	N/A	N/A	
18	Ecuador*	No	N/A	Yes	N/A	Singapore has included this treaty to be covered by MLI. Treaty partner is not an IF member and has not signed MLI. (See Note 1)
19	Egypt	No	N/A	Yes	N/A	Singapore has included this treaty to be covered by MLI. However, treaty partner has not ratified MLI.
20	Estonia	No	N/A	Yes	N/A	Singapore has included this treaty to be covered by MLI. However, treaty partner has not ratified MLI.
21	Ethiopia*	No	N/A	Yes	N/A	Singapore has included this treaty to be covered by MLI. Treaty partner is not an IF member and has not signed MLI. (See Note 1)
22	Fiji*	No	N/A	Yes	N/A	Singapore has included

						this treaty to be covered by MLI. Treaty partner is not an IF member and has not ratified MLI.
23	Finland	Yes	PPT alone	N/A	N/A	
24	France	Yes	PPT alone	N/A	N/A	
25	Georgia	Yes	PPT alone	N/A	N/A	
26	Germany	No	N/A	Yes	N/A	Singapore has included this treaty to be covered by MLI but this treaty has been excluded from MLI by treaty partner. Protocol with BEPS MS signed.
27	Ghana*	No	N/A	Yes	N/A	Singapore has included this treaty to be covered by MLI. Treaty partner is not an IF member and has not signed MLI. (See Note 1)
28	Guernsey	Yes	PPT alone	N/A	N/A	
29	Hungary	No	N/A	Yes	N/A	Singapore has included this treaty to be covered by MLI. However, treaty partner has not ratified MLI.
30	India	Yes	PPT alone	N/A	N/A	
31	Indonesia	No	N/A	Yes	N/A	MLI will enter into force after 30 June 2020. Revised treaty with MS signed.
32	Ireland	Yes	PPT alone	N/A	N/A	
33	Isle of Man	Yes	PPT alone	N/A	N/A	
34	Israel	Yes	PPT alone	N/A	N/A	
35	Italy	No	N/A	Yes	N/A	Singapore has included this treaty to be covered by MLI. However, treaty partner has not ratified MLI.
36	Japan	Yes	PPT alone	N/A	N/A	
37	Jersey	Yes	PPT alone	N/A	N/A	
38	Kazakhstan	No	N/A	Yes	N/A	Singapore has included this treaty to be covered by MLI. However, treaty partner has not ratified MLI.
39	Korea	Yes	PPT alone	N/A	N/A	
40	Kuwait*	No	N/A	Yes	N/A	Singapore has included this treaty to be covered by MLI. Treaty partner is not an IF member and has not ratified MLI.
41	Lao People's Democratic Republic*	No	N/A	Yes	N/A	Singapore has included this treaty to be covered by MLI. Treaty partner is not an IF member and has not signed MLI. (See Note 1)
42	Latvia	No	N/A	Yes	N/A	MLI will enter into effect after 30 June 2020.
43	Libya*	No	N/A	Yes	N/A	Singapore has included this treaty to be covered by MLI. Treaty partner is not an IF member and has not

						signed MLI. (See Note 1)
44	Liechtenstein	No	N/A	Yes	N/A	MLI will enter into effect after 30 June 2020.
45	Lithuania	Yes	PPT alone	N/A	N/A	
46	Luxembourg	Yes	PPT alone	N/A	N/A	
47	Malaysia	No	N/A	Yes	N/A	Singapore has included this treaty to be covered by MLI. However, treaty partner has not ratified MLI.
48	Malta	Yes	PPT alone	N/A	N/A	
49	Mauritius	No	N/A	Yes	N/A	MLI will enter into effect after 30 June 2020.
50	Mexico	No	N/A	Yes	N/A	Singapore has included this treaty to be covered by MLI. However, treaty partner has not ratified MLI.
51	Mongolia	No	N/A	Yes	N/A	Singapore has included this treaty to be covered by MLI. However, treaty partner has not signed MLI.
52	Morocco	No	N/A	Yes	N/A	Singapore has included this treaty to be covered by MLI. However, treaty partner has not ratified MLI.
53	Myanmar*	No	N/A	Yes	N/A	Singapore has included this treaty to be covered by MLI. Treaty partner is not an IF member and has not signed MLI. (See Note 1)
54	Netherlands	Yes	PPT alone	N/A	N/A	
55	New Zealand	Yes	PPT alone	N/A	N/A	
56	Nigeria	No	N/A	Yes	N/A	Singapore has included this treaty to be covered by MLI. However, treaty partner has not ratified MLI.
57	Norway	No	N/A	Yes	N/A	Singapore has included this treaty to be covered by MLI but this treaty has been excluded from MLI by treaty partner. (See Note 1)
58	Oman	No	N/A	Yes	N/A	Singapore has included this treaty to be covered by MLI. However, treaty partner has not ratified MLI.
59	Pakistan	No	N/A	Yes	N/A	Singapore has included this treaty to be covered by MLI. However, treaty partner has not ratified MLI.
60	Panama	No	N/A	Yes	N/A	Singapore has included this treaty to be covered by MLI. However, treaty partner has not ratified MLI.

61	Papua New Guinea	No	N/A	Yes	N/A	Singapore has included this treaty to be covered by MLI. However, treaty partner has not ratified MLI.
62	Philippines*	No	N/A	Yes	N/A	Singapore has included this treaty to be covered by MLI. Treaty partner is not an IF member and has not signed MLI. (See Note 1)
63	Poland	Yes	PPT alone	N/A	N/A	
64	Portugal	No	N/A	Yes	N/A	MLI will enter into effect after 30 June 2020.
65	Qatar	No	N/A	Yes	N/A	MLI will enter into effect after 30 June 2020.
66	Romania	No	N/A	Yes	N/A	Singapore has included this treaty to be covered by MLI. However, treaty partner has not ratified MLI.
67	Russia	No	N/A	Yes	N/A	MLI will enter into effect after 30 June 2020.
68	Rwanda*	No	N/A	Yes	N/A	Singapore has included this treaty to be covered by MLI. Treaty partner is not an IF member and has not signed MLI. (See Note 1)
69	San Marino	No	N/A	Yes	N/A	MLI will enter into force after 30 June 2020.
70	Saudi Arabia	No	N/A	Yes	N/A	MLI will enter into effect after 30 June 2020.
71	Seychelles	No	N/A	Yes	N/A	Singapore has included this treaty to be covered by MLI. However, treaty partner has not ratified MLI.
72	Slovak Republic	Yes	PPT alone	N/A	N/A	
73	Slovenia	Yes	PPT alone	N/A	N/A	
74	South Africa	No	N/A	Yes	N/A	Singapore has included this treaty to be covered by MLI. However, treaty partner has not ratified MLI.
75	Spain	No	N/A	Yes	N/A	Singapore has included this treaty to be covered by MLI. However, treaty partner has not ratified MLI.
76	Sri Lanka	No	N/A	Yes	N/A	Singapore has included this treaty to be covered by MLI. However, treaty partner has not signed MLI.
77	Sweden	No	N/A	Yes	N/A	Singapore has included this treaty to be covered by MLI but this treaty has been excluded from MLI by treaty partner. (See Note 1)
78	Switzerland	No	N/A	Yes	N/A	Singapore has included this treaty to be covered by MLI but this treaty has

						been excluded from MLI by treaty partner. (See Note 1)
79	Thailand	No	N/A	Yes	N/A	Singapore has included this treaty to be covered by MLI. However, treaty partner has not signed MLI.
80	Tunisia	No	N/A	Yes	N/A	Singapore has included this treaty to be covered by MLI. However, treaty partner has not ratified MLI and has not included this treaty to be covered by MLI. Singapore has approached treaty partner to include treaty in its instrument of ratification for the MLI.
81	Turkey	No	N/A	Yes	N/A	Singapore has included this treaty to be covered by MLI. However, treaty partner has not ratified MLI.
82	Turkmenistan*	Yes	PPT alone	N/A	N/A	
83	Ukraine	Yes	PPT alone	N/A	N/A	
84	United Arab Emirates	Yes	PPT alone	N/A	N/A	
85	United Kingdom	Yes	PPT alone	N/A	N/A	
86	Uruguay	No	N/A	Yes	N/A	MLI will enter into effect after 30 June 2020.
87	Uzbekistan*	No	N/A	Yes	N/A	Singapore has included this treaty to be covered by MLI. Treaty partner is not an IF member and has not signed MLI. (See Note 1)
88	Viet Nam	No	N/A	Yes	N/A	Singapore has included this treaty to be covered by MLI. However, treaty partner has not signed MLI.

Note: Discussion to incorporate BEPS MS in treaty is pending / on-going / concluded.

Slovak Republic

A. Progress in the implementation of the minimum standard

The Slovak Republic has 70 tax agreements in force, as reported in its response to the Peer Review questionnaire. Twenty-three of those agreements, the agreements with Australia, Austria, Belgium, Canada, Denmark, Finland, France, Georgia, Iceland, India, Ireland, Israel, Japan, Lithuania, Luxembourg, Malta, the Netherlands, Poland, Serbia, Singapore, Slovenia, Ukraine and the United Kingdom, comply with the minimum standard.

The Slovak Republic signed the MLI in 2017 and deposited its instrument of ratification on 20 September 2018. The MLI entered into force for the Slovak Republic on 1 January 2019. The Slovak Republic has not listed its agreements with Armenia, Mongolia and the United Arab Emirates but indicated in its response to the Peer Review questionnaire that bilateral negotiations would be used with respect to those agreements. Armenia and the United Arab Emirates have listed their agreements with the Slovak Republic under the MLI.

The Slovak Republic is implementing the minimum standard through the inclusion of the preamble statement and the PPT, combined with the LOB.[133]

The agreements modified by the MLI come into compliance with the minimum standard once the provisions of the MLI take effect.

B. Implementation issues

No jurisdiction has raised any concerns about their agreements with the Slovak Republic.

Summary of the jurisdiction response – Slovak Republic

	Treaty partners	Compliance with the standard	If compliant, the alternative implemented	Signature of a complying instrument	The alternative implemented through the complying instrument (if not the MLI)	Comments
1	Armenia	No	N/A	No	N/A	
2	Australia	Yes	PPT alone	N/A	N/A	
3	Austria	Yes	PPT alone	N/A	N/A	
4	Belarus*	No	N/A	Yes	N/A	
5	Belgium	Yes	PPT alone	N/A	N/A	
6	Bosnia-Herzegovina	No	N/A	Yes	N/A	
7	Brazil	No	N/A	Yes	N/A	
8	Bulgaria	No	N/A	Yes	N/A	
9	Canada	Yes	PPT alone	N/A	N/A	
10	China (People's Republic of)	No	N/A	Yes	N/A	
11	Chinese Taipei*	No	N/A	No	N/A	

[133] For its agreements listed under the MLI, the Slovak Republic is implementing the preamble statement (Article 6 of the MLI) and the PPT (Article 7 of the MLI). The Slovak Republic also opted for the simplified LOB under Article 7(6) of the MLI.

12	Croatia	No	N/A	Yes	N/A	
13	Cyprus*	No	N/A	Yes	N/A	
14	Czech Republic	No	N/A	Yes	N/A	
15	Denmark	Yes	PPT and LOB	N/A	N/A	
16	Estonia	No	N/A	Yes	N/A	
17	Ethiopia*	No	N/A	No	N/A	
18	Finland	Yes	PPT alone	N/A	N/A	
19	France	Yes	PPT alone	N/A	N/A	
20	Georgia	Yes	PPT alone	N/A	N/A	
21	Germany	No	N/A	Yes	N/A	
22	Greece	No	N/A	Yes	N/A	
23	Hungary	No	N/A	Yes	N/A	
24	Iceland	Yes	PPT and LOB	N/A	N/A	
25	India	Yes	PPT and LOB	N/A	N/A	
26	Indonesia	No	N/A	Yes	N/A	
27	Iran*	No	N/A	No	N/A	
28	Ireland	Yes	PPT alone	N/A	N/A	
29	Israel	Yes	PPT alone	N/A	N/A	
30	Italy	No	N/A	Yes	N/A	
31	Japan	Yes	PPT alone	N/A	N/A	
32	Kazakhstan	No	N/A	Yes	N/A	
33	Korea	No	N/A	Yes	N/A	
34	Kuwait*	No	N/A	Yes	N/A	
35	Latvia	No	N/A	Yes	N/A	
36	Libya*	No	N/A	Yes	N/A	
37	Lithuania	Yes	PPT alone	N/A	N/A	
38	Luxembourg	Yes	PPT alone	N/A	N/A	
39	Malaysia	No	N/A	Yes	N/A	
40	Malta	Yes	PPT alone	N/A	N/A	
41	Mexico	No	N/A	Yes	N/A	
42	Moldova*	No	N/A	Yes	N/A	
43	Mongolia	No	N/A	No	N/A	
44	Montenegro	No	N/A	Yes	N/A	
45	Netherlands	Yes	PPT alone	N/A	N/A	
46	Nigeria	No	N/A	Yes	N/A	
47	North Macedonia	No	N/A	Yes	N/A	
48	Norway	No	N/A	Yes	N/A	
49	Poland	Yes	PPT alone	N/A	N/A	
50	Portugal	No	N/A	Yes	N/A	
51	Romania	No	N/A	Yes	N/A	
52	Russia	No	N/A	Yes	N/A	
53	Serbia	Yes	PPT alone	N/A	N/A	
54	Singapore	Yes	PPT alone	N/A	N/A	
55	Slovenia	Yes	PPT alone	N/A	N/A	
56	South Africa	No	N/A	Yes	N/A	
57	Spain	No	N/A	Yes	N/A	
58	Sri Lanka	No	N/A	Yes	N/A	
59	Sweden	No	N/A	Yes	N/A	
60	Switzerland	No	N/A	Yes	N/A	
61	Syrian Arab Republic*	No	N/A	Yes	N/A	
62	Tunisia	No	N/A	Yes	N/A	
63	Turkey	No	N/A	Yes	N/A	
64	Turkmenistan*	No	N/A	Yes	N/A	

65	Ukraine	Yes	PPT alone	N/A	N/A	
66	United Arab Emirates	No	N/A	No	N/A	
67	United Kingdom	Yes	PPT alone	N/A	N/A	
68	United States	No	N/A	Yes	N/A	
69	Uzbekistan*	No	N/A	Yes	N/A	
70	Viet Nam	No	N/A	Yes	N/A	

Slovenia

A. Progress in the implementation of the minimum standard

Slovenia has 59 tax agreements in force, as reported in its response to the Peer Review questionnaire. Twenty-four of those agreements, the agreements with Austria, Belgium, Canada, Denmark, Finland, France, Georgia, Iceland, India, Ireland, Israel, Japan, Lithuania, Luxembourg, Malta, the Netherlands, Norway, Poland, Serbia, Singapore, the Slovak Republic, Ukraine, the United Arab Emirates and the United Kingdom, comply with the minimum standard.

Slovenia signed the MLI in 2017 and deposited its instrument of ratification of the MLI on 22 March 2018. The MLI entered into force for Slovenia on 1 July 2018. Slovenia has not listed its agreements with Germany, Montenegro and Sweden but indicated in its response to the Peer Review questionnaire that bilateral negotiations would be used with respect to those agreements

Slovenia is implementing the minimum standard through the inclusion of the preamble statement and the PPT.[134]

The agreements modified by the MLI come into compliance with the minimum standard once the provisions of the MLI take effect.

B. Implementation issues

No jurisdiction has raised any concerns about their agreements with Slovenia.

Summary of the jurisdiction response - Slovenia

	Treaty partners	Compliance with the standard	If compliant, the alternative implemented	Signature of a complying instrument	The alternative implemented through the complying instrument (if not the MLI)	Comments
1	Albania	No	N/A	Yes	N/A	
2	Armenia	No	N/A	Yes	N/A	
3	Austria	Yes	PPT alone	N/A	N/A	
4	Azerbaijan*	No	N/A	Yes	N/A	
5	Belarus*	No	N/A	Yes	N/A	
6	Belgium	Yes	PPT alone	N/A	N/A	
7	Bosnia-Herzegovina	No	N/A	Yes	N/A	
8	Bulgaria	No	N/A	Yes	N/A	
9	Canada	Yes	PPT alone	N/A	N/A	
10	China (People's Republic of)	No	N/A	Yes	N/A	
11	Croatia	No	N/A	Yes	N/A	
12	Cyprus*	No	N/A	Yes	N/A	
13	Czech Republic	No	N/A	Yes	N/A	
14	Denmark	Yes	PPT alone	N/A	N/A	

[134] For its agreements listed under the MLI, Slovenia is implementing the preamble statement (Article 6 of the MLI) and the PPT (Article 7 of the MLI).

15	Estonia	No	N/A	Yes	N/A	
16	Finland	Yes	PPT alone	N/A	N/A	
17	France	Yes	PPT alone	N/A	N/A	
18	Georgia	Yes	PPT alone	N/A	N/A	
19	Germany	No	N/A	No	N/A	
20	Greece	No	N/A	Yes	N/A	
21	Hungary	No	N/A	Yes	N/A	
22	Iceland	Yes	PPT alone	N/A	N/A	
23	India	Yes	PPT/alone	N/A	N/A	
24	Iran*	No	N/A	Yes	N/A	
25	Ireland	Yes	PPT alone	N/A	N/A	
26	Israel	Yes	PPT alone	N/A	N/A	
27	Italy	No	N/A	Yes	N/A	
28	Japan	Yes	PPT alone	N/A	N/A	
29	Kazakhstan	No	N/A	Yes	N/A	
30	Korea	No	N/A	Yes	N/A	
31	Kosovo*	No	N/A	Yes	N/A	
32	Kuwait*	No	N/A	Yes	N/A	
33	Latvia	No	N/A	Yes	N/A	
34	Lithuania	Yes	PPT alone	N/A	N/A	
35	Luxembourg	Yes	PPT alone	N/A	N/A	
36	Malta	Yes	PPT alone	N/A	N/A	
37	Moldova*	No	N/A	Yes	N/A	
38	Montenegro	No	N/A	No	N/A	
39	Netherlands	Yes	PPT alone	N/A	N/A	
40	North Macedonia	No	N/A	Yes	N/A	
41	Norway	Yes	PPT alone	N/A	N/A	
42	Poland	Yes	PPT alone	N/A	N/A	
43	Portugal	No	N/A	Yes	N/A	
44	Qatar	No	N/A	Yes	N/A	
45	Romania	No	N/A	Yes	N/A	
46	Russia	No	N/A	Yes	N/A	
47	Serbia	Yes	PPT alone	N/A	N/A	
48	Singapore	Yes	PPT alone	N/A	N/A	
49	Slovak Republic	Yes	PPT alone	N/A	N/A	
50	Spain	No	N/A	Yes	N/A	
51	Sweden	No	N/A	No	N/A	
52	Switzerland	No	N/A	Yes	N/A	
53	Thailand	No	N/A	Yes	N/A	
54	Turkey	No	N/A	Yes	N/A	
55	Ukraine	Yes	PPT alone	N/A	N/A	
56	United Arab Emirates	Yes	PPT alone	N/A	N/A	
57	United Kingdom	Yes	PPT alone	N/A	N/A	
58	United States	No	N/A	Yes	N/A	
59	Uzbekistan*	No	N/A	Yes	N/A	

South Africa

A. Progress in the implementation of the minimum standard

South Africa has 79 tax agreements in force, as reported in its response to the Peer Review questionnaire.

South Africa signed the MLI in 2017 and has not listed its agreements with Germany, Grenada, Sierra Leone and Zambia. It indicated in its response to the Peer Review questionnaire that bilateral negotiations would be used with respect to its agreements with Brazil, Germany and Zambia. These agreements will therefore not, at this stage, be modified by the MLI.

South Africa is implementing the minimum standard through the inclusion of the preamble statement and the PPT.[135]

The agreements that will be modified by the MLI will come into compliance with the minimum standard once the provisions of the MLI take effect.

B. Implementation issues

South Africa's listed agreements under the MLI will start to be compliant after South Africa' ratification of the MLI. South Africa is encouraged to ratify the MLI as soon as possible.

As mentioned above, South Africa has not listed its agreements with Grenada and Sierra Leone under the MLI. Listing the agreements under the MLI or entering into bilateral renegotiations to implement the minimum standard would ensure that the minimum standard could be implemented in those non-covered agreements.

Summary of the jurisdiction response – South Africa

	Treaty partners	Compliance with the standard	If compliant, the alternative implemented	Signature of a complying instrument	The alternative implemented through the complying instrument (if not the MLI)	Comments
1	Algeria*	No	N/A	Yes	N/A	
2	Australia	No	N/A	Yes	N/A	
3	Austria	No	N/A	Yes	N/A	
4	Belarus*	No	N/A	Yes	N/A	
5	Belgium	No	N/A	Yes	N/A	
6	Botswana	No	N/A	Yes	N/A	
7	Brazil	No	N/A	Yes	N/A	
8	Bulgaria	No	N/A	Yes	N/A	
9	Cameroon	No	N/A	Yes	N/A	
10	Canada	No	N/A	Yes	N/A	
11	Chile	No	N/A	Yes	N/A	
12	China (People's Republic of)	No	N/A	Yes	N/A	
13	Chinese Taipei*	No	N/A	Yes	N/A	

[135] For its agreements listed under the MLI, South Africa is implementing the preamble statement (Article 6 of the MLI) and the PPT (Article 7 of the MLI).

14	Croatia	No	N/A	Yes	N/A	
15	Cyprus*	No	N/A	Yes	N/A	
16	Czech Republic	No	N/A	Yes	N/A	
17	Democratic Republic of the Congo	No	N/A	Yes	N/A	
18	Denmark	No	N/A	Yes	N/A	
19	Egypt	No	N/A	Yes	N/A	
20	Eswatini	No	N/A	Yes	N/A	
21	Ethiopia*	No	N/A	Yes	N/A	
22	Finland	No	N/A	Yes	N/A	
23	France	No	N/A	Yes	N/A	
24	Germany	No	N/A	No	N/A	
25	Ghana*	No	N/A	Yes	N/A	
26	Greece	No	N/A	Yes	N/A	
27	Grenada	No	N/A	No	N/A	
28	Hong Kong (China)	No	N/A	Yes	N/A	
29	Hungary	No	N/A	Yes	N/A	
30	India	No	N/A	Yes	N/A	
31	Indonesia	No	N/A	Yes	N/A	
32	Iran*	No	N/A	Yes	N/A	
33	Ireland	No	N/A	Yes	N/A	
34	Israel	No	N/A	Yes	N/A	
35	Italy	No	N/A	Yes	N/A	
36	Japan	No	N/A	Yes	N/A	
37	Kenya	No	N/A	Yes	N/A	
38	Korea	No	N/A	Yes	N/A	
39	Kuwait*	No	N/A	Yes	N/A	
40	Lesotho*	No	N/A	Yes	N/A	
41	Luxembourg	No	N/A	Yes	N/A	
42	Malawi*	No	N/A	No	N/A	
43	Malaysia	No	N/A	Yes	N/A	
44	Malta	No	N/A	Yes	N/A	
45	Mauritius	No	N/A	Yes	N/A	
46	Mexico	No	N/A	Yes	N/A	
47	Mozambique*	No	N/A	Yes	N/A	
48	Namibia	No	N/A	Yes	N/A	
49	Netherlands	No	N/A	Yes	N/A	
50	New Zealand	No	N/A	Yes	N/A	
51	Nigeria	No	N/A	Yes	N/A	
52	Norway	No	N/A	Yes	N/A	
53	Oman	No	N/A	Yes	N/A	
54	Pakistan	No	N/A	Yes	N/A	
55	Poland	No	N/A	Yes	N/A	
56	Portugal	No	N/A	Yes	N/A	
57	Qatar	No	N/A	Yes	N/A	
58	Romania	No	N/A	Yes	N/A	
59	Russia	No	N/A	Yes	N/A	
60	Rwanda*	No	N/A	Yes	N/A	
61	Saudi Arabia	No	N/A	Yes	N/A	
62	Seychelles	No	N/A	Yes	N/A	
63	Sierra Leone	No	N/A	No	N/A	
64	Singapore	No	N/A	Yes	N/A	
65	Slovak Republic	No	N/A	Yes	N/A	

66	Spain	No	N/A	Yes	N/A	
67	Sweden	No	N/A	Yes	N/A	
68	Switzerland	No	N/A	Yes	N/A	
69	Tanzania*	No	N/A	Yes	N/A	
70	Thailand	No	N/A	Yes	N/A	
71	Tunisia	No	N/A	Yes	N/A	
72	Turkey	No	N/A	Yes	N/A	
73	Uganda*	No	N/A	Yes	N/A	
74	Ukraine	No	N/A	Yes	N/A	
75	United Arab Emirates	No	N/A	Yes	N/A	
76	United Kingdom	No	N/A	Yes	N/A	
77	United States	No	N/A	Yes	N/A	
78	Zambia	No	N/A	No	N/A	
79	Zimbabwe*	No	N/A	Yes	N/A	

Spain

A. Progress in the implementation of the minimum standard

Spain has 92 tax agreements in force, as reported in its response to the Peer Review questionnaire. One of those agreements, the agreement with Mexico complies with the minimum standard.

Spain signed the MLI in 2017 and has not listed its agreements with China (People's Republic of), Japan, the Netherlands, Norway, Sweden and Ukraine. It indicated in its response to the Peer Review questionnaire that bilateral negotiations would be used with respect to those agreements. Ukraine has listed their agreements with Spain under the MLI.

Spain is implementing the minimum standard in its tax agreements through the inclusion of the preamble statement and the PPT, combined with the LOB for its agreement with Japan.[136]

The agreements that will be modified by the MLI will come into compliance with the minimum standard once the provisions of the MLI take effect.

B. Implementation issues

Spain's listed agreements under the MLI will start to be compliant after Spain's ratification of the MLI. Spain is encouraged to ratify the MLI as soon as possible. Spain indicated that the MLI was approved by its Parliament. Spain further indicated that it expected to deposit its instrument of ratification of the MLI in early 2021.

Summary of the jurisdiction response - Spain

	Treaty partners	Compliance with the standard	If compliant, the alternative implemented	Signature of a complying instrument	The alternative implemented through the complying instrument (if not the MLI)	Comments
1	Albania	No	N/A	Yes	N/A	
2	Algeria*	No	N/A	Yes	N/A	
3	Andorra	No	N/A	Yes	N/A	
4	Argentina	No	N/A	Yes	N/A	
5	Armenia	No	N/A	Yes	N/A	
6	Australia	No	N/A	Yes	N/A	
7	Austria	No	N/A	Yes	N/A	
8	Barbados	No	N/A	Yes	N/A	
9	Belgium	No	N/A	Yes	N/A	
10	Bolivia*	No	N/A	Yes	N/A	
11	Bosnia-Herzegovina	No	N/A	Yes	N/A	
12	Brazil	No	N/A	Yes	N/A	
13	Bulgaria	No	N/A	Yes	N/A	

[136] For 87 of its agreements listed under the MLI, Spain is implementing the preamble statement (Article 6 of the MLI). For 86 of its agreements listed under the MLI, Spain is implementing the PPT (Article 7 of the MLI). Spain made a reservation pursuant to Article 6(4) and Article 7(15)(b) of the MLI and three of Spain's agreements are within the scope of this reservation (the agreements with Andorra, Mexico and Romania).

14	Canada	No	N/A	Yes	N/A	
15	Chile	No	N/A	Yes	N/A	
16	China (People's Republic of)	No	N/A	Yes	PPT alone	
17	Colombia	No	N/A	Yes	N/A	
18	Costa Rica	No	N/A	Yes	N/A	
19	Croatia	No	N/A	Yes	N/A	
20	Cuba*	No	N/A	Yes	N/A	
21	Cyprus*	No	N/A	Yes	N/A	
22	Czech Republic	No	N/A	Yes	N/A	
23	Dominican Republic	No	N/A	Yes	N/A	
24	Ecuador*	No	N/A	Yes	N/A	
25	Egypt	No	N/A	Yes	N/A	
26	El Salvador*	No	N/A	Yes	N/A	
27	Estonia	No	N/A	Yes	N/A	
28	Finland	No	N/A	Yes	N/A	
29	France	No	N/A	Yes	N/A	
30	Georgia	No	N/A	Yes	N/A	
31	Germany	No	N/A	Yes	N/A	
32	Greece	No	N/A	Yes	N/A	
33	Hong Kong (China)	No	N/A	Yes	N/A	
34	Hungary	No	N/A	Yes	N/A	
35	Iceland	No	N/A	Yes	N/A	
36	India	No	N/A	Yes	N/A	
37	Indonesia	No	N/A	Yes	N/A	
38	Iran*	No	N/A	Yes	N/A	
39	Ireland	No	N/A	Yes	N/A	
40	Israel	No	N/A	Yes	N/A	
41	Italy	No	N/A	Yes	N/A	
42	Jamaica	No	N/A	Yes	N/A	
43	Japan	No	N/A	Yes	PPT and LOB	
44	Kazakhstan	No	N/A	Yes	N/A	
45	Korea	No	N/A	Yes	N/A	
46	Kuwait*	No	N/A	Yes	N/A	
47	Kyrgyzstan*	No	N/A	Yes	N/A	
48	Latvia	No	N/A	Yes	N/A	
49	Lithuania	No	N/A	Yes	N/A	
50	Luxembourg	No	N/A	Yes	N/A	
51	Malaysia	No	N/A	Yes	N/A	
52	Malta	No	N/A	Yes	N/A	
53	Mexico	Yes	PPT alone	N/A	N/A	
54	Moldova*	No	N/A	Yes	N/A	
55	Morocco	No	N/A	Yes	N/A	
56	Netherlands	No	N/A	No	N/A	
57	New Zealand	No	N/A	Yes	N/A	
58	Nigeria	No	N/A	Yes	N/A	
59	North Macedonia	No	N/A	Yes	N/A	
60	Norway	No	N/A	No	N/A	
61	Oman	No	N/A	Yes	N/A	
62	Pakistan	No	N/A	Yes	N/A	
63	Panama	No	N/A	Yes	N/A	
64	Philippines*	No	N/A	Yes	N/A	
65	Poland	No	N/A	Yes	N/A	

66	Portugal	No	N/A	Yes	N/A
67	Qatar	No	N/A	Yes	N/A
68	Romania	No	N/A	Yes	PPT alone
69	Russia	No	N/A	Yes	N/A
70	Saudi Arabia	No	N/A	Yes	N/A
71	Senegal	No	N/A	Yes	N/A
72	Serbia	No	N/A	Yes	N/A
73	Singapore	No	N/A	Yes	N/A
74	Slovak Republic	No	N/A	Yes	N/A
75	Slovenia	No	N/A	Yes	N/A
76	South Africa	No	N/A	Yes	N/A
77	Sweden	No	N/A	No	N/A
78	Switzerland	No	N/A	Yes	N/A
79	Tajikistan*	No	N/A	Yes	N/A
80	Thailand	No	N/A	Yes	N/A
81	Trinidad and Tobago	No	N/A	Yes	N/A
82	Tunisia	No	N/A	Yes	N/A
83	Turkey	No	N/A	Yes	N/A
84	Turkmenistan*	No	N/A	Yes	N/A
85	Ukraine	No	N/A	No	N/A
86	United Arab Emirates	No	N/A	Yes	N/A
87	United Kingdom	No	N/A	Yes	N/A
88	United States	No	N/A	Yes	N/A
89	Uruguay	No	N/A	Yes	N/A
90	Uzbekistan*	No	N/A	Yes	N/A
91	Venezuela*	No	N/A	Yes	N/A
92	Viet Nam	No	N/A	Yes	N/A

Sri Lanka

A. Progress in the implementation of the minimum standard

Sri Lanka has 47 tax agreements in force, as reported in its response to the Peer Review questionnaire.

None of Sri Lanka's agreements comply with the minimum standard or are subject to a complying instrument.

Sri Lanka has not signed the MLI.

B. Implementation issues

As Sri Lanka has not signed the MLI or implemented anti-treaty-shopping measures in its agreements, the Secretariat will offer its support to design a plan for the implementation of the minimum standard to strengthen its network of agreements.

Summary of the jurisdiction response – Sri Lanka

	Treaty partners	Compliance with the standard	If compliant, the alternative implemented	Signature of a complying instrument	The alternative implemented through the complying instrument (if not the MLI)	Comments
1	Australia	No	N/A	No	N/A	
2	Bahrain	No	N/A	No	N/A	
3	Bangladesh*	No	N/A	No	N/A	
4	Belarus*	No	N/A	No	N/A	
5	Belgium	No	N/A	No	N/A	
6	Bosnia-Herzegovina	No	N/A	No	N/A	
7	Canada	No	N/A	No	N/A	
8	China (People's Republic of)	No	N/A	No	N/A	
9	Croatia	No	N/A	No	N/A	
10	Czech Republic	No	N/A	No	N/A	
11	Denmark	No	N/A	No	N/A	
12	Finland	No	N/A	No	N/A	
13	France	No	N/A	No	N/A	
14	Germany	No	N/A	No	N/A	
15	India	No	N/A	No	N/A	
16	Indonesia	No	N/A	No	N/A	
17	Iran*	No	N/A	No	N/A	
18	Italy	No	N/A	No	N/A	
19	Japan	No	N/A	No	N/A	
20	Korea	No	N/A	No	N/A	
21	Kuwait*	No	N/A	No	N/A	
22	Luxembourg	No	N/A	No	N/A	
23	Malaysia	No	N/A	No	N/A	
24	Mauritius	No	N/A	No	N/A	
25	Montenegro	No	N/A	No	N/A	

26	Nepal*	No	N/A	No	N/A	
27	Netherlands	No	N/A	No	N/A	
28	North Macedonia	No	N/A	No	N/A	
29	Norway	No	N/A	No	N/A	
30	Oman	No	N/A	No	N/A	
31	Pakistan	No	N/A	No	N/A	
32	Philippines*	No	N/A	No	N/A	
33	Poland	No	N/A	No	N/A	
34	Qatar	No	N/A	No	N/A	
35	Romania	No	N/A	No	N/A	
36	Russia	No	N/A	No	N/A	
37	Serbia	No	N/A	No	N/A	
38	Seychelles	No	N/A	No	N/A	
39	Singapore	No	N/A	No	N/A	
40	Slovak Republic	No	N/A	No	N/A	
41	Sweden	No	N/A	No	N/A	
42	Switzerland	No	N/A	No	N/A	
43	Thailand	No	N/A	No	N/A	
44	United Arab Emirates	No	N/A	No	N/A	
45	United Kingdom	No	N/A	No	N/A	
46	United States	No	N/A	No	N/A	
47	Viet Nam	No	N/A	No	N/A	

Sweden

A. Progress in the implementation of the minimum standard

Sweden has 81 tax agreements, as reported in its response to the Peer Review questionnaire, including the multilateral Nordic Convention concluded with Denmark, the Faroe Islands, Finland, Iceland and Norway (the "Nordic Convention").[137] Two of those agreements, the agreement with Russia and the Nordic Convention, comply with the minimum standard.

Sweden signed the MLI in 2017 and deposited its instrument of ratification on 22 June 2018. The MLI entered into force for Sweden on 1 October 2018. Sweden has not listed its agreements with Australia, Austria, Bosnia-Herzegovina, Brazil, Croatia, France, Germany, Montenegro, Portugal, Serbia, Singapore, Slovenia, Spain and Switzerland but indicated in its response to the Peer Review questionnaire that bilateral negotiations would be pursued with respect to its agreements with Brazil, Germany, Portugal Singapore, Slovenia, Spain and Switzerland. Australia, Bosnia-Herzegovina, Croatia, France, Portugal, Serbia and Singapore have listed their agreements with Sweden under the MLI.

The Parties to the Nordic Convention signed a complying instrument in 2018. The protocol entered into force on 28 November 2019 and its provisions took effect on 1 January 2020.

Sweden is implementing the minimum standard through the inclusion of the preamble statement and the PPT.[138]

The agreements that will be modified by the MLI will come into compliance with the minimum standard once the provisions of the MLI take effect.

B. Implementation issues

Sweden has made a reservation under the MLI that delays its entry into effect after completing its internal procedures for this purpose for each of its listed agreements.[139] Sweden has not yet notified that it had completed its internal procedures for any of its listed agreements.

As mentioned above, Sweden has not listed its agreements with Australia, Austria, Bosnia-Herzegovina, Croatia, France, Montenegro and Serbia under the MLI. Listing the agreements under the MLI or entering into bilateral renegotiations to implement the minimum standard would ensure that the minimum standard could be implemented in those non-covered agreements.

---

[137] See the Multilateral convention concluded by Denmark, Finland, the Faroe Islands, Iceland, Norway and Sweden: for the avoidance of double taxation with respect to taxes on income and on capital (1996, 1997, 2008 and 2018). In total, Sweden identified 85 "agreements" in its List of Tax agreements: 80 bilateral agreements and the Nordic Convention concluded with five of its treaty partners.

[138] For its agreements listed under the MLI, Sweden is implementing the preamble statement (Article 6 of the MLI) and the PPT (Article 7 of the MLI).

[139] The reservation was made under Article 35(7)(a) of the MLI.

Summary of the jurisdiction response - Sweden

	Treaty partners	Compliance with the standard	If compliant, the alternative implemented	Signature of a complying instrument	The alternative implemented through the complying instrument (if not the MLI)	Comments
1	Albania	No	N/A	Yes	N/A	
2	Argentina	No	N/A	Yes	N/A	
3	Armenia	No	N/A	Yes	N/A	
4	Australia	No	N/A	No	N/A	
5	Austria	No	N/A	No	N/A	
6	Azerbaijan*	No	N/A	Yes	N/A	
7	Bangladesh*	No	N/A	Yes	N/A	
8	Barbados	No	N/A	Yes	N/A	
9	Belarus*	No	N/A	Yes	N/A	
10	Belgium	No	N/A	Yes	N/A	
11	Bolivia*	No	N/A	Yes	N/A	
12	Bosnia-Herzegovina	No	N/A	No	N/A	
13	Botswana	No	N/A	Yes	N/A	
14	Brazil	No	N/A	Yes	PPT and LOB	
15	Bulgaria	No	N/A	Yes	N/A	
16	Canada	No	N/A	Yes	N/A	
17	Chile	No	N/A	Yes	N/A	
18	China (People's Republic of)	No	N/A	Yes	N/A	
19	Croatia	No	N/A	No	N/A	
20	Cyprus*	No	N/A	Yes	N/A	
21	Czech Republic	No	N/A	Yes	N/A	
22	Denmark	Yes	PPT alone	N/A	N/A	Nordic Convention
23	Egypt	No	N/A	Yes	N/A	
24	Estonia	No	N/A	Yes	N/A	
25	Faroe Islands	Yes	PPT alone	N/A	N/A	Nordic Convention
26	Finland	Yes	PPT alone	N/A	N/A	Nordic Convention
27	France	No	N/A	No	N/A	
28	Gambia*	No	N/A	Yes	N/A	
29	Georgia	No	N/A	Yes	N/A	
30	Germany	No	N/A	No	N/A	
31	Greece	No	N/A	Yes	N/A	
32	Hungary	No	N/A	Yes	N/A	
33	Iceland	Yes	PPT alone	N/A	N/A	Nordic Convention
34	India	No	N/A	Yes	N/A	
35	Indonesia	No	N/A	Yes	N/A	
36	Ireland	No	N/A	Yes	N/A	
37	Israel	No	N/A	Yes	N/A	
38	Italy	No	N/A	Yes	N/A	
39	Jamaica	No	N/A	Yes	N/A	
40	Japan	No	N/A	Yes	N/A	
41	Kazakhstan	No	N/A	Yes	N/A	
42	Kenya	No	N/A	Yes	N/A	
43	Korea	No	N/A	Yes	N/A	
44	Kosovo*	No	N/A	No	N/A	
45	Latvia	No	N/A	Yes	N/A	
46	Lithuania	No	N/A	Yes	N/A	

47	Luxembourg	No	N/A	Yes	N/A	
48	Malaysia	No	N/A	Yes	N/A	
49	Malta	No	N/A	Yes	N/A	
50	Mauritius	No	N/A	Yes	N/A	
51	Mexico	No	N/A	Yes	N/A	
52	Montenegro	No	N/A	No	N/A	
53	Namibia	No	N/A	Yes	N/A	
54	Netherlands	No	N/A	Yes	N/A	
55	New Zealand	No	N/A	Yes	N/A	
56	Nigeria	No	N/A	Yes	N/A	
57	North Macedonia	No	N/A	Yes	N/A	
58	Norway	Yes	PPT alone	N/A	N/A	Nordic Convention
59	Pakistan	No	N/A	Yes	N/A	
60	Philippines*	No	N/A	Yes	N/A	
61	Poland	No	N/A	Yes	N/A	
62	Portugal	No	N/A	Yes	PPT alone	
63	Romania	No	N/A	Yes	N/A	
64	Russia	Yes	PPT alone	N/A	N/A	
65	Saudi Arabia	No	N/A	Yes	N/A	
66	Serbia	No	N/A	No	N/A	
67	Singapore	No	N/A	No	N/A	
68	Slovak Republic	No	N/A	Yes	N/A	
69	Slovenia	No	N/A	No	N/A	
70	South Africa	No	N/A	Yes	N/A	
71	Spain	No	N/A	No	N/A	
72	Sri Lanka	No	N/A	Yes	N/A	
73	Switzerland	No	N/A	Yes	PPT alone	
74	Tanzania*	No	N/A	Yes	N/A	
75	Thailand	No	N/A	Yes	N/A	
76	Trinidad and Tobago	No	N/A	Yes	N/A	
77	Tunisia	No	N/A	Yes	N/A	
78	Turkey	No	N/A	Yes	N/A	
79	Ukraine	No	N/A	Yes	N/A	
80	United Kingdom	No	N/A	Yes	N/A	
81	United States	No	N/A	Yes	N/A	
82	Venezuela*	No	N/A	Yes	N/A	
83	Viet Nam	No	N/A	Yes	N/A	
84	Zambia	No	N/A	Yes	N/A	
85	Zimbabwe*	No	N/A	Yes	N/A	

Switzerland

A. Progress in the implementation of the minimum standard

Switzerland has 106 tax agreements in force, as reported in its response to the Peer Review questionnaire. Four of those agreements, the agreements with Kosovo*, Latvia, the United Kingdom and Zambia, comply with the minimum standard.

Switzerland signed the MLI in 2017 and deposited its instrument of ratification on 29 August 2019. The MLI entered into force for Switzerland on 1 December 2019. Switzerland has listed twelve of its agreements under the MLI and indicated in its response to the Peer Review questionnaire that it would only list an agreement under the MLI if it agrees with its treaty partner on how the MLI modifies their agreement. Switzerland considers that the MLI amends a covered tax agreement like an amending protocol. An agreement with the other contracting jurisdiction on the precise wording of the amendments to the corresponding tax agreement through the MLI is therefore a requirement for Switzerland to include a tax agreement under the MLI.

Switzerland indicated in its response to the Peer Review questionnaire that it has entered or intends to enter into bilateral negotiations with more than 40 of its treaty partners:

- Bilateral complying instruments have been signed with respect to its agreements with Iran*, Ireland, Korea, Kuwait*, the Netherlands, New Zealand, Norway, Sweden and Ukraine; and,
- Bilateral negotiations would be used with respect to agreements with Albania, Algeria*, Armenia, Australia, Belgium, Bulgaria, Canada, China (People's Republic of), Colombia, Côte d'Ivoire, Croatia, Cyprus*, Denmark, Egypt, Estonia, Finland, France, Georgia, Germany, Greece, Hong Kong (China), Hungary, India, Indonesia, Israel, Jamaica, Japan, Kazakhstan, Kyrgyzstan*, Liechtenstein, Malaysia, Malta, Mongolia, Montenegro, Morocco, North Macedonia, Oman, Pakistan, Peru, Poland, Qatar, Romania, Russia, Serbia, Singapore, the Slovak Republic, Slovenia, Spain, Sri Lanka, Thailand, Trinidad and Tobago, Tunisia, the United Arab Emirates, the United States, Uruguay and Viet Nam.[140]

Switzerland also mentioned that it considered that there was no concern for treaty shopping with respect to some of its treaty partners (Anguilla, Antigua and Barbuda, Barbados, Belize, British Virgin Islands, Dominica, Gambia*, Grenada, Malawi*, Montserrat, Saint Kitts and Nevis, Saint Lucia, and Saint Vincent and the Grenadines).

Switzerland has made a reservation under the MLI that delays its entry into effect after completing its internal procedures for this purpose for each of its listed agreements.[141] Switzerland notified that it completed its internal procedures for the entry into effect of the MLI with respect to its agreements with Luxembourg on 27 May 2020 and with respect to its agreements with the Czech Republic and Lithuania on 18 December 2020.

Switzerland is implementing the minimum standard through the inclusion of the preamble statement and the PPT.[142]

---

[140] Each of them has been contacted with a proposal for a protocol amending the tax agreement and corresponding negotiations have been suggested.

[141] The reservation was made under Article 35(7)(a) of the MLI.

[142] For its agreements listed under the MLI, Switzerland is implementing the preamble statement (Article 6 of the MLI) and the PPT (Article 7 of the MLI).

The agreements modified by the MLI come into compliance with the minimum standard once the provisions of the MLI take effect.

B. Implementation issues

No jurisdiction has raised any concerns about their agreements with Switzerland.

Summary of the jurisdiction response - Switzerland

	Treaty partners	Compliance with the standard	If compliant, the alternative implemented	Signature of a complying instrument	The alternative implemented through the complying instrument (if not the MLI)	Comments
1	Albania	No	N/A	No	N/A	
2	Algeria*	No	N/A	No	N/A	
3	Anguilla	No	N/A	No	N/A	
4	Antigua and Barbuda	No	N/A	No	N/A	
5	Argentina	No	N/A	Yes	N/A	
6	Armenia	No	N/A	No	N/A	
7	Australia	No	N/A	No	N/A	
8	Austria	No	N/A	Yes	N/A	
9	Azerbaijan*	No	N/A	No	N/A	
10	Bangladesh*	No	N/A	No	N/A	
11	Barbados	No	N/A	No	N/A	
12	Belarus*	No	N/A	No	N/A	
13	Belgium	No	N/A	No	N/A	
14	Belize	No	N/A	No	N/A	
15	British Virgin Islands	No	N/A	No	N/A	
16	Bulgaria	No	N/A	No	N/A	
17	Canada	No	N/A	No	N/A	
18	Chile	No	N/A	Yes	N/A	
19	China (People's Republic of)	No	N/A	No	N/A	
20	Chinese Taipei*	No	N/A	No	N/A	
21	Colombia	No	N/A	No	N/A	
22	Côte d'Ivoire	No	N/A	No	N/A	
23	Croatia	No	N/A	No	N/A	
24	Cyprus*	No	N/A	No	N/A	
25	Czech Republic	No	N/A	Yes	N/A	
26	Denmark	No	N/A	No	N/A	
27	Dominica	No	N/A	No	N/A	
28	Ecuador*	No	N/A	No	N/A	
29	Egypt	No	N/A	No	N/A	
30	Estonia	No	N/A	No	N/A	
31	Finland	No	N/A	No	N/A	
32	France	No	N/A	No	N/A	
33	Gambia*	No	N/A	No	N/A	
34	Georgia	No	N/A	No	N/A	
35	Germany	No	N/A	No	N/A	
36	Ghana*	No	N/A	No	N/A	

37	Greece	No	N/A	No	N/A	
38	Grenada	No	N/A	No	N/A	
39	Hong Kong (China)	No	N/A	No	N/A	
40	Hungary	No	N/A	No	N/A	
41	Iceland	No	N/A	Yes	N/A	
42	India	No	N/A	No	N/A	
43	Indonesia	No	N/A	No	N/A	
44	Iran*	No	N/A	Yes	PPT alone	
45	Ireland	No	N/A	Yes	PPT alone	
46	Israel	No	N/A	No	N/A	
47	Italy	No	N/A	Yes	N/A	
48	Jamaica	No	N/A	No	N/A	
49	Japan	No	N/A	No	N/A	
50	Kazakhstan	No	N/A	No	N/A	
51	Korea	No	N/A	Yes	PPT alone	
52	Kosovo*	Yes	PPT alone	N/A	N/A	
53	Kuwait*	No	N/A	Yes	PPT alone	
54	Kyrgyzstan*	No	N/A	No	N/A	
55	Latvia	Yes	PPT alone	N/A	N/A	
56	Liechtenstein	No	N/A	No	N/A	
57	Lithuania	No	N/A	Yes	N/A	
58	Luxembourg	No	N/A	Yes	N/A	
59	Malawi*	No	N/A	No	N/A	
60	Malaysia	No	N/A	No	N/A	
61	Malta	No	N/A	No	N/A	
62	Mexico	No	N/A	Yes	N/A	
63	Moldova*	No	N/A	No	N/A	
64	Mongolia	No	N/A	No	N/A	
65	Montenegro	No	N/A	No	N/A	
66	Montserrat	No	N/A	No	N/A	
67	Morocco	No	N/A	No	N/A	
68	Netherlands	No	N/A	Yes	PPT alone	
69	New Zealand	No	N/A	Yes	PPT alone	
70	North Macedonia	No	N/A	No	N/A	
71	Norway	No	N/A	Yes	PPT alone	
72	Oman	No	N/A	No	N/A	
73	Pakistan	No	N/A	No	N/A	PPT, but missing preamble
74	Peru	No	N/A	No	N/A	
75	Philippines*	No	N/A	No	N/A	
76	Poland	No	N/A	No	N/A	
77	Portugal	No	N/A	Yes	N/A	
78	Qatar	No	N/A	No	N/A	
79	Romania	No	N/A	No	N/A	
80	Russia	No	N/A	No	N/A	
81	Saint Kitts and Nevis	No	N/A	No	N/A	
82	Saint Lucia	No	N/A	No	N/A	
83	Saint Vincent and the Grenadines	No	N/A	No	N/A	
84	Serbia	No	N/A	No	N/A	
85	Singapore	No	N/A	No	N/A	
86	Slovak Republic	No	N/A	No	N/A	
87	Slovenia	No	N/A	No	N/A	

88	South Africa	No	N/A	Yes	N/A	
89	Spain	No	N/A	No	N/A	
90	Sri Lanka	No	N/A	No	N/A	
91	Sweden	No	N/A	Yes	PPT alone	
92	Tajikistan*	No	N/A	No	N/A	
93	Thailand	No	N/A	No	N/A	
94	Trinidad and Tobago	No	N/A	No	N/A	
95	Tunisia	No	N/A	No	N/A	
96	Turkey	No	N/A	Yes	N/A	
97	Turkmenistan*	No	N/A	No	N/A	
98	Ukraine	No	N/A	Yes	PPT alone	
99	United Arab Emirates	No	N/A	No	N/A	
100	United Kingdom	Yes	PPT alone	N/A	N/A	
101	United States	No	N/A	No	N/A	
102	Uruguay	No	N/A	No	N/A	
103	Uzbekistan*	No	N/A	No	N/A	
104	Venezuela*	No	N/A	No	N/A	
105	Viet Nam	No	N/A	No	N/A	
106	Zambia	Yes	PPT alone	N/A	N/A	

Thailand

A. Progress in the implementation of the minimum standard

Thailand has 61 tax agreements in force, as reported in its response to the Peer Review questionnaire.

None of Thailand's agreements comply with the minimum standard or are subject to a complying instrument.

Thailand has not signed the MLI.

Thailand indicated in its response to the Peer Review questionnaire that it is currently working towards signing the MLI.

B. Implementation issues

As Thailand has not signed the MLI or implemented anti-treaty-shopping measures in its agreements, the Secretariat will offer its support to design a plan for the implementation of the minimum standard to strengthen its network of agreements.

Summary of the jurisdiction response - Thailand

	Treaty partners	Compliance with the standard	If compliant, the alternative implemented	Signature of a complying instrument	The alternative implemented through the complying instrument (if not the MLI)	Comments
1	Armenia	No	N/A	No	N/A	
2	Australia	No	N/A	No	N/A	
3	Austria	No	N/A	No	N/A	
4	Bahrain	No	N/A	No	N/A	
5	Bangladesh*	No	N/A	No	N/A	
6	Belarus*	No	N/A	No	N/A	
7	Belgium	No	N/A	No	N/A	
8	Bulgaria	No	N/A	No	N/A	
9	Cambodia*	No	N/A	No	N/A	
10	Canada	No	N/A	No	N/A	
11	Chile	No	N/A	No	N/A	
12	China (People's Republic of)	No	N/A	No	N/A	
13	Chinese Taipei*	No	N/A	No	N/A	
14	Cyprus*	No	N/A	No	N/A	
15	Czech Republic	No	N/A	No	N/A	
16	Denmark	No	N/A	No	N/A	
17	Estonia	No	N/A	No	N/A	
18	Finland	No	N/A	No	N/A	
19	France	No	N/A	No	N/A	
20	Germany	No	N/A	No	N/A	
21	Hong Kong (China)	No	N/A	No	N/A	
22	Hungary	No	N/A	No	N/A	
23	India	No	N/A	No	N/A	

24	Indonesia	No	N/A	No	N/A	
25	Ireland	No	N/A	No	N/A	
26	Israel	No	N/A	No	N/A	
27	Italy	No	N/A	No	N/A	
28	Japan	No	N/A	No	N/A	
29	Korea	No	N/A	No	N/A	
30	Kuwait*	No	N/A	No	N/A	
31	Lao People's Democratic Republic*	No	N/A	No	N/A	
32	Luxembourg	No	N/A	No	N/A	
33	Malaysia	No	N/A	No	N/A	
34	Mauritius	No	N/A	No	N/A	
35	Myanmar*	No	N/A	No	N/A	
36	Nepal*	No	N/A	No	N/A	
37	Netherlands	No	N/A	No	N/A	
38	New Zealand	No	N/A	No	N/A	
39	Norway	No	N/A	No	N/A	
40	Oman	No	N/A	No	N/A	
41	Pakistan	No	N/A	No	N/A	
42	Philippines*	No	N/A	No	N/A	
43	Poland	No	N/A	No	N/A	
44	Romania	No	N/A	No	N/A	
45	Russia	No	N/A	No	N/A	
46	Seychelles	No	N/A	No	N/A	
47	Singapore	No	N/A	No	N/A	
48	Slovenia	No	N/A	No	N/A	
49	South Africa	No	N/A	No	N/A	
50	Spain	No	N/A	No	N/A	
51	Sri Lanka	No	N/A	No	N/A	
52	Sweden	No	N/A	No	N/A	
53	Switzerland	No	N/A	No	N/A	
54	Tajikistan*	No	N/A	No	N/A	
55	Turkey	No	N/A	No	N/A	
56	Ukraine	No	N/A	No	N/A	
57	United Arab Emirates	No	N/A	No	N/A	
58	United Kingdom	No	N/A	No	N/A	
59	United States	No	N/A	No	N/A	
60	Uzbekistan*	No	N/A	No	N/A	
61	Viet Nam	No	N/A	No	N/A	

Trinidad and Tobago

A. Progress in the implementation of the minimum standard

Trinidad and Tobago has 17 tax agreements in force, as reported in its response to the Peer Review questionnaire, including the multilateral agreement among the members of the CARICOM concluded with ten treaty partners (the CARICOM Agreement).

None of Trinidad and Tobago's agreements comply with the minimum standard or are subject to a complying instrument.

Trinidad and Tobago has not signed the MLI.

B. Implementation issues

As Trinidad and Tobago has not signed the MLI or implemented anti-treaty-shopping measures in its agreements, the Secretariat will offer its support to design a plan for the implementation of the minimum standard to strengthen its network of agreements.

Trinidad and Tobago is encouraged to bring the CARICOM Agreement up to date by commencing talks among all the treaty partners.[143]

Summary of the jurisdiction response – Trinidad and Tobago

	Treaty partners	Compliance with the standard	If compliant, the alternative implemented	Signature of a complying instrument	The alternative implemented through the complying instrument (if not the MLI)	Comments
1	Antigua and Barbuda	No	N/A	No	N/A	CARICOM
2	Barbados	No	N/A	No	N/A	CARICOM
3	Belize	No	N/A	No	N/A	CARICOM
4	Brazil	No	N/A	No	N/A	
5	Canada	No	N/A	No	N/A	
6	China (People's Republic of)	No	N/A	No	N/A	
7	Denmark	No	N/A	No	N/A	
8	Dominica	No	N/A	No	N/A	CARICOM
9	France	No	N/A	No	N/A	
10	Germany	No	N/A	No	N/A	
11	Grenada	No	N/A	No	N/A	CARICOM
12	Guyana*	No	N/A	No	N/A	CARICOM
13	India	No	N/A	No	N/A	
14	Italy	No	N/A	No	N/A	
15	Jamaica	No	N/A	No	N/A	CARICOM
16	Luxembourg	No	N/A	No	N/A	
17	Norway	No	N/A	No	N/A	
18	Saint Kitts and	No	N/A	No	N/A	CARICOM

143 Revisions to the CARICOM Agreement require an agreement from its eleven treaty partners.

	Nevis					
19	Saint Lucia	No	N/A	No	N/A	CARICOM
20	Saint Vincent and the Grenadines	No	N/A	No	N/A	CARICOM
21	Spain	No	N/A	No	N/A	
22	Sweden	No	N/A	No	N/A	
23	Switzerland	No	N/A	No	N/A	
24	United Kingdom	No	N/A	No	N/A	
25	United States	No	N/A	No	N/A	
26	Venezuela*	No	N/A	No	N/A	

Tunisia

A. Progress in the implementation of the minimum standard

Tunisia has 56 tax agreements in force, as reported in its response to the Peer Review questionnaire, including the Arab Maghreb Union Income Agreement concluded with four treaty partners (the UMA Agreement). [144]

Tunisia signed the MLI in 2018 and has not listed its agreements with Germany and Singapore. It indicated that it would list those agreements in its MLI Position to be submitted upon ratification.

Tunisia implementing the minimum standard through the inclusion of the preamble statement and the PPT.[145]

The agreements that will be modified by the MLI will come into compliance with the minimum standard once the provisions of the MLI take effect.

B. Implementation issues

Tunisia's listed agreements under the MLI will start to be compliant after Tunisia's ratification of the MLI. Tunisia is encouraged to ratify the MLI as soon as possible.

Summary of the jurisdiction response - Tunisia

	Treaty partners	Compliance with the standard	If compliant, the alternative implemented	Signature of a complying instrument	The alternative implemented through the complying instrument (if not the MLI)	Comments
1	Algeria*	No	N/A	Yes	N/A	
2	Austria	No	N/A	Yes	N/A	
3	Belgium	No	N/A	Yes	N/A	
4	Burkina Faso	No	N/A	Yes	N/A	
5	Cameroon	No	N/A	Yes	N/A	
6	Canada	No	N/A	Yes	N/A	
7	China (People's Republic of)	No	N/A	Yes	N/A	
8	Côte d'Ivoire	No	N/A	Yes	N/A	
9	Czech Republic	No	N/A	Yes	N/A	
10	Denmark	No	N/A	Yes	N/A	
11	Egypt	No	N/A	Yes	N/A	
12	Ethiopia*	No	N/A	Yes	N/A	
13	France	No	N/A	Yes	N/A	
14	Germany	No	N/A	No	N/A	The new agreement was signed in 2018 and entered into force as of 16

144 In total, Tunisia identified 58 "agreements" in its List of Tax agreements: 55 bilateral agreements and the UMA Agreement concluded with four of its treaty partners.

145 For its agreements listed under the MLI, Tunisia is implementing the preamble statement (Article 6 of the MLI) and the PPT (Article 7 of the MLI).

						December 2019. It is not listed under the MLI.
15	Greece	No	N/A	Yes	N/A	
16	Hungary	No	N/A	Yes	N/A	
17	Indonesia	No	N/A	Yes	N/A	
18	Iran*	No	N/A	Yes	N/A	
19	Italy	No	N/A	Yes	N/A	
20	Jordan	No	N/A	Yes	N/A	
21	Korea	No	N/A	Yes	N/A	
22	Kuwait*	No	N/A	Yes	N/A	
23	Lebanon*	No	N/A	Yes	N/A	
24	Libya*	No	N/A	Yes	N/A	
25	Luxembourg	No	N/A	Yes	N/A	
26	Mali*	No	N/A	Yes	N/A	
27	Malta	No	N/A	Yes	N/A	
28	Mauritania*	No	N/A	Yes	N/A	
29	Mauritius	No	N/A	Yes	N/A	
30	Morocco	No	N/A	Yes	N/A	
31	Netherlands	No	N/A	Yes	N/A	
32	Norway	No	N/A	Yes	N/A	
33	Oman	No	N/A	Yes	N/A	
34	Pakistan	No	N/A	Yes	N/A	
35	Poland	No	N/A	Yes	N/A	
36	Portugal	No	N/A	Yes	N/A	
37	Qatar	No	N/A	Yes	N/A	
38	Romania	No	N/A	Yes	N/A	
39	Saudi Arabia	No	N/A	Yes	N/A	
40	Senegal	No	N/A	Yes	N/A	
41	Serbia	No	N/A	Yes	N/A	
42	Singapore	No	N/A	No	N/A	The agreement was signed in 2018 and entered into force as of 17 December 2019. It is not listed under the MLI.
43	Slovak Republic	No	N/A	Yes	N/A	
44	South Africa	No	N/A	Yes	N/A	
45	Spain	No	N/A	Yes	N/A	
46	Sudan*	No	N/A	Yes	N/A	
47	Sweden	No	N/A	Yes	N/A	
48	Switzerland	No	N/A	Yes	N/A	
49	Syrian Arab Republic*	No	N/A	Yes	N/A	
50	Turkey	No	N/A	Yes	N/A	
51	United Arab Emirates	No	N/A	Yes	N/A	
52	United Kingdom	No	N/A	Yes	N/A	
53	United States	No	N/A	Yes	N/A	
54	Viet Nam	No	N/A	Yes	N/A	
55	Yemen*	No	N/A	Yes	N/A	
56	Algeria* (UMA)	No	N/A	Yes	N/A	UMA Agreement
57	Libya* (UMA)	No	N/A	Yes	N/A	UMA Agreement
58	Mauritania* (UMA)	No	N/A	Yes	N/A	UMA Agreement
59	Morocco (UMA)	No	N/A	Yes	N/A	UMA Agreement

Turkey

A. Progress in the implementation of the minimum standard

Turkey has 86 tax agreements in force, as reported in its response to the Peer Review questionnaire.

Turkey signed the MLI in 2017, listing its non-compliant agreements.

Turkey is implementing the minimum standard through the inclusion of the preamble statement and the PPT.[146]

The agreements that will be modified by the MLI will come into compliance with the minimum standard once the provisions of the MLI take effect.

B. Implementation issues

Turkey's listed agreements under the MLI will start to be compliant after Turkey's ratification of the MLI. Turkey is encouraged to ratify the MLI as soon as possible.

Summary of the jurisdiction response - Turkey

	Treaty partners	Compliance with the standard	If compliant, the alternative implemented	Signature of a complying instrument	The alternative implemented through the complying instrument (if not the MLI)	Comments
1	Albania	No	N/A	Yes	N/A	
2	Algeria*	No	N/A	Yes	N/A	
3	Australia	No	N/A	Yes	N/A	
4	Austria	No	N/A	Yes	N/A	
5	Azerbaijan*	No	N/A	Yes	N/A	
6	Bahrain	No	N/A	Yes	N/A	
7	Bangladesh*	No	N/A	Yes	N/A	
8	Belarus*	No	N/A	Yes	N/A	
9	Belgium	No	N/A	Yes	N/A	
10	Bosnia-Herzegovina	No	N/A	Yes	N/A	
11	Brazil	No	N/A	Yes	N/A	
12	Bulgaria	No	N/A	Yes	N/A	
13	Canada	No	N/A	Yes	N/A	
14	China (People's Republic of)	No	N/A	Yes	N/A	
15	Croatia	No	N/A	Yes	N/A	
16	Czech Republic	No	N/A	Yes	N/A	
17	Denmark	No	N/A	Yes	N/A	
18	Egypt	No	N/A	Yes	N/A	
19	Estonia	No	N/A	Yes	N/A	
20	Ethiopia*	No	N/A	Yes	N/A	

[146] For its agreements listed under the MLI, Turkey is implementing the preamble statement (Article 6 of the MLI) and the PPT (Article 7 of the MLI).

21	Finland	No	N/A	Yes	N/A
22	France	No	N/A	Yes	N/A
23	Gambia*	No	N/A	Yes	N/A
24	Georgia	No	N/A	Yes	N/A
25	Germany	No	N/A	Yes	N/A
26	Greece	No	N/A	Yes	N/A
27	Hungary	No	N/A	Yes	N/A
28	India	No	N/A	Yes	N/A
29	Indonesia	No	N/A	Yes	N/A
30	Iran*	No	N/A	Yes	N/A
31	Ireland	No	N/A	Yes	N/A
32	Israel	No	N/A	Yes	N/A
33	Italy	No	N/A	Yes	N/A
34	Japan	No	N/A	Yes	N/A
35	Jordan	No	N/A	Yes	N/A
36	Kazakhstan	No	N/A	Yes	N/A
37	Korea	No	N/A	Yes	N/A
38	Kosovo*	No	N/A	Yes	N/A
39	Kuwait*	No	N/A	Yes	N/A
40	Kyrgyzstan*	No	N/A	Yes	N/A
41	Latvia	No	N/A	Yes	N/A
42	Lebanon*	No	N/A	Yes	N/A
43	Lithuania	No	N/A	Yes	N/A
44	Luxembourg	No	N/A	Yes	N/A
45	Malaysia	No	N/A	Yes	N/A
46	Malta	No	N/A	Yes	N/A
47	Mexico	No	N/A	Yes	N/A
48	Moldova*	No	N/A	Yes	N/A
49	Mongolia	No	N/A	Yes	N/A
50	Montenegro	No	N/A	Yes	N/A
51	Morocco	No	N/A	Yes	N/A
52	Netherlands	No	N/A	Yes	N/A
53	New Zealand	No	N/A	Yes	N/A
54	North Macedonia	No	N/A	Yes	N/A
55	Norway	No	N/A	Yes	N/A
56	Oman	No	N/A	Yes	N/A
57	Pakistan	No	N/A	Yes	N/A
58	Philippines*	No	N/A	Yes	N/A
59	Poland	No	N/A	Yes	N/A
60	Portugal	No	N/A	Yes	N/A
61	Qatar	No	N/A	Yes	N/A
62	Romania	No	N/A	Yes	N/A
63	Russia	No	N/A	Yes	N/A
64	Saudi Arabia	No	N/A	Yes	N/A
65	Serbia	No	N/A	Yes	N/A
66	Singapore	No	N/A	Yes	N/A
67	Slovak Republic	No	N/A	Yes	N/A
68	Slovenia	No	N/A	Yes	N/A
69	South Africa	No	N/A	Yes	N/A
70	Spain	No	N/A	Yes	N/A
71	Sudan*	No	N/A	Yes	N/A
72	Sweden	No	N/A	Yes	N/A
73	Switzerland	No	N/A	Yes	N/A

74	Syrian Arab Republic*	No	N/A	Yes	N/A	
75	Tajikistan*	No	N/A	Yes	N/A	
76	Thailand	No	N/A	Yes	N/A	
77	Tunisia	No	N/A	Yes	N/A	
78	Turkish Republic of Northern Cyprus*	No	N/A	Yes	N/A	
79	Turkmenistan*	No	N/A	Yes	N/A	
80	Ukraine	No	N/A	Yes	N/A	
81	United Arab Emirates	No	N/A	Yes	N/A	
82	United Kingdom	No	N/A	Yes	N/A	
83	United States	No	N/A	Yes	N/A	
84	Uzbekistan*	No	N/A	Yes	N/A	
85	Viet Nam	No	N/A	Yes	N/A	
86	Yemen*	No	N/A	Yes	N/A	

Turks and Caicos Islands

A. Progress in the implementation of the minimum standard

The Turks and Caicos Islands has no tax agreements in force, as reported in its response to the Peer Review questionnaire.

B. Implementation issues

No jurisdiction has raised any concerns about the Turks and Caicos Islands.

Ukraine

A. Progress in the implementation of the minimum standard

Ukraine has 75 tax agreements in force, as reported in its response to the Peer Review questionnaire. Twenty of those agreements, the agreements with Belgium, Canada, Denmark, Finland, France, Iceland, India, Ireland, Israel, Japan, Lithuania, Luxembourg, Malta, Poland, Serbia, Singapore, the Slovak Republic, Slovenia, the United Arab Emirates and the United Kingdom, comply with the minimum standard.

Ukraine signed the MLI in 2018 and deposited its instrument of ratification on 8 August 2019. The MLI entered into force for Ukraine on 1 December 2019.

Ukraine signed a bilateral complying instrument with respect to its agreements with the Netherlands, Switzerland and the United Kingdom.

Ukraine is implementing the minimum standard through the inclusion of the preamble statement and the PPT.[147]

The agreements modified by the MLI come into compliance with the minimum standard once the provisions of the MLI take effect.

B. Implementation issues

No jurisdiction has raised any concerns about their agreements with Ukraine.

Summary of the jurisdiction response - Ukraine

	Treaty partners	Compliance with the standard	If compliant, the alternative implemented	Signature of a complying instrument	The alternative implemented through the complying instrument (if not the MLI)	Comments
1	Algeria*	No	N/A	Yes	N/A	
2	Armenia	No	N/A	Yes	N/A	
3	Austria	No	N/A	Yes	N/A	
4	Azerbaijan*	No	N/A	Yes	N/A	
5	Belarus*	No	N/A	Yes	N/A	
6	Belgium	Yes	PPT alone	N/A	N/A	
7	Brazil	No	N/A	Yes	N/A	
8	Bulgaria	No	N/A	Yes	N/A	
9	Canada	Yes	PPT alone	N/A	N/A	
10	China (People's Republic of)	No	N/A	Yes	N/A	
11	Croatia	No	N/A	Yes	N/A	
12	Cuba*	No	N/A	Yes	N/A	
13	Cyprus*	No	N/A	Yes	N/A	
14	Czech Republic	No	N/A	Yes	N/A	
15	Denmark	Yes	PPT alone	N/A	N/A	

[147] For its agreements listed under the MLI, Ukraine is implementing the preamble statement (Article 6 of the MLI) and the PPT (Article 7 of the MLI).

16	Egypt	No	N/A	Yes	N/A	
17	Estonia	No	N/A	Yes	N/A	
18	Finland	Yes	PPT alone	N/A	N/A	
19	France	Yes	PPT alone	N/A	N/A	
20	Georgia	No	N/A	Yes	N/A	
21	Germany	No	N/A	Yes	N/A	
22	Greece	No	N/A	Yes	N/A	
23	Hungary	No	N/A	Yes	N/A	
24	Iceland	Yes	PPT alone	N/A	N/A	
25	India	Yes	PPT alone	N/A	N/A	
26	Indonesia	No	N/A	Yes	N/A	
27	Iran*	No	N/A	Yes	N/A	
28	Ireland	Yes	PPT alone	N/A	N/A	
29	Israel	Yes	PPT alone	N/A	N/A	
30	Italy	No	N/A	Yes	N/A	
31	Japan	Yes	PPT alone	N/A	N/A	
32	Jordan	No	N/A	Yes	N/A	
33	Kazakhstan	No	N/A	Yes	N/A	
34	Korea	No	N/A	Yes	N/A	
35	Kuwait*	No	N/A	Yes	N/A	
36	Kyrgyzstan*	No	N/A	Yes	N/A	
37	Latvia	No	N/A	Yes	N/A	
38	Lebanon*	No	N/A	Yes	N/A	
39	Libya*	No	N/A	Yes	N/A	
40	Lithuania	Yes	PPT alone	N/A	N/A	
41	Luxembourg	Yes	PPT alone	N/A	N/A	
42	Malaysia	No	N/A	Yes	N/A	
43	Malta	Yes	PPT alone	N/A	N/A	
44	Mexico	No	N/A	Yes	N/A	
45	Moldova*	No	N/A	Yes	N/A	
46	Mongolia	No	N/A	Yes	N/A	
47	Montenegro	No	N/A	Yes	N/A	
48	Morocco	No	N/A	Yes	N/A	
49	Netherlands	No	N/A	Yes	PPT alone	
50	North Macedonia	No	N/A	Yes	N/A	
51	Norway	No	N/A	Yes	N/A	
52	Pakistan	No	N/A	Yes	N/A	
53	Poland	Yes	PPT alone	N/A	N/A	
54	Portugal	No	N/A	Yes	N/A	
55	Qatar	No	N/A	No	N/A	
56	Romania	No	N/A	Yes	N/A	
57	Russia	No	N/A	Yes	N/A	
58	Saudi Arabia	No	N/A	Yes	N/A	
59	Serbia	Yes	PPT alone	N/A	N/A	
60	Singapore	Yes	PPT alone	N/A	N/A	
61	Slovak Republic	Yes	PPT alone	N/A	N/A	
62	Slovenia	Yes	PPT alone	N/A	N/A	
63	South Africa	No	N/A	Yes	N/A	
64	Spain	No	N/A	Yes	N/A	
65	Sweden	No	N/A	Yes	N/A	
66	Switzerland	No	N/A	Yes	PPT alone	
67	Syrian Arab Republic*	No	N/A	Yes	N/A	
68	Tajikistan*	No	N/A	Yes	N/A	

69	Thailand	No	N/A	Yes	N/A	
70	Turkey	No	N/A	Yes	N/A	
71	Turkmenistan*	No	N/A	Yes	N/A	
72	United Arab Emirates	Yes	PPT alone	N/A	N/A	
73	United Kingdom	Yes	PPT alone	N/A	N/A	
74	United States	No	N/A	Yes	N/A	
75	Uzbekistan*	No	N/A	Yes	N/A	
76	Viet Nam	No	N/A	Yes	N/A	

United Arab Emirates

A. Progress in the implementation of the minimum standard

The United Arab Emirates has 95 tax agreements in force, as reported in its response to the Peer Review questionnaire. Twenty-one of those agreements, the agreements with Belgium, Canada, Finland, France, India, Ireland, Japan, Jersey, Korea, Lithuania, Luxembourg, Malta, the Netherlands, New Zealand, Poland, Saudi Arabia, Serbia, Singapore, Slovenia, Ukraine and the United Kingdom, comply with the minimum standard.

The United Arab Emirates signed the MLI in 2018 and deposited its instrument of ratification on 29 May 2019. The MLI entered in force for the United Arab Emirates on 1 September 2019. The United Arab Emirates has not listed its agreements with San Marino. These agreements will therefore not, at this stage, be modified by the MLI. San Marino has listed its agreement with the United Arab Emirates under the MLI.

The United Arab Emirates is implementing the minimum standard through the inclusion of the preamble statement and the PPT.[148]

The agreements that modified by the MLI come into compliance with the minimum standard once the provisions of the MLI take effect.

B. Implementation issues

As mentioned above, the United Arab Emirates has not listed its agreement with San Marino under the MLI. Listing the agreement under the MLI or entering into bilateral renegotiations to implement the minimum standard would ensure that the minimum standard could be implemented in that non-covered agreement.

Summary of the jurisdiction response – United Arab Emirates

	Treaty partners	Compliance with the standard	If compliant, the alternative implemented	Signature of a complying instrument	The alternative implemented through the complying instrument (if not the MLI)	Comments
1	Albania	No	N/A	Yes	N/A	
2	Algeria*	No	N/A	Yes	N/A	
3	Andorra	No	N/A	Yes	N/A	
4	Angola*	No	N/A	Yes	N/A	
5	Argentina	No	N/A	Yes	N/A	
6	Armenia	No	N/A	Yes	N/A	
7	Austria	No	N/A	Yes	N/A	
8	Azerbaijan*	No	N/A	Yes	N/A	
9	Bangladesh*	No	N/A	Yes	N/A	
10	Barbados	No	N/A	Yes	N/A	
11	Belarus*	No	N/A	Yes	N/A	
12	Belgium	Yes	PPT alone	N/A	N/A	

148 For its agreements listed under the MLI, the United Arab Emirates is implementing the preamble statement (Article 6 of the MLI) and the PPT (Article 7 of the MLI).

13	Bosnia-Herzegovina	No	N/A	Yes	N/A	
14	Brunei Darussalam	No	N/A	Yes	N/A	
15	Bulgaria	No	N/A	Yes	N/A	
16	Canada	Yes	PPT alone	N/A	N/A	
17	China (People's Republic of)	No	N/A	Yes	N/A	
18	Comoros*	No	N/A	Yes	N/A	
19	Croatia	No	N/A	Yes	N/A	
20	Cyprus*	No	N/A	Yes	N/A	
21	Czech Republic	No	N/A	Yes	N/A	
22	Egypt	No	N/A	Yes	N/A	
23	Estonia	No	N/A	Yes	N/A	
24	Fiji*	No	N/A	Yes	N/A	
25	Finland	Yes	PPT alone	N/A	N/A	
26	France	Yes	PPT alone	N/A	N/A	
27	Georgia	No	N/A	Yes	N/A	
28	Germany	No	N/A	Yes	N/A	
29	Greece	No	N/A	Yes	N/A	
30	Guinea*	No	N/A	Yes	N/A	
31	Hong Kong (China)	No	N/A	Yes	N/A	
32	Hungary	No	N/A	Yes	N/A	
33	India	Yes	PPT alone	N/A	N/A	
34	Indonesia	No	N/A	Yes	N/A	
35	Ireland	Yes	PPT alone	N/A	N/A	
36	Italy	No	N/A	Yes	N/A	
37	Japan	Yes	PPT alone	N/A	N/A	
38	Jersey	Yes	PPT alone	N/A	N/A	
39	Jordan	No	N/A	Yes	N/A	
40	Kazakhstan	No	N/A	Yes	N/A	
41	Kenya	No	N/A	Yes	N/A	
42	Korea	Yes	PPT and LOB	N/A	N/A	
43	Kosovo*	No	N/A	Yes	N/A	
44	Kyrgyzstan*	No	N/A	Yes	N/A	
45	Latvia	No	N/A	Yes	N/A	
46	Lebanon*	No	N/A	Yes	N/A	
47	Liechtenstein	No	N/A	Yes	N/A	
48	Lithuania	Yes	PPT alone	N/A	N/A	
49	Luxembourg	Yes	PPT alone	N/A	N/A	
50	Malaysia	No	N/A	Yes	N/A	
51	Maldives	No	N/A	Yes	N/A	
52	Malta	Yes	PPT alone	N/A	N/A	
53	Mauritius	No	N/A	Yes	N/A	
54	Mexico	No	N/A	Yes	N/A	
55	Moldova*	No	N/A	Yes	N/A	
56	Montenegro	No	N/A	Yes	N/A	
57	Morocco	No	N/A	Yes	N/A	
58	Mozambique*	No	N/A	Yes	N/A	
59	Netherlands	Yes	PPT alone	N/A	N/A	
60	New Zealand	Yes	PPT alone	N/A	N/A	
61	North Macedonia	No	N/A	Yes	N/A	
62	Pakistan	No	N/A	Yes	N/A	
63	Panama	No	N/A	Yes	N/A	
64	Philippines*	No	N/A	Yes	N/A	

65	Poland	Yes	PPT alone	N/A	N/A	
66	Portugal	No	N/A	Yes	N/A	
67	Romania	No	N/A	Yes	N/A	
68	Russia	No	N/A	Yes	N/A	
69	San Marino	No	N/A	No	N/A	
70	Saudi Arabia	Yes	PPT alone	N/A	N/A	
71	Senegal	No	N/A	Yes	N/A	
72	Serbia	Yes	PPT alone	N/A	N/A	
73	Seychelles	No	N/A	Yes	N/A	
74	Singapore	Yes	PPT alone	N/A	N/A	
75	Slovak Republic	No	N/A	Yes	N/A	
76	Slovenia	Yes	PPT alone	N/A	N/A	
77	South Africa	No	N/A	Yes	N/A	
78	Spain	No	N/A	Yes	N/A	
79	Sri Lanka	No	N/A	Yes	N/A	
80	Sudan*	No	N/A	Yes	N/A	
81	Switzerland	No	N/A	Yes	N/A	
82	Syrian Arab Republic*	No	N/A	Yes	N/A	
83	Tajikistan*	No	N/A	Yes	N/A	
84	Thailand	No	N/A	Yes	N/A	
85	Tunisia	No	N/A	Yes	N/A	
86	Turkey	No	N/A	Yes	N/A	
87	Turkmenistan*	No	N/A	Yes	N/A	
88	Ukraine	Yes	PPT alone	N/A	Yes	
90	United Kingdom	Yes	PPT alone	N/A	Yes	
91	Uruguay	No	N/A	Yes	N/A	
92	Uzbekistan*	No	N/A	Yes	N/A	
93	Venezuela*	No	N/A	Yes	N/A	
94	Viet Nam	No	N/A	Yes	N/A	
95	Yemen*	No	N/A	Yes	N/A	

United Kingdom

A. Progress in the implementation of the minimum standard

The United Kingdom has 131 tax agreements in force, as reported in its response to the Peer Review questionnaire. Thirty-five of those agreements, the agreements with Australia, Austria, Belarus*, Belgium, Canada, Colombia, Cyprus*, Denmark, Finland, France, Georgia, Gibraltar, Guernsey, Iceland, India, Ireland, the Isle of Man, Israel, Japan, Jersey, Lithuania, Luxembourg, Malta, the Netherlands, New Zealand, Norway, Poland, Serbia, Singapore, the Slovak Republic, Slovenia, Switzerland, Ukraine, the United Arab Emirates and Uzbekistan*, comply with the minimum standard.

The United Kingdom signed the MLI in 2017 and deposited its instrument of ratification on 29 June 2018. The MLI entered into force for the United Kingdom on 1 October 2018. The United Kingdom has not listed its agreements with Germany but indicated in its response to the Peer Review questionnaire that bilateral negotiations would be used with respect to the agreement.

The United Kingdom's agreements with the Falkland Islands* and Montserrat are not listed under the MLI as they are arrangements with overseas territories. Bilateral negotiations will be used to update these agreements.

The United Kingdom is implementing the minimum standard through the inclusion of the preamble statement and the PPT.[149]

The agreements modified by the MLI come into compliance with the minimum standard once the provisions of the MLI take effect.

B. Implementation issues

No jurisdiction has raised any concerns about their agreements with the United Kingdom.

Summary of the jurisdiction response – United Kingdom

	Treaty partners	Compliance with the standard	If compliant, the alternative implemented	Signature of a complying instrument	The alternative implemented through the complying instrument (if not the MLI)	Comments
1	Albania	No	N/A	Yes	N/A	
2	Algeria*	No	N/A	Yes	N/A	
3	Antigua and Barbuda	No	N/A	Yes	N/A	
4	Argentina	No	N/A	Yes	N/A	
5	Armenia	No	N/A	Yes	N/A	
6	Australia	Yes	PPT alone	N/A	N/A	
7	Austria	Yes	PPT alone	N/A	N/A	

[149] For 117 of its agreements listed under the MLI, the United Kingdom is implementing the preamble statement (Article 6 of the MLI). For its 120 agreements listed under the MLI, the United Kingdom is implementing the PPT (Article 7 of the MLI). The United Kingdom made a reservation pursuant to Article 6(4) of the MLI not to apply Article 6(1) of the MLI with respect to agreements, which already contain the relevant preamble language. Three of the United Kingdom's agreements are within the scope of this reservation.

8	Azerbaijan*	No	N/A	Yes	N/A
9	Bahrain	No	N/A	Yes	N/A
10	Bangladesh*	No	N/A	Yes	N/A
11	Barbados	No	N/A	Yes	N/A
12	Belarus*	Yes	PPT alone	N/A	N/A
13	Belgium	Yes	PPT alone	N/A	N/A
14	Belize	No	N/A	Yes	N/A
15	Bolivia*	No	N/A	Yes	N/A
16	Bosnia-Herzegovina	No	N/A	Yes	N/A
17	Botswana	No	N/A	Yes	N/A
18	Brunei Darussalam	No	N/A	Yes	N/A
19	Bulgaria	No	N/A	Yes	N/A
20	Canada	Yes	PPT alone	N/A	N/A
21	Chile	No	N/A	Yes	N/A
22	China (People's Republic of)	No	N/A	Yes	N/A
23	Chinese Taipei*	No	N/A	No	N/A
24	Colombia	Yes	PPT alone	N/A	N/A
25	Côte d'Ivoire	No	N/A	Yes	N/A
26	Croatia	No	N/A	Yes	N/A
27	Cyprus*	Yes	PPT alone	N/A	N/A
28	Czech Republic	No	N/A	Yes	N/A
29	Denmark	Yes	PPT alone	N/A	N/A
30	Egypt	No	N/A	Yes	N/A
31	Estonia	No	N/A	Yes	N/A
32	Eswatini	No	N/A	Yes	N/A
33	Ethiopia*	No	N/A	Yes	N/A
34	Falkland Islands*	No	N/A	No	N/A
35	Faroe Islands	No	N/A	Yes	N/A
36	Fiji*	No	N/A	Yes	N/A
37	Finland	Yes	PPT alone	N/A	N/A
38	France	Yes	PPT alone	N/A	N/A
39	Gambia*	No	N/A	Yes	N/A
40	Georgia	Yes	PPT alone	N/A	N/A
41	Germany	No	N/A	No	N/A
42	Ghana*	No	N/A	Yes	N/A
43	Gibraltar	Yes	PPT alone	N/A	N/A
44	Greece	No	N/A	Yes	N/A
45	Grenada	No	N/A	Yes	N/A
46	Guernsey	Yes	PPT alone	N/A	N/A
47	Guyana*	No	N/A	Yes	N/A
48	Hong Kong (China)	No	N/A	Yes	N/A
49	Hungary	No	N/A	Yes	N/A
50	Iceland	Yes	PPT alone	N/A	N/A
51	India	Yes	PPT alone	N/A	N/A
52	Indonesia	No	N/A	Yes	N/A
53	Ireland	Yes	PPT alone	N/A	N/A
54	Isle of Man	Yes	PPT alone	N/A	N/A
55	Israel	Yes	PPT alone	N/A	N/A
56	Italy	No	N/A	Yes	N/A
57	Jamaica	No	N/A	Yes	N/A
58	Japan	Yes	PPT and LOB	N/A	N/A
59	Jersey	Yes	PPT alone	N/A	N/A

60	Jordan	No	N/A	Yes	N/A	
61	Kazakhstan	No	N/A	Yes	N/A	
62	Kenya	No	N/A	Yes	N/A	
63	Kiribati*	No	N/A	Yes	N/A	
64	Korea	No	N/A	Yes	N/A	
65	Kosovo*	No	N/A	Yes	N/A	
66	Kuwait*	No	N/A	Yes	N/A	
67	Latvia	No	N/A	Yes	N/A	MLI has effect from 1 January 2021
68	Lesotho*[150]	No	N/A	Yes	N/A	
69	Libya*	No	N/A	Yes	N/A	
70	Liechtenstein	No	N/A	Yes	N/A	MLI has effect from 1 January 2021
71	Lithuania	Yes	PPT alone	N/A	N/A	
72	Luxembourg	Yes	PPT alone	N/A	N/A	
73	Malawi*	No	N/A	Yes	N/A	
74	Malaysia	No	N/A	Yes	N/A	
75	Malta	Yes	PPT alone	N/A	N/A	
76	Mauritius	No	N/A	Yes	N/A	MLI has effect from 1 January 2021
77	Mexico	No	N/A	Yes	N/A	
78	Moldova*	No	N/A	Yes	N/A	
79	Mongolia	No	N/A	Yes	N/A	
80	Montenegro	No	N/A	Yes	N/A	
81	Montserrat	No	N/A	No	N/A	
82	Morocco	No	N/A	Yes	N/A	
83	Myanmar*	No	N/A	Yes	N/A	
84	Namibia	No	N/A	Yes	N/A	
85	Netherlands	Yes	PPT alone	N/A	N/A	
86	New Zealand	Yes	PPT alone	N/A	N/A	
87	Nigeria	No	N/A	Yes	N/A	
88	North Macedonia	No	N/A	Yes	N/A	
89	Norway	Yes	PPT alone	N/A	N/A	
90	Oman	No	N/A	Yes	N/A	
91	Pakistan	No	N/A	Yes	N/A	
92	Panama	No	N/A	Yes	N/A	
93	Papua New Guinea	No	N/A	Yes	N/A	
94	Philippines*	No	N/A	Yes	N/A	
95	Poland	Yes	PPT alone	N/A	N/A	
96	Portugal	No	N/A	Yes	N/A	MLI has effect from 1 January 2021
97	Qatar	No	N/A	Yes	N/A	MLI has effect from 1 January 2021
98	Romania	No	N/A	Yes	N/A	
99	Russia	No	N/A	Yes	N/A	MLI has effect from 1 January 2021
100	Saint Kitts and Nevis	No	N/A	Yes	N/A	
101	Saudi Arabia	No	N/A	Yes	N/A	MLI has effect from 1 January 2021
102	Senegal	No	N/A	Yes	N/A	
103	Serbia	Yes	PPT alone	N/A	N/A	

[150] The agreement is subject to a complying instrument as the new agreement with Lesotho* was listed under the MLI.

104	Sierra Leone	No	N/A	Yes	N/A	
105	Singapore	Yes	PPT alone	N/A	N/A	
106	Slovak Republic	Yes	PPT alone	N/A	N/A	
107	Slovenia	Yes	PPT alone	N/A	N/A	
108	Solomon Islands*	No	N/A	Yes	N/A	
109	South Africa	No	N/A	Yes	N/A	
110	Spain	No	N/A	Yes	N/A	
111	Sri Lanka	No	N/A	Yes	N/A	
112	Sudan*	No	N/A	Yes	N/A	
113	Sweden	No	N/A	Yes	N/A	
114	Switzerland	Yes	PPT alone	N/A	N/A	
115	Tajikistan*	No	N/A	Yes	N/A	
116	Thailand	No	N/A	Yes	N/A	
117	Trinidad and Tobago	No	N/A	Yes	N/A	
118	Tunisia	No	N/A	Yes	N/A	
119	Turkey	No	N/A	Yes	N/A	
120	Turkmenistan*	No	N/A	Yes	N/A	
121	Tuvalu*	No	N/A	Yes	N/A	
122	Uganda*	No	N/A	Yes	N/A	
123	Ukraine	Yes	PPT alone	N/A	N/A	
124	United Arab Emirates	Yes	PPT alone	N/A	N/A	
125	United States	No	N/A	Yes	N/A	
126	Uruguay	No	N/A	Yes	N/A	MLI has effect from 1 January 2021
127	Uzbekistan*	Yes	PPT alone	N/A	N/A	
128	Venezuela*	No	N/A	Yes	N/A	
129	Viet Nam	No	N/A	Yes	N/A	
130	Zambia	No	N/A	Yes	N/A	
131	Zimbabwe*	No	N/A	Yes	N/A	

United States

A. Progress in the implementation of the minimum standard

The United States has 66 tax agreements in force, as reported in its response to the Peer Review questionnaire.

The United States has implemented LOB clauses in most of its agreements. It started to include anti-treaty-shopping measures in 1962,[151] and since the seventies, LOB clauses (which initially targeted investment or holding companies) have appeared in agreements concluded by the United States. All of the United States' agreements are supplemented by its anti-conduit regulations.[152]

The 2016 US Model Convention contains an express statement that the tax treaty should not create opportunities for non-taxation or reduced taxation through tax evasion or avoidance (including through treaty-shopping arrangements aimed at obtaining reliefs provided in this Convention for the indirect benefit of residents of third states).

The United States expects to comply with the minimum standard through a detailed LOB which is not available through the MLI. Therefore, the United States did not sign the MLI and will implement the minimum standard bilaterally.

The United States' agreements with the following 45 jurisdictions contain an LOB and are supplemented by domestic anti-conduit rules: Australia, Austria, Bangladesh*, Barbados, Belgium, Bulgaria, Canada, China (People's Republic of), Cyprus*, Czech Republic, Denmark, Estonia, Finland, France, Germany, Iceland, India, Indonesia, Ireland, Israel, Italy, Jamaica, Japan, Kazakhstan, Latvia, Lithuania, Luxembourg, Malta, Mexico, the Netherlands, New Zealand, Portugal, Russia, the Slovak Republic, Slovenia, South Africa, Spain, Sri Lanka, Sweden, Switzerland, Thailand, Tunisia, Turkey, Ukraine, Venezuela*. Signed conventions with Hungary and Poland contain an LOB and are supplemented by domestic anti-conduit rules. The agreements with Egypt, Korea, Morocco, Norway, and Trinidad and Tobago have a limited anti-treaty shopping rule and are supplemented by domestic anti-conduit rules. The agreement with the United Kingdom contains an LOB and anti-conduit rules and is supplemented by domestic anti-conduit rules.

B. Implementation issues

No jurisdiction has raised any concerns about their agreements with the United States.

[151] With respect to the United States' agreement with Luxembourg.

[152] See I.R.C. §7701(l), added to the Internal Revenue Code by section 13238 of the Omnibus Budget Reconciliation Act of 1993, P.L. 103-66 (allowing the Internal Revenue Service to re-characterise any multiple-party financing transaction as being a transaction directly among any two or more of its parties whenever appropriate to prevent the avoidance of the United States' tax); Treas. Reg. § 1.881-3 (as amended in 2020) (providing additional guidance relating to conduit financing arrangements).

Summary of the jurisdiction response – United States

	Treaty partners	Compliance with the standard	If compliant, the alternative implemented	Signature of a complying instrument	The alternative implemented through the complying instrument (if not the MLI)	Comments
1	Armenia	No	N/A	No	N/A	
2	Australia	No	N/A	No	N/A	LOB supplemented by domestic anti-conduit rules
3	Austria	No	N/A	No	N/A	LOB supplemented by domestic anti-conduit rules
4	Azerbaijan*	No	N/A	No	N/A	
5	Bangladesh*	No	N/A	No	N/A	LOB supplemented by domestic anti-conduit rules
6	Barbados	No	N/A	No	N/A	LOB supplemented by domestic anti-conduit rules
7	Belarus*	No	N/A	No	N/A	
8	Belgium	No	N/A	No	N/A	LOB supplemented by domestic anti-conduit rules
9	Bulgaria	No	N/A	No	N/A	LOB supplemented by domestic anti-conduit rules
10	Canada	No	N/A	No	N/A	LOB supplemented by domestic anti-conduit rules
11	China (People's Republic of)	No	N/A	No	N/A	LOB supplemented by domestic anti-conduit rules
12	Cyprus*	No	N/A	No	N/A	LOB supplemented by domestic anti-conduit rules
13	Czech Republic	No	N/A	No	N/A	LOB supplemented by domestic anti-conduit rules
14	Denmark	No	N/A	No	N/A	LOB supplemented by domestic anti-conduit rules
15	Egypt	No	N/A	No	N/A	Limited anti-treaty shopping rule supplemented by domestic anti-conduit rules
16	Estonia	No	N/A	No	N/A	LOB supplemented by domestic anti-conduit rules
17	Finland	No	N/A	No	N/A	LOB supplemented by domestic anti-conduit rules
18	France	No	N/A	No	N/A	LOB supplemented by domestic anti-conduit rules
19	Georgia	No	N/A	No	N/A	
20	Germany	No	N/A	No	N/A	LOB supplemented by domestic anti-conduit rules
21	Greece	No	N/A	No	N/A	
22	Hungary	No	N/A	No	N/A	LOB in a signed convention, supplemented by domestic anti-conduit rules
23	Iceland	No	N/A	No	N/A	LOB supplemented by domestic anti-conduit rules
24	India	No	N/A	No	N/A	LOB supplemented by domestic anti-conduit rules
25	Indonesia	No	N/A	No	N/A	LOB supplemented by domestic anti-conduit rules
26	Ireland	No	N/A	No	N/A	LOB supplemented by domestic anti-conduit rules
27	Israel	No	N/A	No	N/A	LOB supplemented by

						domestic anti-conduit rules
28	Italy	No	N/A	No	N/A	LOB supplemented by domestic anti-conduit rules
29	Jamaica	No	N/A	No	N/A	LOB supplemented by domestic anti-conduit rules
30	Japan	No	N/A	No	N/A	LOB supplemented by domestic anti-conduit rules
31	Kazakhstan	No	N/A	No	N/A	LOB supplemented by domestic anti-conduit rules
32	Korea	No	N/A	No	N/A	Limited anti-treaty shopping rule supplemented by domestic anti-conduit rules
33	Kyrgyzstan*	No	N/A	No	N/A	
34	Latvia	No	N/A	No	N/A	LOB supplemented by domestic anti-conduit rules
35	Lithuania	No	N/A	No	N/A	LOB supplemented by domestic anti-conduit rules
36	Luxembourg	No	N/A	No	N/A	LOB supplemented by domestic anti-conduit rules
37	Malta	No	N/A	No	N/A	LOB supplemented by domestic anti-conduit rules
38	Mexico	No	N/A	No	N/A	LOB supplemented by domestic anti-conduit rules
39	Moldova*	No	N/A	No	N/A	
40	Morocco	No	N/A	No	N/A	Limited anti-treaty shopping rule supplemented by domestic anti-conduit rules
41	Netherlands	No	N/A	No	N/A	LOB supplemented by domestic anti-conduit rules
42	New Zealand	No	N/A	No	N/A	LOB supplemented by domestic anti-conduit rules
43	Norway	No	N/A	No	N/A	Limited anti-treaty shopping rule supplemented by domestic anti-conduit rules
44	Pakistan	No	N/A	No	N/A	
45	Philippines*	No	N/A	No	N/A	
46	Poland	No	N/A	No	N/A	LOB in a signed convention, supplemented by domestic anti-conduit rules
47	Portugal	No	N/A	No	N/A	LOB supplemented by domestic anti-conduit rules
48	Romania	No	N/A	No	N/A	
49	Russia	No	N/A	No	N/A	LOB supplemented by domestic anti-conduit rules
50	Slovak Republic	No	N/A	No	N/A	LOB supplemented by domestic anti-conduit rules
51	Slovenia	No	N/A	No	N/A	LOB supplemented by domestic anti-conduit rules
52	South Africa	No	N/A	No	N/A	LOB supplemented by domestic anti-conduit rules
53	Spain	No	N/A	No	N/A	LOB supplemented by domestic anti-conduit rules
54	Sri Lanka	No	N/A	No	N/A	LOB supplemented by domestic anti-conduit rules
55	Sweden	No	N/A	No	N/A	LOB supplemented by

						domestic anti-conduit rules
56	Switzerland	No	N/A	No	N/A	LOB supplemented by domestic anti-conduit rules
57	Tajikistan*	No	N/A	No	N/A	
58	Thailand	No	N/A	No	N/A	LOB supplemented by domestic anti-conduit rules
59	Trinidad and Tobago	No	N/A	No	N/A	Limited anti-treaty shopping rule supplemented by domestic anti-conduit rules
60	Tunisia	No	N/A	No	N/A	LOB supplemented by domestic anti-conduit rules
61	Turkey	No	N/A	No	N/A	LOB supplemented by domestic anti-conduit rules
62	Turkmenistan*	No	N/A	No	N/A	.
63	Ukraine	No	N/A	No	N/A	LOB supplemented by domestic anti-conduit rules
64	United Kingdom	No	N/A	No	N/A	LOB and anti-conduit rules in the treaty supplemented by domestic anti-conduit rules
65	Uzbekistan*	No	N/A	No	N/A	
66	Venezuela*	No	N/A	No	N/A	LOB supplemented by domestic anti-conduit rules

Uruguay

A. Progress in the implementation of the minimum standard

Uruguay has 21 tax agreements in force, as reported in its response to the Peer Review questionnaire. Two of those agreements, the agreements with Chile and Paraguay, comply with the minimum standard.

Uruguay signed the MLI in 2017 and deposited its instrument of ratification on 6 February 2020, listing its non-compliant agreements. The MLI entered into force for Uruguay on 1 June 2020.

Uruguay is implementing the minimum standard through the inclusion of the preamble statement and the PPT combined with the LOB.[153]

The agreements that will be modified by the MLI will come into compliance with the minimum standard once the provisions of the MLI take effect.

B. Implementation issues

No jurisdiction has raised any concerns about their agreements with Uruguay.

Summary of the jurisdiction response - Uruguay

	Treaty partners	Compliance with the standard	If compliant, the alternative implemented	Signature of a complying instrument	The alternative implemented through the complying instrument (if not the MLI)	Comments
1	Belgium	No	N/A	Yes	N/A	
2	Chile	Yes	PPT and LOB	N/A	N/A	
3	Ecuador*	No	N/A	Yes	N/A	
4	Finland	No	N/A	Yes	N/A	
5	Germany	No	N/A	Yes	N/A	Germany does not include the DTA with Uruguay as a CTA.
6	Hungary	No	N/A	Yes	N/A	
7	India	No	N/A	Yes	N/A	
8	Korea	No	N/A	Yes	N/A	
9	Liechtenstein	No	N/A	Yes	N/A	
10	Luxembourg	No	N/A	Yes	N/A	
11	Malta	No	N/A	Yes	N/A	
12	Mexico	No	N/A	Yes	N/A	
13	Paraguay	Yes	PPT and LOB	N/A	N/A	
14	Portugal	No	N/A	Yes	N/A	
15	Romania	No	N/A	Yes	N/A	
16	Singapore	No	N/A	Yes	N/A	
17	Spain	No	N/A	Yes	N/A	
18	Switzerland	No	N/A	Yes	N/A	Switzerland does not include the DTA with Uruguay as a CTA.
19	United Arab Emirates	No	N/A	Yes	N/A	
20	United Kingdom	No	N/A	Yes	N/A	
21	Viet Nam	No	N/A	Yes	N/A	

[153] For its agreements listed under the MLI, Uruguay is implementing the preamble statement (Article 6 of the MLI) and the PPT (Article 7 of the MLI). Uruguay also opted for the simplified LOB under Article 7(6) of the MLI.

Viet Nam

A. Progress in the implementation of the minimum standard

Viet Nam has 76 tax agreements in force, as reported in its response to the Peer Review questionnaire.

None of Viet Nam's agreements comply with the minimum standard or are subject to a complying instrument.

Viet Nam has not signed the MLI.

Viet Nam indicated in its response to the Peer Review questionnaire that it is currently working towards signing the MLI.

B. Implementation issues

As Viet Nam has not signed the MLI or implemented anti-treaty-shopping measures in its agreements, the Secretariat will offer its support to design a plan for the implementation of the minimum standard to strengthen its network of agreements.

Summary of the jurisdiction response – Viet Nam

	Treaty partners	Compliance with the standard	If compliant, the alternative implemented	Signature of a complying instrument	The alternative implemented through the complying instrument (if not the MLI)	Comments
1	Australia	No	N/A	No	N/A	
2	Austria	No	N/A	No	N/A	
3	Azerbaijan*	No	N/A	No	N/A	
4	Bangladesh*	No	N/A	No	N/A	
5	Belarus*	No	N/A	No	N/A	
6	Belgium	No	N/A	No	N/A	
7	Brunei Darussalam	No	N/A	No	N/A	
8	Bulgaria	No	N/A	No	N/A	
9	Cambodia*	No	N/A	No	N/A	
10	Canada	No	N/A	No	N/A	
11	China (People's Republic of)	No	N/A	No	N/A	
12	Chinese Taipei*	No	N/A	No	N/A	
13	Croatia	No	N/A	No	N/A	
14	Cuba*	No	N/A	No	N/A	
15	Czech Republic	No	N/A	No	N/A	
16	Democratic People's Republic of Korea*	No	N/A	No	N/A	
17	Denmark	No	N/A	No	N/A	
18	Estonia	No	N/A	No	N/A	
19	Finland	No	N/A	No	N/A	
20	France	No	N/A	No	N/A	
21	Germany	No	N/A	No	N/A	

22	Hong Kong (China)	No	N/A	No	N/A	
23	Hungary	No	N/A	No	N/A	
24	Iceland	No	N/A	No	N/A	
25	India	No	N/A	No	N/A	
26	Indonesia	No	N/A	No	N/A	
27	Iran*	No	N/A	No	N/A	
28	Ireland	No	N/A	No	N/A	
29	Israel	No	N/A	No	N/A	"Mini" PPTs in Article 28
30	Italy	No	N/A	No	N/A	
31	Japan	No	N/A	No	N/A	
32	Kazakhstan	No	N/A	No	N/A	
33	Korea	No	N/A	No	N/A	
34	Kuwait*	No	N/A	No	N/A	
35	Lao People's Democratic Republic*	No	N/A	No	N/A	
36	Latvia	No	N/A	No	N/A	
37	Luxembourg	No	N/A	No	N/A	
38	Macau (China)	No	N/A	No	N/A	
39	Malaysia	No	N/A	No	N/A	
40	Malta	No	N/A	No	N/A	
41	Mongolia	No	N/A	No	N/A	
42	Morocco	No	N/A	No	N/A	
43	Mozambique*	No	N/A	No	N/A	
44	Myanmar*	No	N/A	No	N/A	
45	Netherlands	No	N/A	No	N/A	
46	New Zealand	No	N/A	No	N/A	"Mini" PPTs in dividend, interest, royalty Articles
47	Norway	No	N/A	No	N/A	
48	Oman	No	N/A	No	N/A	"Mini" PPTs in dividend, interest, royalty, technical fees Articles
49	Pakistan	No	N/A	No	N/A	
50	Palestine*	No	N/A	No	N/A	
51	Panama	No	N/A	No	N/A	
52	Philippines*	No	N/A	No	N/A	
53	Poland	No	N/A	No	N/A	
54	Portugal	No	N/A	No	N/A	"Mini" PPT in 1(c) of the Protocol
55	Qatar	No	N/A	No	N/A	
56	Romania	No	N/A	No	N/A	
57	Russia	No	N/A	No	N/A	
58	San Marino	No	N/A	No	N/A	
59	Saudi Arabia	No	N/A	No	N/A	
60	Serbia	No	N/A	No	N/A	
61	Seychelles	No	N/A	No	N/A	
62	Singapore	No	N/A	No	N/A	
63	Slovak Republic	No	N/A	No	N/A	
64	Spain	No	N/A	No	N/A	
65	Sri Lanka	No	N/A	No	N/A	
66	Sweden	No	N/A	No	N/A	
67	Switzerland	No	N/A	No	N/A	
68	Thailand	No	N/A	No	N/A	
69	Tunisia	No	N/A	No	N/A	
70	Turkey	No	N/A	No	N/A	

71	Ukraine	No	N/A	No	N/A	"Mini" PPTs in interest, royalty Articles
72	United Arab Emirates	No	N/A	No	N/A	
73	United Kingdom	No	N/A	No	N/A	"Mini" PPTs in interest and royalty Articles
74	Uruguay	No	N/A	No	N/A	
75	Uzbekistan*	No	N/A	No	N/A	Mini" PPTs in royalty Article
76	Venezuela*	No	N/A	No	N/A	

Zambia

A. Progress in the implementation of the minimum standard

Zambia has 23 tax agreements in force, as reported in its response to the Peer Review questionnaire. One of those agreements, the agreement with Switzerland, complies with the minimum standard.

Zambia has not signed the MLI.

Zambia is implementing the minimum standard through the inclusion of the preamble statement and the PPT.

B. Implementation issues

As Zambia has not signed the MLI or implemented anti-treaty-shopping measures in its agreements, the Secretariat will offer its support to design a plan for the implementation of the minimum standard to strengthen its network of agreements.

Summary of the jurisdiction response - Zambia

	Treaty partners	Compliance with the standard	If compliant, the alternative implemented	Signature of a complying instrument	The alternative implemented through the complying instrument (if not the MLI)	Comments
1	Botswana	No	N/A	No	N/A	
2	Canada	No	N/A	No	N/A	
3	China (People's Republic of)	No	N/A	No	N/A	
4	Denmark	No	N/A	No	N/A	
5	Finland	No	N/A	No	N/A	
6	France	No	N/A	No	N/A	
7	Germany	No	N/A	No	N/A	
8	India	No	N/A	No	N/A	
9	Ireland	No	N/A	No	N/A	
10	Italy	No	N/A	No	N/A	
11	Japan	No	N/A	No	N/A	
12	Kenya	No	N/A	No	N/A	
13	Mauritius	No	N/A	No	N/A	
14	Netherlands	No	N/A	No	N/A	
15	Norway	No	N/A	No	N/A	
16	Romania	No	N/A	No	N/A	
17	Seychelles	No	N/A	No	N/A	
18	South Africa	No	N/A	No	N/A	
19	Sweden	No	N/A	No	N/A	
20	Switzerland	Yes	PPT alone	No	N/A	
21	Tanzania*	No	N/A	No	N/A	
22	Uganda*	No	N/A	No	N/A	
23	United Kingdom	No	N/A	No	N/A	

www.ingramcontent.com/pod-product-compliance
Ingram Content Group UK Ltd.
Pitfield, Milton Keynes, MK11 3LW, UK
UKHW051458290926
15471UKWH00008B/1275

9 789264 707016